C-2587 CAREER EXAMINATION SERIES

This is your
PASSBOOK for...

Associate Court Clerk

Test Preparation Study Guide
Questions & Answers

COPYRIGHT NOTICE

This book is SOLELY intended for, is sold ONLY to, and its use is RESTRICTED to individual, bona fide applicants or candidates who qualify by virtue of having seriously filed applications for appropriate license, certificate, professional and/or promotional advancement, higher school matriculation, scholarship, or other legitimate requirements of education and/or governmental authorities.

This book is NOT intended for use, class instruction, tutoring, training, duplication, copying, reprinting, excerption, or adaptation, etc., by:

1) Other publishers
2) Proprietors and/or Instructors of "Coaching" and/or Preparatory Courses
3) Personnel and/or Training Divisions of commercial, industrial, and governmental organizations
4) Schools, colleges, or universities and/or their departments and staffs, including teachers and other personnel
5) Testing Agencies or Bureaus
6) Study groups which seek by the purchase of a single volume to copy and/or duplicate and/or adapt this material for use by the group as a whole without having purchased individual volumes for each of the members of the group
7) Et al.

Such persons would be in violation of appropriate Federal and State statutes.

PROVISION OF LICENSING AGREEMENTS – Recognized educational, commercial, industrial, and governmental institutions and organizations, and others legitimately engaged in educational pursuits, including training, testing, and measurement activities, may address request for a licensing agreement to the copyright owners, who will determine whether, and under what conditions, including fees and charges, the materials in this book may be used them. In other words, a licensing facility exists for the legitimate use of the material in this book on other than an individual basis. However, it is asseverated and affirmed here that the material in this book CANNOT be used without the receipt of the express permission of such a licensing agreement from the Publishers. Inquiries re licensing should be addressed to the company, attention rights and permissions department.

All rights reserved, including the right of reproduction in whole or in part, in any form or by any means, electronic or mechanical, including photocopying, recording, or by any information storage and retrieval system, without permission in writing from the Publisher.

Copyright © 2025 by
National Learning Corporation

212 Michael Drive, Syosset, NY 11791
(516) 921-8888 • www.passbooks.com
E-mail: info@passbooks.com

PASSBOOK® SERIES

THE *PASSBOOK® SERIES* has been created to prepare applicants and candidates for the ultimate academic battlefield – the examination room.

At some time in our lives, each and every one of us may be required to take an examination – for validation, matriculation, admission, qualification, registration, certification, or licensure.

Based on the assumption that every applicant or candidate has met the basic formal educational standards, has taken the required number of courses, and read the necessary texts, the *PASSBOOK® SERIES* furnishes the one special preparation which may assure passing with confidence, instead of failing with insecurity. Examination questions – together with answers – are furnished as the basic vehicle for study so that the mysteries of the examination and its compounding difficulties may be eliminated or diminished by a sure method.

This book is meant to help you pass your examination provided that you qualify and are serious in your objective.

The entire field is reviewed through the huge store of content information which is succinctly presented through a provocative and challenging approach – the question-and-answer method.

A climate of success is established by furnishing the correct answers at the end of each test.

You soon learn to recognize types of questions, forms of questions, and patterns of questioning. You may even begin to anticipate expected outcomes.

You perceive that many questions are repeated or adapted so that you can gain acute insights, which may enable you to score many sure points.

You learn how to confront new questions, or types of questions, and to attack them confidently and work out the correct answers.

You note objectives and emphases, and recognize pitfalls and dangers, so that you may make positive educational adjustments.

Moreover, you are kept fully informed in relation to new concepts, methods, practices, and directions in the field.

You discover that you are actually taking the examination all the time: you are preparing for the examination by "taking" an examination, not by reading extraneous and/or supererogatory textbooks.

In short, this PASSBOOK®, used directedly, should be an important factor in helping you to pass your test.

ASSOCIATE COURT CLERK

DUTIES

An Associate Court Clerk may perform the following duties:

Assigns work responsibilities to court clerical, office clerical, and court security employees.

Examines court documents such as motions, complex orders, and notes of issue, judgments, petitions, and order-framing issues to ensure their accuracy, completeness, and legal sufficiency.

Prepares the calendar by scheduling a pre-determined number of cases in chronological order from date of filing or as requested.

Calls the calendar and/or motions and annotates said calendar and motions in order to dispose of the daily activity.

Responds to unusual oral and written inquiries from the public and from lawyers and litigants concerning scheduling of cases and court procedures and practices.

Compiles statistical information such as the number of cases pending, the number of cases handled by a particular court part, and calendar entries for submission to the judge, court administrators, and outside public agencies.

Discusses daily court activities such as the scheduling of cases, the calling of the calendar, and court procedures with the judge and court administrators.

Interprets orders, decisions, judgments, motions, and other supporting papers to determine the directives of the judge and the applications and reliefs sought by attorneys and litigants, and performs related duties.

SUBJECT OF EXAMINATION

The multiple-choice written test will cover knowledge, skills.and/or abilities in such areas as:
1. Civil practice laws and rules;
2. Criminal procedure law;
3. Penal law;
4. Family court act;
5. Interpretation of written material of a legal nature; and
6. Supervision.

HOW TO TAKE A TEST

I. YOU MUST PASS AN EXAMINATION

A. WHAT EVERY CANDIDATE SHOULD KNOW

Examination applicants often ask us for help in preparing for the written test. What can I study in advance? What kinds of questions will be asked? How will the test be given? How will the papers be graded?

As an applicant for a civil service examination, you may be wondering about some of these things. Our purpose here is to suggest effective methods of advance study and to describe civil service examinations.

Your chances for success on this examination can be increased if you know how to prepare. Those "pre-examination jitters" can be reduced if you know what to expect. You can even experience an adventure in good citizenship if you know why civil service exams are given.

B. WHY ARE CIVIL SERVICE EXAMINATIONS GIVEN?

Civil service examinations are important to you in two ways. As a citizen, you want public jobs filled by employees who know how to do their work. As a job seeker, you want a fair chance to compete for that job on an equal footing with other candidates. The best-known means of accomplishing this two-fold goal is the competitive examination.

Exams are widely publicized throughout the nation. They may be administered for jobs in federal, state, city, municipal, town or village governments or agencies.

Any citizen may apply, with some limitations, such as the age or residence of applicants. Your experience and education may be reviewed to see whether you meet the requirements for the particular examination. When these requirements exist, they are reasonable and applied consistently to all applicants. Thus, a competitive examination may cause you some uneasiness now, but it is your privilege and safeguard.

C. HOW ARE CIVIL SERVICE EXAMS DEVELOPED?

Examinations are carefully written by trained technicians who are specialists in the field known as "psychological measurement," in consultation with recognized authorities in the field of work that the test will cover. These experts recommend the subject matter areas or skills to be tested; only those knowledges or skills important to your success on the job are included. The most reliable books and source materials available are used as references. Together, the experts and technicians judge the difficulty level of the questions.

Test technicians know how to phrase questions so that the problem is clearly stated. Their ethics do not permit "trick" or "catch" questions. Questions may have been tried out on sample groups, or subjected to statistical analysis, to determine their usefulness.

Written tests are often used in combination with performance tests, ratings of training and experience, and oral interviews. All of these measures combine to form the best-known means of finding the right person for the right job.

II. HOW TO PASS THE WRITTEN TEST

A. NATURE OF THE EXAMINATION

To prepare intelligently for civil service examinations, you should know how they differ from school examinations you have taken. In school you were assigned certain definite pages to read or subjects to cover. The examination questions were quite detailed and usually emphasized memory. Civil service exams, on the other hand, try to discover your present ability to perform the duties of a position, plus your potentiality to learn these duties. In other words, a civil service exam attempts to predict how successful you will be. Questions cover such a broad area that they cannot be as minute and detailed as school exam questions.

In the public service similar kinds of work, or positions, are grouped together in one "class." This process is known as *position-classification*. All the positions in a class are paid according to the salary range for that class. One class title covers all of these positions, and they are all tested by the same examination.

B. FOUR BASIC STEPS

1) Study the announcement

How, then, can you know what subjects to study? Our best answer is: "Learn as much as possible about the class of positions for which you've applied." The exam will test the knowledge, skills and abilities needed to do the work.

Your most valuable source of information about the position you want is the official exam announcement. This announcement lists the training and experience qualifications. Check these standards and apply only if you come reasonably close to meeting them.

The brief description of the position in the examination announcement offers some clues to the subjects which will be tested. Think about the job itself. Review the duties in your mind. Can you perform them, or are there some in which you are rusty? Fill in the blank spots in your preparation.

Many jurisdictions preview the written test in the exam announcement by including a section called "Knowledge and Abilities Required," "Scope of the Examination," or some similar heading. Here you will find out specifically what fields will be tested.

2) Review your own background

Once you learn in general what the position is all about, and what you need to know to do the work, ask yourself which subjects you already know fairly well and which need improvement. You may wonder whether to concentrate on improving your strong areas or on building some background in your fields of weakness. When the announcement has specified "some knowledge" or "considerable knowledge," or has used adjectives like "beginning principles of..." or "advanced ... methods," you can get a clue as to the number and difficulty of questions to be asked in any given field. More questions, and hence broader coverage, would be included for those subjects which are more important in the work. Now weigh your strengths and weaknesses against the job requirements and prepare accordingly.

3) Determine the level of the position

Another way to tell how intensively you should prepare is to understand the level of the job for which you are applying. Is it the entering level? In other words, is this the position in which beginners in a field of work are hired? Or is it an intermediate or advanced level? Sometimes this is indicated by such words as "Junior" or "Senior" in the class title. Other jurisdictions use Roman numerals to designate the level – Clerk I, Clerk II, for example. The word "Supervisor" sometimes appears in the title. If the level is not indicated by the title, check the description of duties. Will you be working under very close supervision, or will you have responsibility for independent decisions in this work?

4) Choose appropriate study materials

Now that you know the subjects to be examined and the relative amount of each subject to be covered, you can choose suitable study materials. For beginning level jobs, or even advanced ones, if you have a pronounced weakness in some aspect of your training, read a modern, standard textbook in that field. Be sure it is up to date and has general coverage. Such books are normally available at your library, and the librarian will be glad to help you locate one. For entry-level positions, questions of appropriate difficulty are chosen – neither highly advanced questions, nor those too simple. Such questions require careful thought but not advanced training.

If the position for which you are applying is technical or advanced, you will read more advanced, specialized material. If you are already familiar with the basic principles of your field, elementary textbooks would waste your time. Concentrate on advanced textbooks and technical periodicals. Think through the concepts and review difficult problems in your field.

These are all general sources. You can get more ideas on your own initiative, following these leads. For example, training manuals and publications of the government agency which employs workers in your field can be useful, particularly for technical and professional positions. A letter or visit to the government department involved may result in more specific study suggestions, and certainly will provide you with a more definite idea of the exact nature of the position you are seeking.

III. KINDS OF TESTS

Tests are used for purposes other than measuring knowledge and ability to perform specified duties. For some positions, it is equally important to test ability to make adjustments to new situations or to profit from training. In others, basic mental abilities not dependent on information are essential. Questions which test these things may not appear as pertinent to the duties of the position as those which test for knowledge and information. Yet they are often highly important parts of a fair examination. For very general questions, it is almost impossible to help you direct your study efforts. What we can do is to point out some of the more common of these general abilities needed in public service positions and describe some typical questions.

1) General information

Broad, general information has been found useful for predicting job success in some kinds of work. This is tested in a variety of ways, from vocabulary lists to questions about current events. Basic background in some field of work, such as sociology or economics, may be sampled in a group of questions. Often these are principles which have become familiar to most persons through exposure rather than through formal training. It is difficult to advise you how to study for these questions; being alert to the world around you is our best suggestion.

2) Verbal ability

An example of an ability needed in many positions is verbal or language ability. Verbal ability is, in brief, the ability to use and understand words. Vocabulary and grammar tests are typical measures of this ability. Reading comprehension or paragraph interpretation questions are common in many kinds of civil service tests. You are given a paragraph of written material and asked to find its central meaning.

3) Numerical ability

Number skills can be tested by the familiar arithmetic problem, by checking paired lists of numbers to see which are alike and which are different, or by interpreting charts and graphs. In the latter test, a graph may be printed in the test booklet which you are asked to use as the basis for answering questions.

4) Observation

A popular test for law-enforcement positions is the observation test. A picture is shown to you for several minutes, then taken away. Questions about the picture test your ability to observe both details and larger elements.

5) Following directions

In many positions in the public service, the employee must be able to carry out written instructions dependably and accurately. You may be given a chart with several columns, each column listing a variety of information. The questions require you to carry out directions involving the information given in the chart.

6) Skills and aptitudes

Performance tests effectively measure some manual skills and aptitudes. When the skill is one in which you are trained, such as typing or shorthand, you can practice. These tests are often very much like those given in business school or high school courses. For many of the other skills and aptitudes, however, no short-time preparation can be made. Skills and abilities natural to you or that you have developed throughout your lifetime are being tested.

Many of the general questions just described provide all the data needed to answer the questions and ask you to use your reasoning ability to find the answers. Your best preparation for these tests, as well as for tests of facts and ideas, is to be at your physical and mental best. You, no doubt, have your own methods of getting into an exam-taking mood and keeping "in shape." The next section lists some ideas on this subject.

IV. KINDS OF QUESTIONS

Only rarely is the "essay" question, which you answer in narrative form, used in civil service tests. Civil service tests are usually of the short-answer type. Full instructions for answering these questions will be given to you at the examination. But in case this is your first experience with short-answer questions and separate answer sheets, here is what you need to know:

1) Multiple-choice Questions

Most popular of the short-answer questions is the "multiple choice" or "best answer" question. It can be used, for example, to test for factual knowledge, ability to solve problems or judgment in meeting situations found at work.

A multiple-choice question is normally one of three types—
- It can begin with an incomplete statement followed by several possible endings. You are to find the one ending which *best* completes the statement, although some of the others may not be entirely wrong.
- It can also be a complete statement in the form of a question which is answered by choosing one of the statements listed.

- It can be in the form of a problem – again you select the best answer.

Here is an example of a multiple-choice question with a discussion which should give you some clues as to the method for choosing the right answer:

When an employee has a complaint about his assignment, the action which will *best* help him overcome his difficulty is to
- A. discuss his difficulty with his coworkers
- B. take the problem to the head of the organization
- C. take the problem to the person who gave him the assignment
- D. say nothing to anyone about his complaint

In answering this question, you should study each of the choices to find which is best. Consider choice "A" – Certainly an employee may discuss his complaint with fellow employees, but no change or improvement can result, and the complaint remains unresolved. Choice "B" is a poor choice since the head of the organization probably does not know what assignment you have been given, and taking your problem to him is known as "going over the head" of the supervisor. The supervisor, or person who made the assignment, is the person who can clarify it or correct any injustice. Choice "C" is, therefore, correct. To say nothing, as in choice "D," is unwise. Supervisors have and interest in knowing the problems employees are facing, and the employee is seeking a solution to his problem.

2) True/False Questions

The "true/false" or "right/wrong" form of question is sometimes used. Here a complete statement is given. Your job is to decide whether the statement is right or wrong.

SAMPLE: A roaming cell-phone call to a nearby city costs less than a non-roaming call to a distant city.

This statement is wrong, or false, since roaming calls are more expensive.

This is not a complete list of all possible question forms, although most of the others are variations of these common types. You will always get complete directions for answering questions. Be sure you understand *how* to mark your answers – ask questions until you do.

V. RECORDING YOUR ANSWERS

Computer terminals are used more and more today for many different kinds of exams.
For an examination with very few applicants, you may be told to record your answers in the test booklet itself. Separate answer sheets are much more common. If this separate answer sheet is to be scored by machine – and this is often the case – it is highly important that you mark your answers correctly in order to get credit.
An electronic scoring machine is often used in civil service offices because of the speed with which papers can be scored. Machine-scored answer sheets must be marked with a pencil, which will be given to you. This pencil has a high graphite content which responds to the electronic scoring machine. As a matter of fact, stray dots may register as answers, so do not let your pencil rest on the answer sheet while you are pondering the correct answer. Also, if your pencil lead breaks or is otherwise defective, ask for another.

Since the answer sheet will be dropped in a slot in the scoring machine, be careful not to bend the corners or get the paper crumpled.

The answer sheet normally has five vertical columns of numbers, with 30 numbers to a column. These numbers correspond to the question numbers in your test booklet. After each number, going across the page are four or five pairs of dotted lines. These short dotted lines have small letters or numbers above them. The first two pairs may also have a "T" or "F" above the letters. This indicates that the first two pairs only are to be used if the questions are of the true-false type. If the questions are multiple choice, disregard the "T" and "F" and pay attention only to the small letters or numbers.

Answer your questions in the manner of the sample that follows:

32. The largest city in the United States is
    A. Washington, D.C.
    B. New York City
    C. Chicago
    D. Detroit
    E. San Francisco

1) Choose the answer you think is best. (New York City is the largest, so "B" is correct.)
2) Find the row of dotted lines numbered the same as the question you are answering. (Find row number 32)
3) Find the pair of dotted lines corresponding to the answer. (Find the pair of lines under the mark "B.")
4) Make a solid black mark between the dotted lines.

VI. BEFORE THE TEST

Common sense will help you find procedures to follow to get ready for an examination. Too many of us, however, overlook these sensible measures. Indeed, nervousness and fatigue have been found to be the most serious reasons why applicants fail to do their best on civil service tests. Here is a list of reminders:

- Begin your preparation early – Don't wait until the last minute to go scurrying around for books and materials or to find out what the position is all about.
- Prepare continuously – An hour a night for a week is better than an all-night cram session. This has been definitely established. What is more, a night a week for a month will return better dividends than crowding your study into a shorter period of time.
- Locate the place of the exam – You have been sent a notice telling you when and where to report for the examination. If the location is in a different town or otherwise unfamiliar to you, it would be well to inquire the best route and learn something about the building.
- Relax the night before the test – Allow your mind to rest. Do not study at all that night. Plan some mild recreation or diversion; then go to bed early and get a good night's sleep.
- Get up early enough to make a leisurely trip to the place for the test – This way unforeseen events, traffic snarls, unfamiliar buildings, etc. will not upset you.
- Dress comfortably – A written test is not a fashion show. You will be known by number and not by name, so wear something comfortable.

- Leave excess paraphernalia at home – Shopping bags and odd bundles will get in your way. You need bring only the items mentioned in the official notice you received; usually everything you need is provided. Do not bring reference books to the exam. They will only confuse those last minutes and be taken away from you when in the test room.
- Arrive somewhat ahead of time – If because of transportation schedules you must get there very early, bring a newspaper or magazine to take your mind off yourself while waiting.
- Locate the examination room – When you have found the proper room, you will be directed to the seat or part of the room where you will sit. Sometimes you are given a sheet of instructions to read while you are waiting. Do not fill out any forms until you are told to do so; just read them and be prepared.
- Relax and prepare to listen to the instructions
- If you have any physical problem that may keep you from doing your best, be sure to tell the test administrator. If you are sick or in poor health, you really cannot do your best on the exam. You can come back and take the test some other time.

VII. AT THE TEST

The day of the test is here and you have the test booklet in your hand. The temptation to get going is very strong. Caution! There is more to success than knowing the right answers. You must know how to identify your papers and understand variations in the type of short-answer question used in this particular examination. Follow these suggestions for maximum results from your efforts:

1) Cooperate with the monitor

The test administrator has a duty to create a situation in which you can be as much at ease as possible. He will give instructions, tell you when to begin, check to see that you are marking your answer sheet correctly, and so on. He is not there to guard you, although he will see that your competitors do not take unfair advantage. He wants to help you do your best.

2) Listen to all instructions

Don't jump the gun! Wait until you understand all directions. In most civil service tests you get more time than you need to answer the questions. So don't be in a hurry. Read each word of instructions until you clearly understand the meaning. Study the examples, listen to all announcements and follow directions. Ask questions if you do not understand what to do.

3) Identify your papers

Civil service exams are usually identified by number only. You will be assigned a number; you must not put your name on your test papers. Be sure to copy your number correctly. Since more than one exam may be given, copy your exact examination title.

4) Plan your time

Unless you are told that a test is a "speed" or "rate of work" test, speed itself is usually not important. Time enough to answer all the questions will be provided, but this does not mean that you have all day. An overall time limit has been set. Divide the total time (in minutes) by the number of questions to determine the approximate time you have for each question.

5) Do not linger over difficult questions

If you come across a difficult question, mark it with a paper clip (useful to have along) and come back to it when you have been through the booklet. One caution if you do this – be sure to skip a number on your answer sheet as well. Check often to be sure that you have not lost your place and that you are marking in the row numbered the same as the question you are answering.

6) Read the questions

Be sure you know what the question asks! Many capable people are unsuccessful because they failed to *read* the questions correctly.

7) Answer all questions

Unless you have been instructed that a penalty will be deducted for incorrect answers, it is better to guess than to omit a question.

8) Speed tests

It is often better NOT to guess on speed tests. It has been found that on timed tests people are tempted to spend the last few seconds before time is called in marking answers at random – without even reading them – in the hope of picking up a few extra points. To discourage this practice, the instructions may warn you that your score will be "corrected" for guessing. That is, a penalty will be applied. The incorrect answers will be deducted from the correct ones, or some other penalty formula will be used.

9) Review your answers

If you finish before time is called, go back to the questions you guessed or omitted to give them further thought. Review other answers if you have time.

10) Return your test materials

If you are ready to leave before others have finished or time is called, take ALL your materials to the monitor and leave quietly. Never take any test material with you. The monitor can discover whose papers are not complete, and taking a test booklet may be grounds for disqualification.

VIII. EXAMINATION TECHNIQUES

1) Read the general instructions carefully. These are usually printed on the first page of the exam booklet. As a rule, these instructions refer to the timing of the examination; the fact that you should not start work until the signal and must stop work at a signal, etc. If there are any *special* instructions, such as a choice of questions to be answered, make sure that you note this instruction carefully.

2) When you are ready to start work on the examination, that is as soon as the signal has been given, read the instructions to each question booklet, underline any key words or phrases, such as *least, best, outline, describe* and the like. In this way you will tend to answer as requested rather than discover on reviewing your paper that you *listed without describing*, that you selected the *worst* choice rather than the *best* choice, etc.

3) If the examination is of the objective or multiple-choice type – that is, each question will also give a series of possible answers: A, B, C or D, and you are called upon to select the best answer and write the letter next to that answer on your answer paper – it is advisable to start answering each question in turn. There may be anywhere from 50 to 100 such questions in the three or four hours allotted and you can see how much time would be taken if you read through all the questions before beginning to answer any. Furthermore, if you come across a question or group of questions which you know would be difficult to answer, it would undoubtedly affect your handling of all the other questions.

4) If the examination is of the essay type and contains but a few questions, it is a moot point as to whether you should read all the questions before starting to answer any one. Of course, if you are given a choice – say five out of seven and the like – then it is essential to read all the questions so you can eliminate the two that are most difficult. If, however, you are asked to answer all the questions, there may be danger in trying to answer the easiest one first because you may find that you will spend too much time on it. The best technique is to answer the first question, then proceed to the second, etc.

5) Time your answers. Before the exam begins, write down the time it started, then add the time allowed for the examination and write down the time it must be completed, then divide the time available somewhat as follows:
    - If 3-1/2 hours are allowed, that would be 210 minutes. If you have 80 objective-type questions, that would be an average of 2-1/2 minutes per question. Allow yourself no more than 2 minutes per question, or a total of 160 minutes, which will permit about 50 minutes to review.
    - If for the time allotment of 210 minutes there are 7 essay questions to answer, that would average about 30 minutes a question. Give yourself only 25 minutes per question so that you have about 35 minutes to review.

6) The most important instruction is to *read each question* and make sure you know what is wanted. The second most important instruction is to *time yourself properly* so that you answer every question. The third most important instruction is to *answer every question*. Guess if you have to but include something for each question. Remember that you will receive no credit for a blank and will probably receive some credit if you write something in answer to an essay question. If you guess a letter – say "B" for a multiple-choice question – you may have guessed right. If you leave a blank as an answer to a multiple-choice question, the examiners may respect your feelings but it will not add a point to your score. Some exams may penalize you for wrong answers, so in such cases *only*, you may not want to guess unless you have some basis for your answer.

7) Suggestions
    a. Objective-type questions
        1. Examine the question booklet for proper sequence of pages and questions
        2. Read all instructions carefully
        3. Skip any question which seems too difficult; return to it after all other questions have been answered
        4. Apportion your time properly; do not spend too much time on any single question or group of questions

5. Note and underline key words – *all, most, fewest, least, best, worst, same, opposite,* etc.
6. Pay particular attention to negatives
7. Note unusual option, e.g., unduly long, short, complex, different or similar in content to the body of the question
8. Observe the use of "hedging" words – *probably, may, most likely,* etc.
9. Make sure that your answer is put next to the same number as the question
10. Do not second-guess unless you have good reason to believe the second answer is definitely more correct
11. Cross out original answer if you decide another answer is more accurate; do not erase until you are ready to hand your paper in
12. Answer all questions; guess unless instructed otherwise
13. Leave time for review

  b. Essay questions
1. Read each question carefully
2. Determine exactly what is wanted. Underline key words or phrases.
3. Decide on outline or paragraph answer
4. Include many different points and elements unless asked to develop any one or two points or elements
5. Show impartiality by giving pros and cons unless directed to select one side only
6. Make and write down any assumptions you find necessary to answer the questions
7. Watch your English, grammar, punctuation and choice of words
8. Time your answers; don't crowd material

8) Answering the essay question

Most essay questions can be answered by framing the specific response around several key words or ideas. Here are a few such key words or ideas:

M's: manpower, materials, methods, money, management
P's: purpose, program, policy, plan, procedure, practice, problems, pitfalls, personnel, public relations

  a. Six basic steps in handling problems:
1. Preliminary plan and background development
2. Collect information, data and facts
3. Analyze and interpret information, data and facts
4. Analyze and develop solutions as well as make recommendations
5. Prepare report and sell recommendations
6. Install recommendations and follow up effectiveness

  b. Pitfalls to avoid
1. *Taking things for granted* – A statement of the situation does not necessarily imply that each of the elements is necessarily true; for example, a complaint may be invalid and biased so that all that can be taken for granted is that a complaint has been registered

2. *Considering only one side of a situation* – Wherever possible, indicate several alternatives and then point out the reasons you selected the best one
3. *Failing to indicate follow up* – Whenever your answer indicates action on your part, make certain that you will take proper follow-up action to see how successful your recommendations, procedures or actions turn out to be
4. *Taking too long in answering any single question* – Remember to time your answers properly

IX. AFTER THE TEST

Scoring procedures differ in detail among civil service jurisdictions although the general principles are the same. Whether the papers are hand-scored or graded by machine we have described, they are nearly always graded by number. That is, the person who marks the paper knows only the number – never the name – of the applicant. Not until all the papers have been graded will they be matched with names. If other tests, such as training and experience or oral interview ratings have been given, scores will be combined. Different parts of the examination usually have different weights. For example, the written test might count 60 percent of the final grade, and a rating of training and experience 40 percent. In many jurisdictions, veterans will have a certain number of points added to their grades.

After the final grade has been determined, the names are placed in grade order and an eligible list is established. There are various methods for resolving ties between those who get the same final grade – probably the most common is to place first the name of the person whose application was received first. Job offers are made from the eligible list in the order the names appear on it. You will be notified of your grade and your rank as soon as all these computations have been made. This will be done as rapidly as possible.

People who are found to meet the requirements in the announcement are called "eligibles." Their names are put on a list of eligible candidates. An eligible's chances of getting a job depend on how high he stands on this list and how fast agencies are filling jobs from the list.

When a job is to be filled from a list of eligibles, the agency asks for the names of people on the list of eligibles for that job. When the civil service commission receives this request, it sends to the agency the names of the three people highest on this list. Or, if the job to be filled has specialized requirements, the office sends the agency the names of the top three persons who meet these requirements from the general list.

The appointing officer makes a choice from among the three people whose names were sent to him. If the selected person accepts the appointment, the names of the others are put back on the list to be considered for future openings.

That is the rule in hiring from all kinds of eligible lists, whether they are for typist, carpenter, chemist, or something else. For every vacancy, the appointing officer has his choice of any one of the top three eligibles on the list. This explains why the person whose name is on top of the list sometimes does not get an appointment when some of the persons lower on the list do. If the appointing officer chooses the second or third eligible, the No. 1 eligible does not get a job at once, but stays on the list until he is appointed or the list is terminated.

X. HOW TO PASS THE INTERVIEW TEST

The examination for which you applied requires an oral interview test. You have already taken the written test and you are now being called for the interview test – the final part of the formal examination.

You may think that it is not possible to prepare for an interview test and that there are no procedures to follow during an interview. Our purpose is to point out some things you can do in advance that will help you and some good rules to follow and pitfalls to avoid while you are being interviewed.

What is an interview supposed to test?

The written examination is designed to test the technical knowledge and competence of the candidate; the oral is designed to evaluate intangible qualities, not readily measured otherwise, and to establish a list showing the relative fitness of each candidate – as measured against his competitors – for the position sought. Scoring is not on the basis of "right" and "wrong," but on a sliding scale of values ranging from "not passable" to "outstanding." As a matter of fact, it is possible to achieve a relatively low score without a single "incorrect" answer because of evident weakness in the qualities being measured.

Occasionally, an examination may consist entirely of an oral test – either an individual or a group oral. In such cases, information is sought concerning the technical knowledges and abilities of the candidate, since there has been no written examination for this purpose. More commonly, however, an oral test is used to supplement a written examination.

Who conducts interviews?

The composition of oral boards varies among different jurisdictions. In nearly all, a representative of the personnel department serves as chairman. One of the members of the board may be a representative of the department in which the candidate would work. In some cases, "outside experts" are used, and, frequently, a businessman or some other representative of the general public is asked to serve. Labor and management or other special groups may be represented. The aim is to secure the services of experts in the appropriate field.

However the board is composed, it is a good idea (and not at all improper or unethical) to ascertain in advance of the interview who the members are and what groups they represent. When you are introduced to them, you will have some idea of their backgrounds and interests, and at least you will not stutter and stammer over their names.

What should be done before the interview?

While knowledge about the board members is useful and takes some of the surprise element out of the interview, there is other preparation which is more substantive. It *is* possible to prepare for an oral interview – in several ways:

1) Keep a copy of your application and review it carefully before the interview

This may be the only document before the oral board, and the starting point of the interview. Know what education and experience you have listed there, and the sequence and dates of all of it. Sometimes the board will ask you to review the highlights of your experience for them; you should not have to hem and haw doing it.

2) Study the class specification and the examination announcement

Usually, the oral board has one or both of these to guide them. The qualities, characteristics or knowledges required by the position sought are stated in these documents. They offer valuable clues as to the nature of the oral interview. For example, if the job involves supervisory responsibilities, the announcement will usually indicate that knowledge of modern supervisory methods and the qualifications of the candidate as a supervisor will be tested. If so, you can expect such questions, frequently in the form of a hypothetical situation which you are expected to solve. NEVER go into an oral without knowledge of the duties and responsibilities of the job you seek.

3) Think through each qualification required

Try to visualize the kind of questions you would ask if you were a board member. How well could you answer them? Try especially to appraise your own knowledge and background in each area, *measured against the job sought*, and identify any areas in which you are weak. Be critical and realistic – do not flatter yourself.

4) Do some general reading in areas in which you feel you may be weak

For example, if the job involves supervision and your past experience has NOT, some general reading in supervisory methods and practices, particularly in the field of human relations, might be useful. Do NOT study agency procedures or detailed manuals. The oral board will be testing your understanding and capacity, not your memory.

5) Get a good night's sleep and watch your general health and mental attitude

You will want a clear head at the interview. Take care of a cold or any other minor ailment, and of course, no hangovers.

What should be done on the day of the interview?

Now comes the day of the interview itself. Give yourself plenty of time to get there. Plan to arrive somewhat ahead of the scheduled time, particularly if your appointment is in the fore part of the day. If a previous candidate fails to appear, the board might be ready for you a bit early. By early afternoon an oral board is almost invariably behind schedule if there are many candidates, and you may have to wait. Take along a book or magazine to read, or your application to review, but leave any extraneous material in the waiting room when you go in for your interview. In any event, relax and compose yourself.

The matter of dress is important. The board is forming impressions about you – from your experience, your manners, your attitude, and your appearance. Give your personal appearance careful attention. Dress your best, but not your flashiest. Choose conservative, appropriate clothing, and be sure it is immaculate. This is a business interview, and your appearance should indicate that you regard it as such. Besides, being well groomed and properly dressed will help boost your confidence.

Sooner or later, someone will call your name and escort you into the interview room. *This is it.* From here on you are on your own. It is too late for any more preparation. But remember, you asked for this opportunity to prove your fitness, and you are here because your request was granted.

What happens when you go in?

The usual sequence of events will be as follows: The clerk (who is often the board stenographer) will introduce you to the chairman of the oral board, who will introduce you to the other members of the board. Acknowledge the introductions before you sit down. Do not be surprised if you find a microphone facing you or a stenotypist sitting by. Oral interviews are usually recorded in the event of an appeal or other review.

Usually the chairman of the board will open the interview by reviewing the highlights of your education and work experience from your application – primarily for the benefit of the other members of the board, as well as to get the material into the record. Do not interrupt or comment unless there is an error or significant misinterpretation; if that is the case, do not hesitate. But do not quibble about insignificant matters. Also, he will usually ask you some question about your education, experience or your present job – partly to get you to start talking and to establish the interviewing "rapport." He may start the actual questioning, or turn it over to one of the other members. Frequently, each member undertakes the questioning on a particular area, one in which he is perhaps most competent, so you can expect each member to participate in the examination. Because time is limited, you may also expect some rather abrupt switches in the direction the questioning takes, so do not be upset by it. Normally, a board member will not pursue a single line of questioning unless he discovers a particular strength or weakness.

After each member has participated, the chairman will usually ask whether any member has any further questions, then will ask you if you have anything you wish to add. Unless you are expecting this question, it may floor you. Worse, it may start you off on an extended, extemporaneous speech. The board is not usually seeking more information. The question is principally to offer you a last opportunity to present further qualifications or to indicate that you have nothing to add. So, if you feel that a significant qualification or characteristic has been overlooked, it is proper to point it out in a sentence or so. Do not compliment the board on the thoroughness of their examination – they have been sketchy, and you know it. If you wish, merely say, "No thank you, I have nothing further to add." This is a point where you can "talk yourself out" of a good impression or fail to present an important bit of information. Remember, *you close the interview yourself*.

The chairman will then say, "That is all, Mr. _____, thank you." Do not be startled; the interview is over, and quicker than you think. Thank him, gather your belongings and take your leave. Save your sigh of relief for the other side of the door.

How to put your best foot forward

Throughout this entire process, you may feel that the board individually and collectively is trying to pierce your defenses, seek out your hidden weaknesses and embarrass and confuse you. Actually, this is not true. They are obliged to make an appraisal of your qualifications for the job you are seeking, and they want to see you in your best light. Remember, they must interview all candidates and a non-cooperative candidate may become a failure in spite of their best efforts to bring out his qualifications. Here are 15 suggestions that will help you:

1) Be natural – Keep your attitude confident, not cocky

If you are not confident that you can do the job, do not expect the board to be. Do not apologize for your weaknesses, try to bring out your strong points. The board is interested in a positive, not negative, presentation. Cockiness will antagonize any board member and make him wonder if you are covering up a weakness by a false show of strength.

2) Get comfortable, but don't lounge or sprawl

Sit erectly but not stiffly. A careless posture may lead the board to conclude that you are careless in other things, or at least that you are not impressed by the importance of the occasion. Either conclusion is natural, even if incorrect. Do not fuss with your clothing, a pencil or an ashtray. Your hands may occasionally be useful to emphasize a point; do not let them become a point of distraction.

3) Do not wisecrack or make small talk

This is a serious situation, and your attitude should show that you consider it as such. Further, the time of the board is limited – they do not want to waste it, and neither should you.

4) Do not exaggerate your experience or abilities
In the first place, from information in the application or other interviews and sources, the board may know more about you than you think. Secondly, you probably will not get away with it. An experienced board is rather adept at spotting such a situation, so do not take the chance.

5) If you know a board member, do not make a point of it, yet do not hide it
Certainly you are not fooling him, and probably not the other members of the board. Do not try to take advantage of your acquaintanceship – it will probably do you little good.

6) Do not dominate the interview
Let the board do that. They will give you the clues – do not assume that you have to do all the talking. Realize that the board has a number of questions to ask you, and do not try to take up all the interview time by showing off your extensive knowledge of the answer to the first one.

7) Be attentive
You only have 20 minutes or so, and you should keep your attention at its sharpest throughout. When a member is addressing a problem or question to you, give him your undivided attention. Address your reply principally to him, but do not exclude the other board members.

8) Do not interrupt
A board member may be stating a problem for you to analyze. He will ask you a question when the time comes. Let him state the problem, and wait for the question.

9) Make sure you understand the question
Do not try to answer until you are sure what the question is. If it is not clear, restate it in your own words or ask the board member to clarify it for you. However, do not haggle about minor elements.

10) Reply promptly but not hastily
A common entry on oral board rating sheets is "candidate responded readily," or "candidate hesitated in replies." Respond as promptly and quickly as you can, but do not jump to a hasty, ill-considered answer.

11) Do not be peremptory in your answers
A brief answer is proper – but do not fire your answer back. That is a losing game from your point of view. The board member can probably ask questions much faster than you can answer them.

12) Do not try to create the answer you think the board member wants
He is interested in what kind of mind you have and how it works – not in playing games. Furthermore, he can usually spot this practice and will actually grade you down on it.

13) Do not switch sides in your reply merely to agree with a board member
Frequently, a member will take a contrary position merely to draw you out and to see if you are willing and able to defend your point of view. Do not start a debate, yet do not surrender a good position. If a position is worth taking, it is worth defending.

14) Do not be afraid to admit an error in judgment if you are shown to be wrong

The board knows that you are forced to reply without any opportunity for careful consideration. Your answer may be demonstrably wrong. If so, admit it and get on with the interview.

15) Do not dwell at length on your present job

The opening question may relate to your present assignment. Answer the question but do not go into an extended discussion. You are being examined for a *new* job, not your present one. As a matter of fact, try to phrase ALL your answers in terms of the job for which you are being examined.

Basis of Rating

Probably you will forget most of these "do's" and "don'ts" when you walk into the oral interview room. Even remembering them all will not ensure you a passing grade. Perhaps you did not have the qualifications in the first place. But remembering them will help you to put your best foot forward, without treading on the toes of the board members.

Rumor and popular opinion to the contrary notwithstanding, an oral board wants you to make the best appearance possible. They know you are under pressure – but they also want to see how you respond to it as a guide to what your reaction would be under the pressures of the job you seek. They will be influenced by the degree of poise you display, the personal traits you show and the manner in which you respond.

ABOUT THIS BOOK

This book contains tests divided into Examination Sections. Go through each test, answering every question in the margin. We have also attached a sample answer sheet at the back of the book that can be removed and used. At the end of each test look at the answer key and check your answers. On the ones you got wrong, look at the right answer choice and learn. Do not fill in the answers first. Do not memorize the questions and answers, but understand the answer and principles involved. On your test, the questions will likely be different from the samples. Questions are changed and new ones added. If you understand these past questions you should have success with any changes that arise. Tests may consist of several types of questions. We have additional books on each subject should more study be advisable or necessary for you. Finally, the more you study, the better prepared you will be. This book is intended to be the last thing you study before you walk into the examination room. Prior study of relevant texts is also recommended. NLC publishes some of these in our Fundamental Series. Knowledge and good sense are important factors in passing your exam. Good luck also helps. So now study this Passbook, absorb the material contained within and take that knowledge into the examination. Then do your best to pass that exam.

EXAMINATION SECTION

EXAMINATION SECTION
TEST 1

DIRECTIONS: Each question or incomplete statement is followed by several suggested answers or completions. Select the one that BEST answers the question or completes the statement. *PRINT THE LETTER OF THE CORRECT ANSWER IN THE SPACE AT THE RIGHT.*

1. Forcible touching is classified as a
   A. Class A Misdemeanor
   B. Class B Misdemeanor
   C. Class C Misdemeanor
   D. Felony

   1.____

2. Inciting to riot is classified as a
   A. Class B Misdemeanor
   B. Grand Felony
   C. Class A Misdemeanor
   D. Felony

   2.____

3. A misdemeanor is defined as an offense, other than a traffic infraction, for which a sentence to a term of imprisonment in excess of _____ day(s) may be imposed, but for which a sentence to a term of imprisonment in excess of _____ year(s) cannot be imposed.
   A. six; one
   B. five; one
   C. fifteen; two
   D. fifteen; one

   3.____

4. Fortune telling, falser personation and creating a hazard are all classified as
   A. felonies
   B. misdemeanors
   C. violations
   d. minor infractions

   4.____

5. A motorist, Jan, ran a traffic light at the intersection of Buffalo Avenue and Rochester Way. Jan is afraid that she has committed a misdemeanor because she was applying lipstick as she was driving and nearly hit a fire hydrant after she realized she blew the light.
   What is Jan guilty of committing?
   A. A traffic infraction, which is not a misdemeanor
   B. A traffic infraction, also known as a misdemeanor
   C. A Class A Misdemeanor
   D. A Class B Misdemeanor

   5.____

6. If James is sentenced to a period of probation, which of the following is MOST likely to accompany the sentence?
   A. The conditions of the sentence, including not leaving the state or abstaining from alcohol
   B. The address of James's probation officer and how to get there from James's home address
   C. The address of the judge presiding over James's probation hearing
   D. The jury instructions which were given to the jury in James's trial

   6.____

7. For a Class A Misdemeanor, other than sexual assault, what is the MAXIMUM period of probation?
   A. Two years   B. Three years   C. Four years   D. Five years

8. For a Class A Misdemeanor sexual assault, the period of probation is _____ years.
   A. four   B. five   C. six   D. seven

9. The conditions of probation or conditional discharge shall be determined by the
   A. jury
   B. parole officer
   C. court
   D. prosecuting attorney

10. When imposing a sentence of probation or conditional discharge, the court may consider restitution and require which of the following?
    A. The defendant avoid injurious habits
    B. Work in a respectable retail environment
    C. Study to become a nurse or other healthcare professional
    D. Participate in an alcohol or substance abuse program of the defendant's family's choosing

11. If Bill has been convicted of a traffic violation which caused the serious physical injury or death of another person, which of the following may the court require as a condition of probation?
    A. Anger management course
    B. Motor vehicle accident prevention course
    C. Defense driving course
    D. Motor skills and research methodology course

12. Unconditional discharge may be imposed for a felony as long as the court sets forth the
    A. actions the defendant has taken not to repeat his or her illicit behavior
    B. reasons for its actions
    C. skills or other licenses of the defendant
    D. other crimes the defendant is alleged to have committed

13. Pursuant to Article 65 of the New York Penal Law, as a condition of probation for sex offenders, the court may impose which of the following additional conditions?
    Reasonable limitation on
    A. food obtained from local grocery stores
    B. his or her use of the internet
    C. the amount of money expended on gaming devices
    D. extracurricular activities

14. Pursuant to Article 70 of the New York Penal Law, the court must inquire that parents of a minor committed to the Department of Corrections grant the minor the capacity to consent to
    A. routine dental treatment
    B. mental health treatment, but only if needed
    C. routine medical treatment, but only if required
    D. routine medical, dental, and mental health services and treatment

14._____

15. If a defendant is given a sentence of life imprisonment without parole, where will the defendant be committed?
    A. Custody of the City Department of Corrections
    B. Custody of the State Department of Corrections
    C. Custody of the State Department of Corrections and community supervisions for the remainder of the life of the defendant
    D. Rikers Island

15._____

16. A court sentence may run
    A. concurrently or consecutively
    B. concurrently or contemporaneously
    C. consecutively or respectively
    D. concurrently or coincidentally

16._____

17. Rich has been convicted of a felony murder of his cousin, Eric. While released on $5,000,000 bail, he is alleged to have murdered a shopkeeper in Albany. Rich is convicted of 25 years for the murder of Eric and 30 years for the murder of the shopkeeper. The sentences will run _____ for a total of _____ years incarceration.
    A. consecutively; 30
    B. consecutively; 55
    C. concurrently; 55
    D. contemporaneously; 30

17._____

Questions 18-19.

DIRECTIONS: Questions 18 and 19 are to be answered on the basis of the following information.

Paul and Amy have filed for divorce. Amy has been granted $450 per month in alimony, but Paul has not paid in over seven months. Amy has been living with her sister, Meredith, for over a year and because Paul has not paid Amy alimony, Amy has not been able to pay Meredith rent.

18. May Meredith petition the court to enforce the judgment against Paul?
    A. Yes, because Meredith is materially affected by Paul's nonpayment.
    B. Yes, because Meredith is Amy's sibling and thereby part of her nuclear family.
    C. No, because Amy has only been living with Meredith for a part of Paul's period of noncompliance with the court order.
    D. No.

18._____

19. A petition to enforce the judgment against Paul would need to be brought in which court?
    A. State of New York
    B. Supreme Court or a Court of Competent Jurisdiction
    C. Manhattan Family Court
    D. Criminal Court

20. During a support proceeding in family court, which of the following will MOST likely be accompanied to a sworn statement of net worth?
    A. Pay stubs from the year the individual earned the most, and the least, amount of money
    B. Tax return without any accompanying documentation
    C. W-2 tax and wage statements
    D. Current paycheck stub, most recently filed income tax returns, and the W-2 wage and income statements

Questions 21-22.

DIRECTIONS: Questions 21 and 22 are to be answered on the basis of the following information.

Candace filed for divorce from Jason last January. Jason and Candace have agreed to a support arrangement between themselves. Jason will pay Candace $300 per month, except during the summer months of June, July, and August, when Jason is temporarily out of work due to his occupation as a teaching paraprofessional.

21. What must Candace produce to the Court for approval?
    A. The agreement itself which must be reduced to writing
    B. Jason's bank statements, proving he can afford to pay $300 per month
    C. Jason's pay stubs, proving he is customarily out of work during the summer months
    D. The agreement is automatically approved given that the parties arranged the details themselves.

22. Who will approve the document Candace produces to the Court?
    A. The jury
    B. The attorney(s) representing Jason
    C. The court only
    D. The court or support magistrate

23. A summons was served on Jamal requiring him to appear for a family court proceeding involving his sister and father. Jamal failed to appear. The court may issue a(n) _____ directing that Jamal be arrested and brought before the court.
    A. indictment   B. subpoena   C. issue   D. warrant

24. With respect to the finding of the court and according to the New York Family Court Act, the effect of the issuance of a temporary order of protection is
    A. essentially a finding of guilt
    B. admission by the parties that the defendant will harm his or herself and others
    C. not a finding of wrongdoing
    D. a precursor to a felony conviction

24.____

25. Assume that a warrant is issued for Daniel in Richmond County. Where will Daniel be taken if he is taken into custody in Suffolk County?
    A. A family judge in Suffolk County
    B. A family judge in Richmond County
    C. A family judge in New York City
    D. The Supreme Court

25.____

KEY (CORRECT ANSWERS)

1.	A		11.	B
2.	C		12.	B
3.	D		13.	B
4.	B		14.	D
5.	A		15.	C
6.	A		16.	A
7.	B		17.	B
8.	C		18.	D
9.	C		19.	B
10.	A		20.	D

21. A
22. D
23. D
24. C
25. A

TEST 2

DIRECTIONS: Each question or incomplete statement is followed by several suggested answers or completions. Select the one that BEST answers the question or completes the statement. *PRINT THE LETTER OF THE CORRECT ANSWER IN THE SPACE AT THE RIGHT.*

1. Which of the following is a defendant the LEAST likely to hear when being brought before the court pursuant to a warrant?
   He or she will be
   A. informed of the contents of the petition
   B. given the opportunity to present witnesses
   C. advised of their right to counsel
   D. given the option of having the public hear the case

2. If the initial return of a summons or warrant is before a judge of the court, when support is an issue, the judge must make a(n) _____ order, either temporary or permanent with regard to support.
   A. reasonable   B. timely   C. immediate   D. seasoned

3. Kevin has petitioned the court for temporary child support for his daughter, Maddie, from his ex-wife Katie. Katie objects to any determination of child support even though Maddie lives with Kevin full time. Katie argues that Kevin makes more money than her and there is no outstanding emergency or other issue that warrants the need for child support.
   May the court make an order for temporary child support?
   A. No, because Kevin earns more than Katie.
   B. No, because there is no impending emergency or issue warranting support.
   C. Yes, because Maddie lives with Kevin.
   D. Yes, because the court may make an order for temporary support sufficient to meet the needs of the child without a showing of immediate need.

4. Dante is deemed an "eligible offender" because of his prior conviction of armed robbery. An eligible offender is an individual
   A. with a prior conviction
   B. with a prior conviction of a felony with a deadly weapon
   C. who has a prior conviction of an offense, but has not been convicted of more than once of a felony
   D. with at least one prior felony conviction

5. How many votes are required from the State Board of Parole to issue a certificate of good conduct for an eligible offender?
   _____ unanimous votes
   A. Two   B. Three   C. Five   D. Four

6. Jim is interested in obtaining a certificate of good conduct from the New York State Board of Parole after serving time for a Class C Felony.
What is the MINIMUM amount of time that must pass before the Parole Board can grant Jim a certificate of good conduct, assuming he satisfies all other requirements of the Board?
   A. One year
   B. Eighteen months
   C. Two years
   D. Three years

7. Leandra's Law specifies that no person shall operate a motor vehicle while impaired or otherwise intoxicated with a child aged _____ years or less as a passenger.
   A. twelve
   B. thirteen
   C. fifteen
   D. eighteen

8. Liam was convicted of driving under the influence of alcohol when he was nineteen in California, his home state. In an attempt to escape his license suspension of one year, he moved to New York to live with his aunt.
Is Liam's license still suspended?
   A. Yes, his license is suspended in California only
   B. Yes, his license is suspended in New York and California
   C. Yes, his license is suspended in all states
   D. No

9. An adult driving under the combination of drugs and alcohol for the first time will MOST likely be convicted of a
   A. traffic infraction
   B. sanction offense
   C. misdemeanor
   D. felony

10. James has been hired as a marketing assistant for a local pharmaceutical company. After he received his offer letter from the Human Resources Department with his starting salary and start date, he received a call from Sylvia, the HR Coordinator. She informed James that a mistake had been made and the company did not realize James had a criminal record. She rescinded the employment offer and apologized to James for the inconvenience.
Did the company violate any law?
   A. No, the company is permitted to rescind the offer since James is a felon
   B. No, the company informed James of the situation before he started his employment
   C. Yes, the company should have completed his background search prior to sending his offer of employment
   D. Yes

11. Before Daniel started law school, he became a licensed HVAC technician working for his father's air conditioning repair business. After law school, he became a licensed attorney. Daniel also owns a handgun for which he has a permit. Which of the following are considered "licenses" under the New York Corrections Law Article 23-a?
   A. HVAC license only
   B. HVAC and Bar licenses only
   C. HVAC and Firearm licenses only
   D. HVAC, Bar and Firearm licenses

12. When Marissa was 19, she began working for a local accountant, Bill. After one year as an intern, she began to steal cash and other gifts Bill received from his clients. Bill reported her to authorities and she was convicted of larceny. Seven years later, Marissa is denied employment as an accountant with a local CPA firm.
    Why is this permitted under the New York Corrections Law?
    A. There is a direct relationship between the offense she committed and the employment she is seeking.
    B. Denial of employment is only permitted after ten years has passed since the conviction, not seven years.
    C. Marissa was not a minor when she committed the crime.
    D. The CPA firm is not permitted to deny Marissa employment in this situation.

13. Once a child custody determination has been decided, it is conclusive unless and until the
    A. parents move out of state
    B. child moves out of state with one of the parents
    C. order is modified or changed
    D. judge nullifies the order due to noncompliance

14. When Bob and Sharon were dating, they lived in Connecticut and moved to Westchester County after they got married. They had their son, Jayden, soon after and when Jayden turned six years old, Bob and Sharon divorced. Bob moved back to Connecticut and has petitioned the court for full legal and physical custody of Jayden. The child custody determination hearings have started in New York and Bob would like his sister, Michelle, to testify on his behalf at the hearing. Michelle lives in Connecticut.
    May Bob's sister testify?
    A. No
    B. No, because she lives in Connecticut
    C. Yes, even though she lives in Connecticut
    D. Yes, because she is a material witness to Bob and Sharon's marriage

15. A private placement adoption is MOST accurately defined as any adoption
    A. of a minor other than that placed by an authorized agency
    B. organized by three or more parties
    C. of a minor organized directly by the parties of the adoptee child
    D. of a minor other than that placed by a government agency

16. James wants to adopt his stepdaughter, Stephanie, so that he can include her in his will. James is still married to Stephanie's mother, Diane.
    May James adopt Stephanie?
    A. It cannot be determined because it is not known if Stephanie is a minor.
    B. Yes, because James has a legitimate reason for adopting Stephanie.
    C. No, because James requires Diane's signature or consent to adopt Stephanie.
    D. No, because James cannot adopt Stephanie for the purpose of inheritance or support rights.

17. Which of the following individuals will be entitled to notice of adoption pursuant to the New York Domestic Relations Law?
    A. A person determined by a court to be the father of the child
    B. The great-aunt of the child
    C. The doctor, midwife, or other person who delivered the child
    D. The maternal grandfather of the child

    17.____

18. Grounds for divorce in New York include all of the following EXCEPT
    A. Cruel and inhuman treatment of the plaintiff by the defendant
    B. Abandonment of the plaintiff for a period of one or more years
    C. Confinement of the defendant in prison for a period of three or more consecutive years after the marriage of the plaintiff and defendant
    D. The dissolution of the common law marriage between the plaintiff and defendant

    18.____

Questions 19-20.

DIRECTIONS: Questions 19 and 20 are to be answered on the basis of the following information.

Amanda wants to file for divorce from Todd on the grounds of adultery. Todd carried on an affair with Amanda's co-worker, Rebecca, nearly six years ago. When Amanda discovered the affair six years ago, she immediately moved out.

19. Will Amanda's petition for divorce be granted?
    A. Yes, because adultery is a ground for divorce in the State of New York.
    B. No, because the affair was forgiven.
    C. No, because Amanda allowed Todd to have an affair and implicitly forgave him by living with him at the time the affair began.
    D. No, because Amanda's petition for divorce was not commenced within five years after the discovery of the affair.

    19.____

20. Does Amanda have the right to a trial by jury on the issues concerning the grounds for granting her divorce from Todd?
    A. No, because the adulterous affair is settled as fact
    B. No, because the affair is presumed to have ended and/or become immaterial once the divorce petition is filed
    C. No, because there is no right to a trial by jury for divorce cases
    D. Yes, because there is a right to trial by jury of the issues of the grounds for divorce.

    20.____

21. According to the New York Criminal Procedure Law, the prosecution of a petty offense must be commenced within _____ year(s).
    A. one   B. two   C. three   D. four

    21.____

22. According to the New York Criminal Procedure Law, the prosecution for a misdemeanor must be commenced within _____ year(s).
    A. one   B. two   C. three   D. four

    22.____

23. Joel, the treasurer for ABC Limited, Inc., has been stealing from the company for approximately three years. The CEO of ABC Limited, Billy, discovered the larceny nearly two years ago. Billy fired Joel but never brought charges for the theft.
    Will Billy be able to prosecute Joel for larceny?
    A. Yes, because prosecution for larceny committed by a person in violation of a fiduciary duty may be commenced within three years
    B. Yes, because prosecution for larceny committed by a person in violation of a fiduciary duty may be commenced within two years
    C. No, because prosecution for larceny committed by a person in violation of a fiduciary duty must commence within one year
    D. No.

24. After a criminal action is commenced, the defendant is entitled to a _____ trial.
    A. deliberate   B. quick   C. thorough   D. speedy

25. Must the court furnish a defendant with a copy of the felony complaint during arraignment?
    A. No, because a court may furnish this information but is not required to
    B. No, because a court must furnish the complaint before trial but not at arraignment
    C. No, because the court must determine whether the defendant is to be held for grand jury
    E. Yes

KEY (CORRECT ANSWERS)

1.	D		11.	B
2.	C		12.	A
3.	D		13.	C
4.	C		14.	C
5.	B		15.	A
6.	D		16.	D
7.	C		17.	A
8.	A		18.	D
9.	C		19.	D
10.	D		20.	D

21. A
22. B
23. D
24. D
25. D

TEST 3

DIRECTIONS: Each question or incomplete statement is followed by several suggested answers or completions. Select the one that BEST answers the question or completes the statement. *PRINT THE LETTER OF THE CORRECT ANSWER IN THE SPACE AT THE RIGHT.*

1. Aggravated criminal contempt, aggravated family offense, and absconding from a community treatment facility are classified as 1.____
   A. E Felonies
   B. Violent Felonies
   C. Misdemeanors
   D. Felonies

2. Aggravated harassment in the second degree and arson in the fifth degree are examples of 2.____
   A. Felonies
   B. Misdemeanors
   C. A Misdemeanors
   D. Violent Felonies

3. Murder in the first degree will always be classified as a(n) 3.____
   A. Misdemeanor
   B. E Felony
   C. Felony
   D. Minor Felony

4. A "child born out of wedlock" is 4.____
   A. any child of marriage unless dissolved
   B. any children born after the parents are married
   C. a child born after the marriage license is obtained, but before the parents are legally married
   D. any children born between two consenting adults

5. The social welfare law maintains that in the case of neglect or inability of the parents to provide for the support and education of the child, the child is supported by the 5.____
   A. next closest kin to the mother
   B. next closest kin to the father
   C. child welfare agency of the state
   D. county, city, or town chargeable under the provision of the social welfare law

6. The district attorney who conducts a hearing upon a felony complaint represents, or hears, the case on behalf of the 6.____
   A. county   B. city   C. people   D. government

7. If after a hearing on a felony complaint there is a reasonable cause to believe that a defendant committed an offense that was not a felony, the court may 7.____
   A. reduce the charge but keep the felony charge on record
   B. keep the felony charge on record until the defendant is proven innocent of the lesser crime
   C. reduce the charge to one for such non-felony offense
   D. release the defendant on his or her own recognizance

8. May a court order the removal of an action that begins in criminal court to family court?
   A. Yes, but only if the court states on record the factors upon which the determination is based
   B. Yes, but only if there are two related parties at issue
   C. Yes, but only if the complaining party consents to such a removal
   D. Yes, but only justice is better served if the case were removed to family court

9. Proceedings to establish paternity may be originated in which court? The court in the
   A. county where the mother or child resides or in the county where the putative father resides or is found
   B. city where the birth father lives
   C. county where the mother lives
   D. county where the mother birthed the child

10. If a juvenile offender defendant waives a hearing upon a felony complaint, the court must order that the defendant be held for
    A. the action of the grand jury
    B. capacity hearings
    C. guardianship determination
    D. the results of paternity

11. Bail is defined as
    A. cash or deposit
    B. deposit or bail
    C. cash or bail
    D. bail or cash

12. For the purposes recognizance, bail and commitment, an "obliger" is MOST appropriately defined as the
    A. defendant
    B. person who executes the bail bond on behalf of the defendant, assuming the undertaking
    C. co-defendant
    D. person who signs a contract indicating that they intend to post bail bond in the future

13. An appearance bond is a bail bond in which the only obligor is the
    A. defendant or principal
    B. property secured therewith
    C. defendant's co-conspirators, if any
    D. contract of appearance of the defendant

Questions 14-15.

DIRECTIONS: Questions 14 and 15 are to be answered on the basis of the following information.

Ed's mother has posted bail in the amount of $250,000 for Ed's release after he was charged with aggravated assault. The court imposed the condition that Ed appear for subsequent hearings related to the charges. Ed failed to appear for the second hearing before Judge O'Connor, who then issued a warrant for his arrest. Ed claimed his mother became gravely ill which is why he did not appear for his hearing.

14. What is the effect of Ed's failure to appear on the bail previously posted? 14.____
The bail is
 A. unequivocally forfeited.
 B. generally forfeited, unless the court finds Ed had sufficient excuse for missing his appearance.
 C. reduced given the nature of Ed's mother's health condition.
 D. forfeited unless Ed's mother can produce a doctor's note.

15. Assume that the bail has been forfeited. The local criminal must pay the forfeited bail to the 15.____
 A. local village justice
 B. treasurer or other financial officer if it is a city court or the state comptroller if it is a town or village court
 C. chief justice directly
 D. treasurer of the junior congressional member of the State of New York

16. What does Leandra's Law prohibit? 16.____
 A. Driving while intoxicated with a person less than 15 years of age as a passenger in the vehicle
 B. Driving while under the influence of alcohol with other passengers in the vehicle
 C. Driving while under the influence of drugs or alcohol with a passenger less than 12 years of age in the vehicle
 D. Driving while intoxicated

17. An elderly gentleman, Dave, was assaulted at his 70th birthday celebration by another elderly man, Frank, who is ten years younger than Dave. Dave suffered various minor injuries. 17.____
What is the MOST appropriate charge against Frank?
 A. Assault 3   B. Assault 2
 C. Harassment   D. Violent misdemeanor

18. According to the New York Civil Practice Law and Rules, when a defendant has failed to appear, plead, or proceed to trial of an action, what is the MOST appropriate remedy for a plaintiff? 18.____
 A. Resume judgment   B. Dismissal action
 C. Default judgment   D. Increase in charge

19. The party responsible for adopting rules of the courts including the preparation and publication of court calendars of the unified court system is the
    A. chief justice of the Civil Courts
    B. chief administrator of the courts
    C. comptroller of the currency
    D. bailiff of the unified court system

20. Katie sues Terry for breach of contract after Terry failed to appear for Katie's baby shower and deliver food as the contracted caterer. Terry filed a cross-claim against Samuel, whom she hired to drive her to the venue of Katie's shower. Terry alleges that because Samuel never picked her up as agreed upon, she failed to perform the catering contract for Katie.
    The action to join the claims is also known as
    A. correction of claims
    B. severance of claims
    C. joinder of claims
    D. class action

21. Generally, when actions involving a common question of law or fact are pending before the court, the court may order the actions be _____ to avoid unnecessary costs or delay.
    A. combined
    B. categorized
    C. classified
    D. consolidated

22. Justice O'Connor has ordered that certain claims in an action before the court be heard separately, or severed, from one another.
    Who is now responsible for determining the order of when each of the newly severed claims are heard?
    A. The chief justice, if not Justice O'Connor
    B. The constable
    C. The court
    D. The attorneys of record

23. Which of the following is a prerequisite to the filing of a class action?
    A. The class is so numerous that joinder of all members is impracticable.
    B. The attorneys for each class member approves the joinder of the class.
    C. Less than 500 persons embody the entire class.
    D. The class acts as a whole and accept the settlement paid as a lump sum.

24. The order permitting a class action shall do which of the following?
    A. Describe the class
    B. Set out the demand for the class
    C. Name the attorneys of record
    D. Detail the action generally

25. A class action cannot be dismissed, discontinued, or compromised without the
    A. consent of the attorneys of record
    B. approval of the court
    C. approval of the class
    D. approval of the court after a full hearing on the merits of the defense

KEY (CORRECT ANSWERS)

1.	D		11.	C
2.	B		12.	B
3.	C		13.	A
4.	B		14.	B
5.	D		15.	B
6.	C		16.	A
7.	C		17.	B
8.	A		18.	C
9.	A		19.	B
10.	A		20.	C

21. D
22. C
23. A
24. A
25. B

TEST 4

DIRECTIONS: Each question or incomplete statement is followed by several suggested answers or completions. Select the one that BEST answers the question or completes the statement. *PRINT THE LETTER OF THE CORRECT ANSWER IN THE SPACE AT THE RIGHT.*

1. During a criminal trial, where an error or other legal defect in the proceedings occurs that prejudices the defendant, the court must declare a _____ upon motion of the defendant.
   A. hung jury
   B. recantation
   C. mistrial
   D. error of motion

   1.____

2. Which party can file a motion for mistrial if it is physically impossible to proceed with the trial in conformity with the law?
   A. Defendant
   B. Plaintiff
   C. The court
   D. All of the above

   2.____

3. After issuing a trial order of dismissal which has the effect of dismissing the entire indictment, the court does which of the following immediately?
   A. Discharge the defendant from custody or exonerate the bail.
   B. Notify the defendant's next of kin
   C. Notify the complaining witness and/or victim of the dismissal
   D. Arrange for a possible appeal from the plaintiff and/or the people

   3.____

4. Generally, when the court has imposed a sentence of imprisonment, when is the last time the sentence can be changed, suspended, or interrupted?
   A. Before the sentence has commenced
   B. After the sentence has been served
   C. After the arraignment, but before the conclusion of the trial
   D. After the instructions on the charge(s) are read to the jury

   4.____

5. Judge Smith rendered a verdict in a criminal case in Essex County. However, the court did not have jurisdiction over the case. The PROPER remedy is
   A. dismissal
   B. hung jury
   C. mistrial
   D. vacate judgment

   5.____

6. The court may vacate a judgment, upon motion of the defendant, for which of the following grounds?
   A. The judgment was procured by duress.
   B. The material evidence at trial was true, but presented in a way that painted the defendant in a negative light.
   C. Material evidence was obtained for trial via search warrant or other lawful device.
   D. All of the above

   6.____

7. Rachel, a licensed eighth grade teacher, was recently convicted of felony larceny. Who must be notified of Rachel's felony conviction?
   A. Rachel's next of kin
   B. The New York Comptroller, who must garnish Rachel's pay
   C. The Department of Education
   D. The Parole Board of New York

8. Jamal knowingly filed a false financing statement for his contractor business, indicating that he owes more money than he actually does to his bank lender. Jamal was convicted of intentionally filing a false financing statement under the Uniform Commercial Code (UCC).
   Who must be notified of Jamal's conviction?
   A. The Office of the UCC
   B. The New York Secretary of State
   C. The Chief Justice
   D. The Parole Board of New York

9. During jury selection, Dawn's lawyer did not object to any potential jurors. Once the trial began, Dawn's attorney raised the objection that juror number 3, Richard, may be biased against Dawn.
   What is the MOST appropriate response to Dawn's attorney's objection?
   A. A challenge to the jury panel must be made before the selection of the jury commences, therefore overruled
   B. A challenge to the jury panel must be made before the selection of the jury ends, therefore overruled
   C. A challenge to the jury panel must be made before the selection of the jury commences, therefore accepted
   D. Sustained

10. A criminal trial jury consists of not less than _____ members.
    A. fourteen   B. nine   C. six   D. twelve

11. Pursuant to Article 270 of the New York Criminal Procedure Law, either party may examine prospective jurors regarding their qualifications to serve as jurors. However, the court cannot allow the questioning to
    A. become repetitious, irrelevant, or involve questioning of a juror's knowledge of the rules of law
    B. reduce to questioning of the individual's family history or other background
    C. involve asking the prospective juror about his prior service on a jury
    D. contain questions that are relevant to the case, but asked in a rude or belittling manner

12. How many peremptory challenges may either side exercise during jury selection?
    A. One   B. Two
    C. Three   D. Dependent on the type of case

13. A challenge for cause of a prospective juror which is not made before he is sworn as a trial juror shall be deemed to be
    A. accepted   B. rebuked   C. waived   D. refuted

14. According to Section 270.16 of the New York Criminal Procedure Law, the examination of prospective jurors by either party is permitted to take place outside the presence of other prospective jurors for which type of case?
    A. Matrimonial cases, involving the adoption of a stepchild or adopted child
    B. Surrogates cases, involving complicated estates
    C. Capital cases, in which the crime charged may be punishable by death
    D. All such cases as long as the defense moves first

15. A peremptory challenge is defined as a(n)
    A. objection to a prospective juror for which no reason need be assigned
    B. objection to a prospective juror for which there must be a reason assigned
    C. objection to a prospective juror for justified cause
    D. trial objection

16. At what point in a trial is the jury provided with general instructions concerning its basic functions, duties, and conduct?
    After the jury has been sworn _____ opening address.
    A. but before the people's
    B. and after the people's
    C. but before the defense's
    D. and after the defense's

17. Pursuant to Section 270.45 of the New York Criminal Procedure Law, the court may in its discretion either permit a jury to _____ during recesses and/or adjournments or direct that they be continuously kept together during such periods under the supervision of an appropriate public servant.
    A. not communicate with one another
    B. not make eye contact with one another
    C. refrain from using their mobile phones
    D. separate

18. If a defendant pleads not responsible by reason of mental disease or defect, the court will ask him or her which of the following?
    A. About the offense or offenses charged in the indictment
    B. Family background
    C. Feelings or mental state at the time of the hearing
    D. Additional information not previously asked by counsel

19. Assuming the same facts as Question 18, by answering the questions posed by the court, the defendant has effectively
    A. lost his right to appeal by waiver
    B. waived his or her right to not be compelled to incriminate him or herself
    C. harmed him or herself
    D. waived his or her rights under the Second Amendment

20. Before accepting a plea of not responsible by reason of mental disease or defect, the court must find and state which of the following on record in detail?
    A. That the affirmative defense of lack of criminal responsibility by reason of mental disease or defect would be proven by the defendant at trial by a preponderance of the evidence
    B. That the defendant entered the plea under duress
    C. That the court is satisfied the defendant has been diagnosed with a generally accepted mental disease
    D. That the defendant can speak for himself

21. Intermittent imprisonment is defined as
    A. revocable sentence of imprisonment to be served on days or during certain periods of days, or both, specified by the court
    B. irrevocable sentence of imprisonment to be served part time
    C. revocable sentence of imprisonment to be served on weekends only
    D. another form of irrevocable release based on one's own recognizance

22. If John is currently serving an intermittent sentence of imprisonment and is then sentenced to a definite sentence of three years, when will he begin his definite sentence?
    A. After the conclusion of his intermittent sentence
    B. After a hearing of the court to determine which sentence takes priority
    C. After thirty days
    D. Immediately

23. Burglary in the first, second, and third degree is classified as a
    A. misdemeanor
    B. minor infraction
    C. felony
    D. subordinate crime

24. The crime of conspiracy is
    A. always classified as a felony
    B. always classified as a misdemeanor
    C. sometimes classified as a felony, but in other instances classified as a misdemeanor
    D. not a crime

25. The criminal sale of a firearm is
    A. always classified as a felony
    B. always classified as a violent felony
    C. sometimes classified as a felony, but in other instances classified as a misdemeanor
    D. not a crime if there is no buyer

KEY (CORRECT ANSWERS)

1. C
2. D
3. A
4. A
5. D

6. A
7. C
8. B
9. A
10. D

11. A
12. D
13. C
14. C
15. A

16. A
17. D
18. A
19. B
20. A

21. A
22. D
23. C
24. C
25. D

EXAMINATION SECTION
TEST 1

DIRECTIONS: Each question or incomplete statement is followed by several suggested answers or completions. Select the one that BEST answers the question or completes the statement. *PRINT THE LETTER OF THE CORRECT ANSWER IN THE SPACE AT THE RIGHT.*

Questions 1-5.

DIRECTIONS: Questions 1 through 5 are to be answered on the basis of the following fact pattern.

Bill initiated a lawsuit against his landlord, Amy, last year. Bill claims Amy did not upkeep common areas in the four-apartment building where Bill resides. These common areas include the hallway, entryway, and parking lot of the building. Bill is not represented by an attorney, but Amy is represented by Maureen. The parties have failed to settle the matter outside of court. Bill, Amy, and Maureen are ready to move forward with court proceedings.

1. The magistrate judge sets the pre-trial conference between the parties for March 30 at 9:30 A.M. The parties required to attend the pretrial conference are
    A. Maureen, Bill, and the judge
    B. the judge only
    C. Bill and Amy
    D. Bill, Amy, and Maureen

    1._____

2. During the pre-trial conference, the judge wants the parties to stipulate to as many issues as possible before trial. The judge instructs the parties to focus on undisputed facts. An example of a stipulation would be:
    A. Both parties agree the parking lot is not a common area
    B. Maureen files a motion to vacate
    C. Bill wants to expedite the case and start trial the following Monday]
    D. Amy files a counterclaim against Bill for failure to pay rent on time

    2._____

3. A pre-trial conference is attended by the required parties if the case does not settle before trial. However, a pre-trial conference cannot be set until
    A. the jury is selected
    B. the attorneys have entered appearances
    C. initial pleadings, including the complaint and answer, have been filed
    D. the court clerk is selected

    3._____

4. Which deadline is MOST likely to be set by the judge during the pre-trial conference?
    The deadline
    A. to decide which juror will serve as foreperson
    B. to decide which courthouse the trial will take place
    C. for all discovery to be completed
    D. for the judge to select a law clerk to transcribe court proceedings

    4._____

5. Bill will be appearing as a 5.____
   A. defendant
   B. pro se litigant
   C. respondent
   D. en banc party

Questions 6-9.

DIRECTIONS: Questions 6 through 9 are to be answered on the basis of the following fact pattern.

Adam, Barbara, Cameron, and David appear for jury duty on June 15. Adam and Barbara have each served on a trial before; Adam served on a criminal trial while Barbara served on a civil trial. The trial Adam served on lasted three months, and he would prefer not to serve on a trial ever again. Cameron and David have never served on a trial before and are unsure of what to expect.

6. While prospective jurors wait to be called by the clerk, Adam and Cameron 6.____
   spark up a conversation. Adam tells Cameron that if he were selected to be a juror Cameron may be isolated from his family and friends for weeks.
   What is Adam referring to?
   A. Ex-parte communications, which prohibit jurors from speaking with anyone else during the trial
   B. Voir dire, which may require one to be questioned in judge's chambers about past dealings
   C. Jury sequestration or juror isolation from the public to prevent contact with outside influences
   D. Individual depositions of jurors prior to the start of a trial

7. Barbara overhears the conversation between Adam and Cameron and 7.____
   interjects. She explains that not all juries operate the same way. She explains that in the middle of the trial in which she served, the defendant filed a motion requesting a bench trial.
   A bench trial is a trial without a
   A. plaintiff's attorney
   B. jury
   C. defendant's attorney
   D. bailiff

8. The court's clerk finally begins jury selection. He or she calls how many jurors 8.____
   from the jury selection list?
   A. 9   B. 6   C. 10   D. 12

9. Cameron and David are selected and take a seat in the jury box. The judge 9.____
   provides an overview of the case and tells the prospective jurors that the case involves armed robbery. As a teenager, David was mugged at gunpoint while walking home from school. He raises his hand and tells the judge he may be biased in the trial because of his personal experience.
   The defendant's attorney will ask that David be excused
   A. with good reason
   B. for cause
   C. without prejudice
   D. with prejudice

3 (#1)

10. Which of the following does NOT occur during the judge's charge to the jury? 10.____
    A. A discussion of the standard of proof jurors should apply to the case
    B. A reminder that opening and closing arguments are considered evidence
    C. A note that jurors should base their conclusions on the evidence presented at trial
    D. A reminder that jurors are required to adhere to the relevant laws in rendering a verdict

11. Which of the following does the court reporter NOT record 11.____
    A. testimony of the witnesses
    B. objections made by the attorneys
    C. the judge's respective rulings of objections
    D. ex-parte communications

Questions 12-16.

DIRECTIONS: Questions 12 through 16 are to be answered on the basis of the following fact pattern.

Michael is accused of felony theft of an automobile. The vehicle was taken from an 18-unit apartment building parking lot sometime during the night of August 15. The vehicle was driven for approximately five miles before the driver crashed it into a parked car. The driver fled the scene. The owner of the vehicle, Jeffrey, was asleep in his apartment during the time the vehicle was stolen. Michael and Jeffrey are represented by counsel.

12. Given the charge of felony theft of an automobile, Michael now faces how long a term of incarceration? 12.____
    A. One year or more   B. One year or less
    C. Six months   D. Five years or more

13. During Jeffrey's testimony, one of the jurors, Samantha, realizes she was in 13.____
    the building where the car was stolen on the night of the theft. She was sleeping over her sister's apartment for the night and remembers seeing a bright blue Porsche – Jeffrey's car – in the parking lot before bed. She immediately informs the bailiff who tells the judge.
    How will the judge MOST likely move forward in the case?
    A. Declare a mistrial
    B. Acquit Michael of all charges
    C. Excuse the juror and replace here with an alternate juror and continue the trial
    D. Demand the attorneys in the case submit post-hearing briefs on the issue

14. In open court, the judge asks Samantha details about why she was in the 14.____
    apartment at the time Michael allegedly stole Jeffrey's car and what, if anything, she remembers about that night. Samantha says she did not see or hear anything suspicious, but does remember Michael being in the apartment building in one of the common areas. Michael's attorney files a motion for a mistrial after Samantha's testimony to the court. Why?

A. Samantha's testimony has substantially prejudiced the other jurors who heard Michael was in the building on the night of the theft.
   B. There is not enough substantive evidence to continue the trial against Michael.
   C. Samantha should have been removed as a juror at the beginning of the trial.
   D. The case must be filed in the court closest to where the car was found, not where it was allegedly taken.

15. If the judge declares a mistrial, what effect would that determination have on the jury verdict?
   A. No effect; the jury must still render a decision on the merits
   B. The jury need only to determine damages.
   C. The jury does not need to render a verdict.
   D. Only six jurors need to serve after the judge declares a mistrial.

16. After all evidence has been presented, it is clear Michael did not commit the crime. Michael was in another state at the time of the theft and could not have committed felony theft of Jeffrey's automobile. Before the case is submitted to a jury, Michael's attorney submits a motion that argues no reasonable jury could find for Jeffrey. Michael's attorney asks the judge to instruct the jury to find Michael not guilty.
   Michael's attorney is requesting a(n) _____, because Michael clearly did not commit the crime.
   A. reduced charge
   B. substitute charge
   C. acquittal
   D. directed verdict

17. During the direct examination of one of the plaintiff's witnesses, the defendant's attorney objects. Defendant's attorney believes opposing counsel asked a leading question. The judge sustains defendant's objection.
   How must plaintiff's counsel proceed?
   A. The witness may answer the question as asked.
   B. Plaintiff's counsel must re-phrase the question in a proper form or ask another question.
   C. Plaintiff's counsel must stop his or her line of questioning completely.
   D. The witness may step down.

18. An expert is permitted to
   A. review the plaintiff's evidence, draw a reasonable conclusion, and give testimony to that effect
   B. review the defendant's evidence, draw a reasonable conclusion, and submit his or her opinion in writing to the judge
   C. give his or her opinion based on the facts in evidence and provide the reasoning for that opinion
   D. provide an opinion in open court

19. Which party, as a matter of right, is entitled to a rebuttal in closing arguments?
    A. The plaintiff
    B. The defense
    C. The defense, but only after the plaintiff has given their closing argument
    D. The defense, but only if the plaintiff waives their right to make a closing argument

20. When a jury cannot agree on a verdict, a(n) _____ occurs and the result is a(n) _____.
    A. mistrial; acquittal
    B. mistrial; hung jury
    C. hung jury; mistrial
    D. acquittal; mistrial

21. Generally speaking, the role of the foreperson, also known as the presiding juror, is to
    A. announce the verdict
    B. preside over discussion of the jurors
    C. preside over the votes of the jurors
    D. all of the above

22. A request to poll the jury serves what purpose?
    Jury polling
    A. ensures the verdict to be recorded is accurate
    B. allows jurors to resolve any conflicts of interests prior to the start of trial
    C. helps the jury selection process move faster
    D. allows the judge to ensure each juror will be impartial and unbiased while hearing evidence

23. In which of the following scenarios would a bailiff MOST likely intervene?
    A. The plaintiff and defense attorneys are chatting with one another outside the courtroom.
    B. The judge and his or her law clerk are overheard talking about the case in judge's chambers.
    C. One of the jurors is talking with the defense attorney inside the courtroom before others have entered the room.
    D. The plaintiff and the defendant's attorney are heard talking in the hallway.

24. Which of the following would be submitted only after a verdict is rendered?
    A. Motion to dismiss
    B. Motion in limine
    C. Motion to exclude
    D. Motion in arrest of judgment

25. In many jurisdictions, a motion for a new trial must be filed before a party can file a(n)
    A. exculpatory plea
    B. motion for mistrial
    C. acquittal by default
    D. appeal

KEY (CORRECT ANSWERS)

1. A
2. A
3. C
4. C
5. B

6. C
7. B
8. D
9. B
10. B

11. D
12. A
13. C
14. A
15. C

16. D
17. B
18. C
19. A
20. C

21. D
22. A
23. C
24. D
25. D

TEST 2

DIRECTIONS: Each question or incomplete statement is followed by several suggested answers or completions. Select the one that BEST answers the question or completes the statement. *PRINT THE LETTER OF THE CORRECT ANSWER IN THE SPACE AT THE RIGHT.*

Questions 1-5.

DIRECTIONS: Questions 1 through 5 are to be answered on the basis of the following fact pattern.

James and Sean started an accounting practice five years ago. Business quickly soured and James and Sean decided to each start their own competing business practices. While James' business flourished, Sean's practice has floundered. Sean believes James spoke poorly about him to their mutual friends, ruining his professional reputation, and went behind his back to steal clients. Sean now wants to sue James civilly.

1. How would Sean begin a civil suit against James?
    A. Sean needs to file an interpleader to compel James to court.
    B. Sean must file a motion to compel proceedings.
    C. Sean must file a complaint against Sean in the proper court.
    D. Sean can outline the facts of his case to the clerk who will transcribe the issues.

2. Sean must also file a summons with the clerk.
   What is the role of the summons in initiating a lawsuit?
    A. It puts the other party on notice that a lawsuit has been filed against them.
    B. It compels discovery in a court of proper jurisdiction.
    C. It requires the other party to answer by initiating a cross-motion.
    D. It gives the other party extended time to file a counterclaim.

3. Sean's attorney and James' attorney begin the process of exchanging information about the witnesses each side plans to call and the evidence that will be presented at trial.
   This process is called
    A. interrogation   B. discovery   C. compulsion   D. demurrer

4. One of James' and Sean's former clients is moving to London. James' and Sean's attorneys agree to take her deposition now and use it at trial in the event she will not be able to appear.
   At trial, her testimony will be _____ and part of the record.
    A. read into evidence   B. ex parte
    C. sequestered   D. assumed credible

5. After being notified that a lawsuit has been filed against him, James has an opportunity to answer the _____ that has been filed against him.
    A. pleadings   B. motion to compel
    C. interpleader   D. complaint

1.____

2.____

3.____

4.____

5.____

6. Venue refers to the district or county within a state where the
   A. lawsuit began
   B. lawsuit must be heard
   C. plaintiff resides
   D. plaintiff is domiciled

7. After both parties have agreed on a jury, the jurors are _____ by the court clerk before they are impaneled.
   A. instructed to take notes
   B. sworn in
   C. fingerprinted
   D. arranged

8. Can the prosecution compel a defendant in a criminal trial to take the stand and testify?
   A. Yes; he or she must explain what happened in open court
   B. Yes; he or she must take the stand and testify they are using their Fifth Amendment right against self-incrimination.
   C. Yes; he or she must take the stand but they can refuse to answer any question they choose.
   D. No.

9. Criminal charges are brought against a person in all of the following ways, EXCEPT
   A. citation   B. information   C. indictment   D. subpoena

Questions 10-15.

DIRECTIONS: Questions 10 through 15 are to be answered on the basis of the following fact pattern.

Jason's brother, Andrew, has been arrested. Jason appears at the courthouse as soon as he hears this news. He does not know why Andrew has been arrested, but suspects it may be related to his tumultuous relationship with his ex-girlfriend, who has filed a temporary restraining order against Andrew.

10. If Andrew was not arrested on a warrant, when will he be able to file a plea of guilty, not guilty, or no contest?
    A. At arraignment
    B. At trial
    C. At a preliminary conference
    D. At indictment

11. If Andrew is released from custody without a payment of money on the promise that he will appear for all hearings and for trial, the judge has released Andrew
    A. on his own recognizance
    B. with time served
    C. after a concurrent term
    D. on exculpatory evidence

12. In the alternative, if the judge sets bail for Andrew's release, he or she does so with the intent of
    A. punishing Andrew
    B. ensuring Andrew will appear for trial and all pre-trial hearings for which he must be present
    C. setting a fine dependent on the type of crime alleged
    D. releasing Andrew into the custody of his responsible brother, Jason

13. Which of the following should NOT be a factor a judge may use in deciding the amount of Andrew's bail?
    A. The risk of Andrew's fleeing
    B. The type of crime Andrew is alleged to have committed
    C. Andrew's age, race, and sex
    D. The safety of the community

14. During Andrew's initial appearance, the judge explains to Andrew that he has a right to a trial by jury.
    If Andrew does not want a trial by jury, what type of trial will he receive?
    A. An expedited trial
    B. A bench trial
    C. A summation
    D. An information

15. Andrew pleads no contest to the charges in his initial appearance.
    Andrew is effectively
    A. not admitting guilt or disputing the charge alleged
    B. admitting guilt
    C. denying the charge but admitting he will pay any fines incurred
    D. deferring his plea until a later date

Questions 16-19.

DIRECTIONS: Questions 16 through 19 are to be answered on the basis of the following fact pattern.

Jameson and Avery are neighbors. Jameson moved and purchased a home in the lot next to Avery's lot three months ago. Avery is suing Jameson for building a fence on Avery's property. Jameson attests the fence is actually being built on his own property and there is no boundary dispute. Jameson and Avery are both represented by counsel. A number of motions are filed by each party and discovery has been a lengthy process thus far.

16. Both parties serve each other requests to answer questions in writing under oath. Avery's attorney demands Jameson answer questions about the purchase of his home and dealings with the contractors building the fence. Jameson demands Avery answer questions about the property line dividing their property.
    This type of discovery is called
    A. interrogatories
    B. demands
    C. summons
    D. written decision

17. Avery's attorney would like to depose the property surveyor, Abe.
    Can Jameson and/or Jameson's attorney attend Abe's deposition?
    A. No, because Abe will be Avery's witness
    B. No, because Avery can share the information with Jameson's counsel at a later date
    C. No, because Abe's testimony may not be inadmissible in court so Jameson's presence would be futile
    D. Yes

18. Which of the following will NOT occur at the pre-trial conference between the parties?
    A. A deadline for discovery will be set.
    B. A trial date will be set.
    C. The judge will encourage stipulations between the parties.
    D. The judge will ask for oral arguments.

19. During discovery, both parties ascertain that Jameson built the fence on his side of the property line. Jameson's attorney asks the court to dismiss the case because there is no longer a legally sound basis to proceed.
    This request to the court is a motion to
    A. relinquish   B. dismiss   C. vacate   D. suppress

20. Which type of evidence suggests a fact by implication or inference?
    A. Exculpatory   B. Demandable
    C. Circumstantial   D. Ascertainable

21. Sam sued David civilly last September. Sam prevailed in the original suit. David has appealed. David is now the _____ and Sam is the _____.
    A. petitionery; respondent   B. appellant; appellee
    C. appellant; petitioner   D. respondent; appellee

22. If an appellate court remands a case back to the lower trial court, which of the following instructions may be imposed on the trial court.
    A. A new trial be held
    B. The trial court's judgment be modified or corrected
    C. The trial court reconsider the facts and/or the evidence presented
    D. All of the above

23. Which of the following motions may only be filed after all of the evidence has been presented?
    A. Motion in limine   B. Motion for directed verdict
    C. Motion for summary judgment   D. Motion for admission

24. When is it permissible for parties to settle a suit?
    A. Before the trial begins   B. During the trial
    c. While the jury is deliberating D. All of the above

5 (#2)

25. Summations are typically a part of _____ and discuss the evidence and the inferences that can be drawn from that evidence. 25._____
    A. closing arguments
    B. indictments
    C. hearings on the merits
    D. ex-parte communications

KEY (CORRECT ANSWERS)

1.	C	11.	A
2.	A	12.	B
3.	B	13.	C
4.	A	14.	B
5.	D	15.	A
6.	B	16.	A
7.	B	17.	D
8.	D	18.	D
9.	D	19.	B
10.	A	20.	C

21. B
22. D
23. B
24. D
25. A

TEST 3

DIRECTIONS: Each question or incomplete statement is followed by several suggested answers or completions. Select the one that BEST answers the question or completes the statement. *PRINT THE LETTER OF THE CORRECT ANSWER IN THE SPACE AT THE RIGHT.*

Questions 1-4.

DIRECTIONS: Questions 1 through 4 are to be answered on the basis of the following fact pattern.

Steven is on trial for embezzlement. The case is complex; there are eight witnesses for the prosecution and twelve witnesses for the defense, including character witnesses. Steven has filed a cross-claim against his former employer, and plaintiff, ABC Corp., Inc. for defamation of character. Steven maintains that he never stole a dime from ABC Corp., Inc. and wants ABC Corp., Inc. to issue him a public apology when the trial is over.

1. The BEST place to refer back to the testimony of one witness is   1.____
   A. the docket
   B. the judge's notes
   C. the stenographer's transcript
   D. clerk notes

2. Steven's attorney presents evidence that his client was not working on the   2.____
   days the theft from ABC Corp. allegedly occurred.
   What kind of evidence is Steven's counsel presenting to the court?
   A. Alibi
   B. Exculpatory
   C. Exclusionary
   D. Exemplary

3. Alexandra, a friend of Steven, testifies for the prosecution in Steven's case.   3.____
   Alexandra testifies that Steven told her that he embezzled money from ABC Corp. Steven's attorney objects to Alexandra's testimony because it is
   A. exculpatory   B. hearsay   C. untrue   D. impeachment

4. At the close of Steven's trial, oral arguments are made by _____ to the   4.____
   court, summarizing their position on the evidence that has been presented and their theories on the case in its entirety.
   A. jurors   B. plaintiffs   C. attorneys   D. defense

Questions 5-8.

DIRECTIONS: Questions 5 through 8 are to be answered on the basis of the following fact pattern.

April 16 is turning out to be a very busy day at the courthouse. In the morning, three cases were withdrawn by the plaintiff without a hearing, six cases were dismissed without prejudice by the judge, and two cases were settled out of court.

5. How many were decided by the judge on April 16?   5.____
   A. 0   B. 2   C. 6   D. 3

6. How many cases were heard before the judge? 6.____
   A. 3   B. 6   C. 2   D. 8

7. How many cases would the court reporter need to be present for? 7.____
   A. 6   B. 3   C. 2   D. 8

8. How many of the cases were awarded damages? 8.____
   A. 2   B. 6   C. 3   D. 0

Questions 9-12.

DIRECTIONS: Questions 9 through 12 are to be answered on the basis of the following fact pattern.

Miranda has initiated a lawsuit against her former friend, Anne, for breach of contract. Miranda referred Anne's interior design services to Miranda's boss. Anne went to Miranda's boss' house for an initial consultation and, even though Anne agreed to design three rooms in the house, she never followed through with the contract. Miranda is incredibly embarrassed by the entire situation. Anne, however, maintains that she has a reasonable excuse for not finishing the work.

9. In addition to money damages, Miranda would also like the court to compel Anne to execute the contract or, in other words, actually design the rooms. This remedy is deemed 9.____
   A. compulsion under order
   B. specific performance
   C. remedy at law
   D. joint and several liability

10. Miranda alleges that she suffered pain and suffering from Anne's inability to execute the contract. 10.____
    What type of damages are pain and suffering categorized as?
    A. Punitive   B. Special   C. Specific   D. Compensatory

11. Miranda lives in New York. Anne lives in New Jersey. Miranda's boss lives in Connecticut. When Miranda files suit in New York, the judge initially indicates that she does not have 11.____
    A. authority   B. jurisdiction   C. venue   D. domicile

12. The contract that is alleged to have been breached exists between Anne and Miranda's boss, not Miranda. Therefore, there is no legal cause of action for the case to proceed. Miranda's boss is free to file the claim against Anne at a later date if she so chooses. 12.____
    The court will
    A. dismiss the action without prejudice
    B. deny the action without prejudice
    C. sustain the action
    D. abdicate as necessary

13. Nominal damages are
    A. damages awarded in name only, indicating no substantial harm was done
    B. damages to recompense the injured for the infliction of emotional distress
    C. damages to recompense the initiator of the lawsuit
    D. a reimbursement of filing fees, awarded to the person who can prove they are injured

14. The type of recovery being sought by the plaintiff is known as the
    A. order   B. punishment   C. remedy   D. issue

15. Robert approaches the clerk's desk in a panic. He says that he filed a lawsuit against his cousin, Mike, but neglected to add his cousin's friend, Roy, to the suit.
    What action is Robert attempting to take?
    A. Amending the complaint
    B. Adding an addendum to the summons
    C. Re-issuing a summons
    D. Redacting the answer

Questions 16-20.

DIRECTIONS: Questions 16 through 20 are to be answered on the basis of the following fact pattern.

Daniel and Patrick sue one another civilly. Daniel sues Patrick for intentional infliction of emotional distress and Patrick countersues Daniel for assault. Both causes of action stem from a physical altercation which took place at a youth hockey game where Daniel's and Patrick's sons played against one another. At trial, the judge found that Daniel started the fight and attacked Patrick and found, by extension, that Patrick was not a contributor in the altercation.
Daniel appealed the decision to an appellate court. Daniel's attorney argued that the trial court erred, as a matter of law, in finding that Daniel was the sole initiator of the altercation and ignored evidence to the contrary. Appellate courts generally render decisions by a panel. The panel in Daniel's appeal was comprised of three justices. The appellate court agreed with the trial court's finding of fault.

16. The ultimate disposition of this case was the appellate court
    A. affirmed the lower court's decision
    B. remanded the lower court's decision
    C. reversed the lower court's decision
    D. acquitted Daniel of all charges

17. An opinion from the entire panel of justices is known as a
    A. per curiam decision   B. affirmative decision
    C. stare decisis   D. en banc order

18. One of the judges agrees with the decision of the court, but disagrees with the reasoning of the conclusion. This judge decides to write his own opinion. This is deemed a
    A. dissenting opinion
    B. remedial decision
    C. concurring opinion
    D. recurrent opinion

19. Suppose that one of the judges disagrees entirely with the ruling. How will the judgment be altered because of the disagreement?
    The judgment
    A. is unaffected because the majority voted in agreement with the trial court
    B. is unaffected because this judge did not author a dissenting opinion
    C. is unaffected because oral arguments were not made before the panel
    D. will be overturned

20. The appellate court still requires _____, even if it is established by the trial court, known as original _____.
    A. domicile; venue
    B. venue; jurisdiction
    C. jurisdiction; jurisdiction
    D. jurisdiction; domicile

21. The legal theory upon which a case is based is called a
    A. basis
    B. decisis
    C. cause of action
    D. precedent

Questions 22-25.

DIRECTIONS: Questions 22 through 25 are to be answered on the basis of the following fact pattern.

Last July, Sarah stole Alexis's car and took it for a joyride along Main Street. After a long joyride, Sarah decided to pick up Ashley at Ashley's apartment. Although Ashley asked when Sarah bought a new car, Sarah lied and told Ashley that it was her aunt's car that she borrowed with permission. Sarah and Ashley went on another joyride, this time driving up to 90 miles per hour on the highways around town. After three hours, Ashley asked to go home and Sarah obliged. After Sarah dropped Ashley back off at her apartment, Sarah sped through a busy intersection and crashed the car. The car was totaled.
Alexis has filed a lawsuit against both Sarah and Ashley.

22. Alexis is determined to sue both Sarah and Ashley for conversion, or the wrongful act of dominion or control over another person's property. However, after meeting with her attorney, Alexis decided she may not be able to prove each _____ of the alleged crime against Ashley.
    A. stage   B. element   C. circumstance   D. remedy

23. After Alexis initiated her lawsuit against Sarah and Ashley, Ashley requested the court remove her from the lawsuit altogether. She attested that she could not have participated in a crime if she did not know the car was stolen. Her request to the court will come in the form of a(n)
    A. notice   B. motion   C. termination   D. demand

24. Ashley's attorney asks the judge to instruct the jury that it can consider mitigating factors in rendering a verdict against Ashley.
    An example of a mitigating factor in this scenario would MOST likely be
    A. Ashley does not known Alexis
    B. Sarah is no longer friends with Alexis
    C. Ashley asked Sarah about the origins of the car and Sarah's reply was untruthful
    D. Ashley and Sarah were working in cahoots to steal Alexis's car

    24.____

25. During the time of the crime Sarah was a minor. A minor is legally defined as
    A. someone who cannot think for themselves
    B. anyone under 21
    C. a legally emancipated individual
    D. an infant or individual under the age of legal competence

    25.____

KEY (CORRECT ANSWERS)

1.	C		11.	B
2.	B		12.	A
3.	B		13.	A
4.	C		14.	C
5.	C		15.	A
6.	B		16.	A
7.	A		17.	A
8.	D		18.	C
9.	B		19.	A
10.	D		20.	C

21.	C
22.	B
23.	B
24.	C
25.	D

TEST 4

DIRECTIONS: Each question or incomplete statement is followed by several suggested answers or completions. Select the one that BEST answers the question or completes the statement. *PRINT THE LETTER OF THE CORRECT ANSWER IN THE SPACE AT THE RIGHT.*

Questions 1-4.

DIRECTIONS: Questions 1 through 4 are to be answered on the basis of the following fact pattern.

A complex civil litigation suit is set to begin between ABC Insurance Corp. and DEF Indemnity Corp. Adam represents ABC Insurance and Jane represents DEF Indemnity Corp. Multiple extensions have been granted to either side to conduct more extensive discovery. At the last conference scheduled before trial, the presiding judge is notably frustrated at the requested delays from both Adam and Jane. The presiding judge would like both parties to stipulate to as many points as possible.

1. Adam and Jane appear in the permanent record as _____ unless either are withdrawn or are otherwise removed from the case.
   A. attorneys in time
   B. attorneys of record
   C. attorneys of the case
   D. permanent attorneys

2. The judge asks whether the parties have attempted to settle this matter in another forum, such as binding _____.
   A. decision-making
   B. arbitration
   C. neutral court
   D. judgment arena

3. While the judge would like the parties to settle, he quickly realizes that it is not a possibility between these two parties. Adam and Jane continue to argue about various issues including expert witnesses. Adam argues that Jane's expert witness, who will testify about financial crimes, is a quack. In response, Jane offers that her witness be _____, or testify under oath at a date prior to trial.
   A. sworn in   B. indemnified   C. deposed   D. saddled

4. Which of the following is the LEAST appropriate behavior of the judge during a pre-trial conference?
   A. Providing advice on Adam or Jane's legal strategy for trial
   B. Asking the parties to stipulate to the facts
   C. Remaining indifferent about the witnesses each party plans to call at trial
   D. Setting a date for trial more than three months away

5. A lawsuit with a single cause of action being breach of contract will be classified as what type of suit?
   A. Criminal   B. Divisional   C. Situational   D. Civil

1.____

2.____

3.____

4.____

5.____

39

6. Sheila's mother passed away last week. She comes to the courthouse and asks about the probate process. You inform her that probate may not be necessary if she is the person named in the will as the individual who will administer her mother's estate. This individual is otherwise known as the
    A. administrator   B. guarantor   C. creditor   D. executor

7. Brandy would like her juvenile record expunged. What is she seeking to do? She is requesting
    A. her record, or a portion of her record, be removed
    B. her record be sealed
    C. her record be unsealed
    D. to make her record unavailable to creditors

8. Having never met Jamie, a pro se litigant, Judge Smith strikes up a friendly conversation about the recent political climate in the elevator with him on the way to the courtroom. In the courtroom that afternoon, Jamie enters his appearance and says, "You and I are clearly already on the same page, Judge" in open court. Jamie's adversary, Courtney, requests that the judge recuses himself from the case. Why?
    A. Jamie and Judge Smith's political affiliations are unsavory.
    B. Judge Smith is clearly biased as evidenced by Jamie's comment.
    C. Judge Smith and Jamie have partaken in en banc communications.
    D. Judicial discrimination is appropriate if a conflict of interest would affect a judge's ruling.

9. Emily appears at court with a crumbled notice in her hands. She has a complaint in her hands and indicates that she never answered or responded to the complaint, hoping it would go away or resolve itself.
    Emily is currently
    A. in default   B. owes restitution
    C. in declaratory judgment   D. subsidiary

10. A conditional release from incarceration is known as
    A. an expungement   B. a restitution
    C. parole   D. reduced sentence

11. Tom paid a contractor to cut down a large pine tree in front of his house. The tree had grown so tall that it has started to interfere with the power lines running parallel to the street. As the contractor cut down the tree, a large gust of wind blew and the tree crashed down on top of his neighbor, Dane's, roof. Dane is suing Tom for failure to exercise the degree of care that a reasonable person would have exercised in the same circumstance.
    Dane is suing Tom for
    A. lack of judgment   B. breach of contract
    C. negligence   D. conversion

12. Lawyers are generally prohibited from asking _____ questions of their own witnesses because they are suggestive, or prompt, the witness to answer in a certain way.
    A. leading   B. direct   C. cross   D. sustainable

13. One process that is generally private, and not heard in open court, is(are)
    A. testimony of expert witnesses   B. swearing in of jurors
    C. objections   D. plea bargaining

14. The burden of proof in a civil case is _____ stringent than that in a criminal case.
    A. less   B. more   C. equally   D. substantially

15. May jurors consider arguments made during an attorney's opening or closing arguments as evidence or fact?
    A. Yes, but only if compelling
    B. Yes, but only under the circumstances explained by the judge
    C. Yes, unconditionally
    D. No

16. In reviewing the court transcript, which of the following is the attorney LEAST likely to find?
    A. The judge's opinions on the case   B. Testimony of the petitioner
    C. Attorneys of record   D. Names of the expert witnesses

17. A mandatory injunction has the effect of
    A. requiring a party to do a particular act
    B. providing the option of a party to do a particular act
    C. requiring a party to report their actions
    D. providing the party an option to report their actions

18. James approaches the clerk's desk and asks how, generally, judges make their decisions on legal matters.
    The MOST correct answer would be: Based on
    A. case law, or the body of all court decisions which govern or provide precedent on the same legal issue before the judge
    B. case law, personal opinion, and oral arguments by attorneys
    C. case law, oral arguments by attorneys, and the defendant's rap sheet
    D. "stare decisis" or that which has already been decided

19. Which of the following individuals is LEAST likely to serve on a jury?
    A. Susan, who has been called numerous times but never served on a jury
    B. Bill, a supporter of labor unions and freelance political columnist
    C. Gary, who served on a murder trial 10 years ago
    D. Amy, a 16-year-old genius who just finished her junior year of college

20. If a grand jury decides there is enough evidence to move forward with criminal charges against a group or individual, they return a(n)
    A. information   B. indictment   C. warrant   D. seizure

21. When an attorney attempts to reduce the credibility of the other side's witness, they are said to be trying to _____ the witness.
    A. objectify   B. anger   C. impeach   D. frustrate

    21.____

22. During a lengthy murder trial, it is discovered that two of the jurors have been romantically involved. They have conspired with one another to enter votes of "not guilty" and attempt to sway other jurors in their favor in an attempt to close out deliberations early.
    What is the likely outcome of the trial?
    A. Hung jury   B. Mistrial
    C. Acquittal   D. Defensive charge

    22.____

23. The judge's charge to the jury is also known as
    A. voir dire   B. en banc
    C. jury instructions D. sua sponte

    23.____

24. Who is MOST likely to deliver the sentence to the convicted?
    A. Bailiff   B. Jury
    C. Judge   D. Jury foreperson

    24.____

25. A motion for directed verdict is made
    A. without the jury present
    B. with only the jury foreperson present
    C. with the entire jury present
    D. with only the alternate jurors present

    25.____

KEY (CORRECT ANSWERS)

1.	B	11.	C
2.	B	12.	A
3.	C	13.	D
4.	A	14.	A
5.	D	15.	D
6.	D	16.	A
7.	A	17.	A
8.	D	18.	A
9.	A	19.	D
10.	C	20.	B

21.	C
22.	B
23.	C
24.	C
25.	A

EXAMINATION SECTION
TEST 1

DIRECTIONS: Each question or incomplete statement is followed by several suggested answers or completions. Select the one that BEST answers the question or completes the statement. *PRINT THE LETTER OF THE CORRECT ANSWER IN THE SPACE AT THE RIGHT.*

Questions 1-5.

DIRECTIONS: Questions 1 through 5 are to be answered on the basis of the following fact pattern.

When Family Court opens on Monday morning, Desiree rushes to the clerk's desk in a panic. Her ex-boyfriend, Alex, has made threats against her and her children and she would like to file a restraining order as soon as possible. She has never been in court before and does not have any idea of what to expect or what she may need, but she is in fear of her and her children's lives.

1. While Desiree fears for her safety, she cannot obtain a final order of protection against Alex. Why?
   A. A judge has not yet been assigned to the case.
   B. A judge has not been assigned, so there has been no finding of a family offense being committed and Alex has not agreed to the order.
   C. Desiree's children should be present for the request to the court unless they are under age 18.
   D. Alex has not agreed to the order.

1.____

2. A temporary restraining order only lasts until
   A. the close of the case
   B. the beginning of an appeal
   C. the next time the petitioner is in court
   D. it is extended indefinitely

2.____

3. Desiree asks how long a final order of protection lasts. The MOST appropriate response is
   A. two or ten years   B. two or five years
   C. one year   D. six months

3.____

4. Which party is responsible for drafting the petition to the judge for a temporary restraining order?
   A. The judge   B. The party seeking the order
   C. The clerk   D. A spectator

4.____

2 (#1)

5. After Desiree starts her case, Alex is served with a summons. Three weeks later, Desiree returns to the courthouse to say that she has changed her mind and no longer fears for her safety.
Desiree must
   A. withdraw her petition for a restraining order
   B. start an anger management program
   C. withdraw her petition with prejudice as she will not be able to file again
   D. recuse herself

6. Jamie has hired legal counsel to represent him in the purchase of commercial buildings across New York State. With his attorney's help, he has secured the purchase of nine different office buildings totaling $2 million. Last week, Jamie discovered that his attorney forged his signature on the sale of four of those properties and collected the proceedings. Assume the threshold for filing a suit in Albany County is $50,000, Nassau County is $200,000, and New York County is $500,000.
Where can Jamie sue his attorney for malpractice?
   A. New York County
   B. Albany County
   C. Nassau County
   D. All of the above

7. Which of the following matters is LEAST likely to be heard in the Albany County – Commercial Division?
   A. Commercial class actions
   B. Transactions governed by the Uniform Commercial Code
   C. Divorce
   D. Shareholder derivate action

8. Which of the following matters is LEAST likely to be heard in Suffolk County District Court?
   A. Small claims matter of $1,000,000
   B. Arraignment in a felony case
   C. Petty larceny (theft of $200)
   D. Shoplifting

9. Which of the following is LEAST likely to be heard in the Landlord and Tenant Court?
   A. Non-payment proceedings
   B. Hold-over proceedings
   C. Evictions
   D. Adoptions

10. Dave approaches the clerk's desk and insists that he has a tenant in his building who refuses to pay rent and will not vacate the premises.
Dave seeks assistance on initiating _____ proceedings.
   A. Annulment   B. Hold-over   C. Numeration   D. Abandonment

11. John and Jill need to file for bankruptcy and would like to do so together.
John and Jill would file which type of petition?
   A. Separate   B. Tenants   C. Survivor   D. Joint

12. Rich would like to know what advice he can give his brother who was arrested last night for driving under the influence of alcohol. Rich's brother is scheduled to be arraigned this morning. While you may not be authorized to give legal advice, it is prudent to know that a plea of nolo contendere has the same effect as a plea of _____, but is not an admission of guilt.
    A. acquittal B. remorse C. not guilty D. guilty

13. Emily arrives in court for her bankruptcy hearing. Emily is not working, does not have any savings. She does not own any property, jewelry, collectibles, or other precious items of value.
    Emily's bankruptcy petition will MOST likely be classified as a _____ case.
    A. nolo contendere
    B. no asset
    C. no prohibition
    D. Chapter 13

14. Assume the same facts as above. Emily is a full-time student and took out a student loan before filing bankruptcy.
    The trustee has informed Emily her student loan is a _____ debt.
    A. dischargeable
    B. non-dischargeable
    C. immediate
    D. short term

15. A party in interest in bankruptcy is defined as a party who
    A. has standing to be heard in a matter to be decided in the bankruptcy case
    B. standing to disrupt the court
    C. intends to file a brief
    D. intends to petition for early release

16. A petty offense is one that is punishable by _____ or less in prison.
    A. six months B. one year C. three years D. four years

17. Town and village courts have jurisdiction over
    A. vehicle and traffic matters
    B. small claims
    C. civil matters
    D. all of the above

18. The highest civil court in New York is the
    A. Supreme Court
    B. City Court
    C. Civil Court
    D. Court of Appeals

19. The highest criminal court in New York is the
    A. New York City Criminal Court
    B. Court of Appeals
    C. County Courts
    D. Village Courts

Questions 20-23.

DIRECTIONS: Questions 20 through 23 are to be answered on the basis of the following fact pattern.

Amy is a Guardians ad Litem ("GAL") for the New York Housing Court. She volunteered for the Court because she wanted to help people resolve their housing disputes. The judge has appointed Amy as Gerald's GAL in his case. Gerald is involved in a minor dispute with his landlord.

20. Amy believes that Gerald's housing issues stem from his poor money management. Can Amy manage Gerald's checkbook and other personal finances as they relate to his housing case?
    A. Yes, because his finances relate to his housing case
    B. Yes, because he clearly cannot manage his money on his own
    C. Yes, but only if Gerald asks her to
    D. No

21. Amy is NOT allowed to do which of the following things?
    A. Meet with Gerald
    B. Meet with Gerald's landlord
    C. Allow Gerald's landlord into Gerald's apartment
    D. Ensure the landlord completes repairs as promised

22. A GAL works in which party's best interest?
    A. Gerald's landlord
    B. Gerald
    C. The appointed party
    D. The judge

23. Amy has fallen ill and cannot meet her obligations as a GAL. Which party can remove Amy as Gerald's GAL?
    A. Gerald
    B. Gerald's landlord
    C. The judge
    D. The clerk

24. Pro per is another term for _____ or a self-represented person.
    A. pro tem
    B. pro se
    C. qui tam
    D. quid pro

25. Sanctions are defined as a
    A. penalty or other type of enforcement used to bring about compliance with the law
    B. penalty specific to international trade law
    C. federal penalty reserved for those who lie under oath
    D. misdemeanor crime punishable by more than four years in prison

KEY (CORRECT ANSWERS)

1. A
2. C
3. B
4. C
5. A

6. D
7. C
8. A
9. D
10. B

11. D
12. D
13. B
14. B
15. A

16. A
17. D
18. D
19. B
20. D

21. C
22. C
23. C
24. B
25. A

TEST 2

DIRECTIONS: Each question or incomplete statement is followed by several suggested answers or completions. Select the one that BEST answers the question or completes the statement. *PRINT THE LETTER OF THE CORRECT ANSWER IN THE SPACE AT THE RIGHT.*

Questions 1-5.

DIRECTIONS: Questions 1 through 5 are to be answered on the basis of the following fact pattern.

Edwin has been served with a lawsuit from his former accountant, Bob. Bob claims Edwin never paid him for his accounting services after he filed Edwin's personal income tax and business income tax returns. Edwin has come to the clerk's desk confused and angry.

1. Edwin wants to know what the basis of Bob's legal claim is against him. Where can Edwin find more information about the case?
   A. The internet
   B. The complaint
   C. The subpoena
   D. The arraignment

2. Edwin claims that he was audited by the IRS shortly after Bob filed his personal income taxes. Edwin wants to sue Bob in connection with his being audited. In order to do so, Edwin would need to
   A. re-sue
   B. re-file
   C. countersue
   D. cross-claim

3. Bob filed taxes for Edwin and Edwin's wife. While Edwin's wife is not listed on the Complaint in Edwin's suit against Bob, Edwin's wife would also like to appear as a party to the case. Is this possible?
   A. No, because Edwin's wife may be unavailable for trial
   B. No, because Edwin's wife is not initiating the suit
   C. No, because Edwin can only sue Bob himself
   D. Yes

4. Which of the following courts is MOST appropriate for Edwin's suit against Bob?
   A. Housing Court
   B. Surrogates Court
   C. Civil Court
   D. Criminal Court

5. Which of the following is MOST likely to be the legal basis of Bob's suit against Edwin?
   A. Breach of contract
   B. Negligence
   C. Assault
   D. Defamation

6. The Housing Court is made of parts. The resolution part presides over all pre-trial matters in a case and attempts to settle the case. Jeremy appears at Housing Court for his trial that begins this morning.
   Is Jeremy's case appropriate for the pre-trial part of the Housing Court?
   A. Yes, as pre-trial matters preclude this
   B. Yes, as a check in before the trial can start
   C. No, the trial part is separate and distinct from the pre-trial part of Housing Court
   D. No, the trial part only hears cases on Mondays

6.____

Questions 7-8.

DIRECTIONS: Questions 7 and 8 are to be answered on the basis of the following text.

Jenny received a notice from the marshal that she is being evicted from her apartment. She wants to ignore the notice, but comes to the courthouse at the urging of her boyfriend.

7. Her boyfriend warns her that if she does not take care of the notice, she and her _____ may be _____ from the apartment.
   A. property; removed
   B. removed; property
   C. property; removal
   D. assets; removed

7.____

8. At the courthouse, the clerk instructs Jenny to complete an affidavit in support of a(n)
   A. order for removal
   B. petition
   C. order to show cause
   D. justification

8.____

9. Because Jenny never answered the original petition for eviction from her landlord, her landlord obtained a _____ judgment against her. Jenny now needs to complete an affidavit in support of an order to show cause to _____ a judgment based on failure to answer.
   A. vacate; default
   B. vacate; demand
   C. default; vacate
   D. default; validate

9.____

10. A clerk in the Resolution Part of Housing Court can do all of the following EXCEPT
    A. answer questions about the court calendar
    B. answer questions about the judge's rules
    C. assist the judge as necessary
    D. provide detailed legal analysis and/or advice

10.____

11. A judge may direct parties in a dispute to mediation, which is a form of
    A. neutrality
    B. alternative dispute resolution
    C. alternative judgment
    D. non-binding analysis of the legal dispute

11.____

12. Joel and Rachel would like to place their daughter into foster care. Do Joel and Rachel need an attorney to represent them in court?
    A. Yes, as foster care placements are complicated
    B. Yes, unless they do not have money to hire a lawyer
    C. No, legal representation is not required but they do have a right to have the court appoint an attorney if they cannot afford one
    D. No, unless they change their minds after the placement has taken place

13. The New York Court of Claims is the only court where one can seek damages against
    A. the State of New York or other state-related agencies
    B. New York City
    C. municipalities in Richmond County
    D. New York State colleges

14. While City Courts such as Binghamton City Court handle criminal and civil matters, the amount in dispute can only be up to
    A. $20,000,000   B. $15,000   C. $1,000,000   D. $5,000,000

15. Beatrice is having issues understanding her mother's will. Her mother is living, but Beatrice wants to ensure she understands all of the terms of the will while her mother is still alive.
    Beatrice is not the named executor, which is defined as
    A. someone named in the will appointed to wind up the affairs of the deceased person
    B. the person who inherits all of the deceased person's property
    C. the attorney of the estate
    D. the judge who presides over the estate

16. A person who is named in the will to inherit money or other property is the
    A. executrix   B. devisee   C. custodian   D. beneficiary

17. Matters of will and probate are heard in which court?
    A. Civil Court   B. Family Court
    C. Surrogates Court   D. Criminal Court

18. A revocable trust is a trust that can be
    A. rescinded by the grantor after creation
    B. overruled by a judge
    C. nullified by the beneficiaries
    D. canceled outright without warning to the trust remainders

19. James approaches the clerk's desk seeking assistance regarding a child support matter. James lost his job a few months ago and can no longer pay his child support.
    What is the LEAST appropriate advice you can give James?
    A. He is prudent for coming to the court to seek assistance as there are serious penalties for non-payment of child support.
    B. A support order can be modified.

C. Without income, he cannot possibly pay child support, so he should wait until he is found in contempt of court.
D. Penalties for non-payment include interception of tax refunds, suspension of personal and business licenses, and seizure of bank accounts.

20. As a clerk for the New York Court of Appeals, you are asked to determine whether a case from one of the trial courts has been upheld or reversed. If the case has been upheld, it is recorded in the docket as
    A. remanded   b. retained   C. affirmed   D. affiant

21. If a case has been reversed or sent back to the trial court from the New York Court of Appeals, the word _____ will be recorded in the docket.
    A. retained   B. reversed   C. remanded   D. replevin

22. Sue does not agree with the finding of the Family Court. She asks if an order can be appealed.
    The MOST appropriate response is:
    A. No, as all orders are final
    B. No, as Family Court does not pose any legal issues requiring appeal
    C. No, given that Sue is not represented by an attorney
    D. Yes, she may appeal from an order

23. Joe, John, and Beth are involved in a paternity suit. Joe believes he is the father of Beth's baby, Sarah, but John maintains that he is the father.
    What document would be MOST helpful for the court in resolving this matter?
    A. John and Beth's marriage license
    B. Joe and Beth's marriage license
    C. Sarah's birth certificate
    D. Beth's medical records

24. Abel is concerned that his cousin, Ted, is not able to afford legal representation in his trial for armed robbery. Ted must be considered _____ or otherwise unable to afford to hire a lawyer before defense counsel is appointed by the court.
    A. responsible   B. indigent   C. not guilty   D. petty

25. Which of the following is heard and determined outside of the courtroom?
    A. Hearing   B. Plea bargain
    C. Testimony   D. Evidence

KEY (CORRECT ANSWERS)

1.	B		11.	B
2.	C		12.	C
3.	D		13.	A
4.	C		14.	B
5.	A		15.	A
6.	C		16.	D
7.	A		17.	C
8.	C		18.	A
9.	C		19.	C
10.	D		20.	C

21. C
22. D
23. C
24. B
25. B

EXAMINATION SECTION
TEST 1

DIRECTIONS: Each question or incomplete statement is followed by several suggested answers or completions. Select the one that BEST answers the question or completes the statement. *PRINT THE LETTER OF THE CORRECT ANSWER IN THE SPACE AT THE RIGHT.*

1. Which of the following parties is authorized to administer oaths? 1.____
   A. All court clerks
   B. Court bailiffs
   C. Judges only
   D. Judge's clerks only

2. Janelle has been retained as Stephanie's defense attorney. Stephanie is charged with felony burglary in the first degree. 2.____
   When must Janelle file a notice of appearance with the court?
   A. Before opening argument
   B. Before her first appearance in court or 10 days after her appointment, whichever is sooner
   C. 10 days after her appointment as Stephanie's attorney
   D. No later than Stephanie's first scheduled arraignment

3. Tony is a new associate at the law offices of Deck & Decker, LLP. He needs to file a motion to dismiss for his managing attorney's client and is unsure of where to deliver the papers for the court's consideration. 3.____
   Unless directed to do directly by the court, papers for consideration of the court should be delivered to
   A. the presiding judge
   B. the clerk's office of the trial court in the appropriate courtroom
   C. any of the judges in the appropriate courtroom
   D. the bailiff or court officer on duty

4. How many terms of court are in one year? 4.____
   A. 12   B. 13   C. 26   D. 52

5. Upon otherwise excluded from a courtroom by the judge, the Family Court is open to the 5.____
   A. families having business in the court only
   B. extended families having business in the court only
   C. public
   D. judge's law clerks and court officers only

6. Which of the following is a factor the judge may consider in excluding someone from the courtroom during a Family Court proceeding? 6.____
   The person is
   A. causing or likely to cause a disruption in the proceedings
   B. related to a member of the family in the court
   C. related to the judge or other clerk
   D. an alternate court officer

2 (#1)

7. Which of the following are appropriate considerations for a pre-trial conference? 7.____
   A. Completion of discovery
   B. Admissions of fact
   C. Possibilities for settlement
   D. All of the above

8. In any proceeding to determine temporary or permanent custody or visitation, once a hearing or trial is commenced, it shall proceed to conclusion within _____ days. 8.____
   A. 30   B. 60   C. 90   D. 120

Questions 9-12.

DIRECTIONS: Questions 9 through 12 are to be answered on the basis of the following fact pattern.

Tim and Kat have two children together. After their divorce, Tim was ordered to pay child support in the amount of $480 per month. Soon after divorcing, Tim lost his job as a paralegal with a local law firm but quickly found another job that paid more than double his paralegal salary. Tim has not paid child support in over six months. Kat recently learned that Tim has been earning more than enough money to pay the monthly support obligation as well as the amount Tim owes in arrears.

9. What must Kat file in order to schedule a hearing to determine nonpayment of child support? 9.____
   A. A petition that alleges willful violation of an order of support
   B. A subpoena that requires Tim to hand over his bank statements
   C. A summons that requires Tim to hand over his bank statements
   D. A notice of deposition to inform Tim that a complaint will follow

10. After the judge or support magistrate commences a hearing to determine whether Tim is purposefully evading paying child support, how many adjournments can each side request? 10.____
    A. Unlimited
    B. Up to two adjournments each
    C. Only one adjournment can be permitted, and only to secure counsel
    D. No adjournments are permitted

11. The hearing must conclude within how many days of commencement? 11.____
    A. 30   B. 60   C. 90   D. 120

12. Assume that testimony must be taken in the hearing between Tim and Kat. The testimony will be given by Tim's former employer, Bob, who has recently moved to Idaho. 12.____
    Can Bob provide testimony by telephone or other electronic means?
    A. Yes, with court approval and if the request is completed using an official form
    B. Yes, if Kat and Tim both consent to the method of testimony delivery

56

C. Yes, if Kat and Tim both consent in writing at least fifteen days prior to the scheduled hearing date
D. No

13. Which of the following must be submitted with a petition to terminate the birth mother's rights?
    A. Sworn written statement by the mother naming the father
    B. A blood sample of the child's maternal grandmother
    C. A blood or other DNA sample of the child's paternal grandmother
    D. A sworn written statement by any individual familiar with both the mother and father who can attest to the identity of both parties

14. When a child is placed in foster care, he or she comes under the jurisdiction of the _____ Court.
    A. Surrogates   B. Civil   C. Criminal   D. Family

15. Judge Slater presided over the hearing regarding Baby Jay's foster care placement. In a subsequent proceeding, Baby Jay's mother has decided to voluntarily terminate her parental rights.
    Will Judge Slater be assigned to the parental rights hearing?
    A. No
    B. Yes, if practicable
    C. Yes, if specifically requested by Baby Jay's current guardian
    D. Yes, if specifically requested by the parent requesting her rights be terminated

16. If a child in a custody proceeding is Native American, that child is subject to which of the following?
    A. Social Services Law
    B. Indian Child Welfare Act
    C. Child Welfare Act of Natives
    D. Division of American Children

17. Which of the following papers is required in an adoption proceeding?
    A. Certified copy of the birth certificate of the adoptive child
    B. Certified marriage certificate, where the adoptive parents are married
    C. A proposed order of adoption
    D. All of the above

18. The court may determine the best interests of the child in an adoption proceeding factoring in which of the following?
    A. The sexual orientation of the adoptive parents
    B. The race or ethnicity of the adoptive parents
    C. The age of the adoptive child
    D. None of the above

19. At any scheduled call of a calendar or at any conference, if all parties do not appear, the court may note the _____ on the record.
    A. dismissal   B. acquittal
    C. acquiescence   D. default

20. In any discontinued action, the attorney for the defendant shall file a stipulation or statement of discontinuance with the county clerk within _____ day(s) of such continuance.
    A. one   B. ten   C. fifteen   D. twenty

21. Unless the court otherwise provides, where the attorney of record for any party arranges for another attorney to conduct the trial, the trial counsel must be identified in writing to the court and all parties no later than 15 days after the pretrial conference or, if there is not a pretrial conference, at least _____ days before trial.
    A. 10   B. 5   C. 15   D. 30

22. A preliminary examination of a witness or juror by a judge or counsel prior to trial is known as the process of
    A. de jure
    B. benchmarking
    C. voir dire
    D. stare decisis

23. Which two pieces of information are attorneys prohibited from sharing in the process identified in Question 22?
    Counsel may not
    A. read from any pleadings or information potential jurors of the amount of money at issue
    B. identify their client or provide any background to the dispute at issue
    C. reveal their true identities or provide any detail as to where the dispute at issue took place
    D. provide any details about the case but may provide details on the identity of their client

24. A bifurcated trial is MOST appropriate in which of the following circumstances?
    A. A bar owner serves alcohol to a minor and may be both criminally liable and civilly liable for the damages to the minor
    B. A disgruntled neighbor who yells at his neighbor and kicks over his garden gnomes is sued
    C. A civil dispute between Amy and her former employer has come to the surface after Amy accuses her employer of sexual harassment
    D. A dispute between friends that is settled outside of court

25. Each attorney appearing in a proceeding shall file a
    A. written notice of appearance
    B. written order of appearance
    C. oral notice of appearance
    D. written issue of notice

KEY (CORRECT ANSWERS)

1.	A		11.	B
2.	B		12.	A
3.	B		13.	A
4.	B		14.	D
5.	C		15.	B
6.	A		16.	B
7.	D		17.	D
8.	C		18.	D
9.	A		19.	D
10.	C		20.	D

21. A
22. C
23. A
24. A
25. A

TEST 2

DIRECTIONS: Each question or incomplete statement is followed by several suggested answers or completions. Select the one that BEST answers the question or completes the statement. *PRINT THE LETTER OF THE CORRECT ANSWER IN THE SPACE AT THE RIGHT.*

1. Mark wants to postpone determination of his visitation rights to see his daughter, Maddie. He believes he has a better chance of getting to see Maddie more if he lives within an hour of Maddie's mother and Mark is not moving until the end of next month.
Generally, what is the time limitation on custody and/or visitation determination once a hearing is commenced?
   A. 30 days   B. 60 days   C. 90 days   D. 120 days

   1._____

2. Which party assigns criminal actions to judges?
   A. Chief Justice of the New York Supreme Court
   B. Nassau County Supreme Court
   C. The Presiding Judge in the district of jurisdiction
   D. The Chief Administrator of the Courts

   2._____

3. A _____ of court is a designated unit of the court in which specified business of the court is to be conducted by a judge or quasi-judicial officer.
   A. unit   B. division   C. part   D. sequence

   3._____

4. Tim has escaped from the Child Center in Albany. When a child absconds from a facility to which he or she was duly remanded, what action must an authorized representative of the facility take?
Written notice must be given to the clerk of the court from which the remand was made within _____ hours.
   A. 24   B. 36   C. 48   D. 72

   4._____

5. Which of the following individuals is qualified to serve as a Support Magistrate?
   A. Margaret, a senior paralegal with the Utica Family Court
   B. Jamal, a former court bailiff who has been an acting family law attorney for the last six years
   C. Sharon, a Colorado criminal court chief justice
   D. Amy, a New York City police officer who is family with child custody issues

   5._____

6. Support magistrates shall be appointed as nonjudicial employees of the Unified Court System on a full-time basis for a term of _____ years and, in the discretion of the Chief Administrator, may be reappointed for a subsequent _____-year terms.
   A. 1; 2   B. 3; 5   C. 3; 3   D. 3; 6

   6._____

7. Ed and Elizabeth were married for eight years and four children together. Ed filed for divorce, alleging that Elizabeth had an affair with one of Ed's coworkers, Tom. Ed is seeking full custody of all four children and wants the court to deny Elizabeth alimony and child support.
   Which of the following statements is a finding of fact?
   A. Elizabeth is most likely having an affair with Tom.
   B. Elizabeth is more than likely an adulterous spouse.
   C. Ed and Elizabeth were married for eight years.
   D. Elizabeth's request for child support is frivolous.

8. A certified copy of the birth certificate of the child must accompany which of the following hearings?
   A. An adoption proceeding
   B. Petition to terminate a birth mother's rights
   C. Extra-judicial surrender of a child
   D. All of the above

9. Which of the following qualify as a "special application" which must be made in writing and accompanied by affidavits setting forth the reason(s) for the application?
   A. Dispense with the statutorily required personal appearance
   B. Period of residence of a child
   C. Period of waiting after filing of the adoption petition
   D. All of the above

10. Rachel, a probation officer, has been asked to conduct an investigation into the guardianship of McKenzie, a recently orphaned four-year-old girl, in foster care. The court would like to appoint a guardian but needs a disinterested person to interview McKenzie's next of kin before rendering a decision.
    Is Rachel authorized to conduct such an investigation?
    A. No, because Rachel is not an attorney
    B. No, because Rachel is not a certified private investigator
    C. Yes, because Rachel is presumably over the age of 18
    D. Yes, because an investigation by a disinterested person is authorized if requested by the court

11. When a petition for temporary guardianship has been filed by an adoptive parent, the clerk of the court in which the petition has been filed shall distribute a written notice to the adoptive parents and lawyers who have appeared, and to the Commissioner of _____ or the Director of the _____, as appropriate.
    A. Mental Health; Family Court
    B. Court Services; Child Welfare Services
    C. Social Services; Probation Service
    D. Social Services; Family Court Services

12. Bella would like to terminate her parental rights and surrender her daughter to foster care. Bella, however, is unsure of how to proceed and is nervous to speak with any of the court officers or court clerks. Bella currently lives in Utica County, New York.
Which of the following individuals is designated to speak with Bella about bringing a proceeding under the Family Court Act before the proceeding is commenced?
   A. Commanding officer of any law enforcement agency providing police service in Utica County
   B. Utica County district attorney
   C. The clerk of the Family Court and the clerk of the criminal court of Utica County
   D. All of the above

Questions 13-15.

DIRECTIONS: Questions 13 through 15 are to be answered on the basis of the following fact pattern.

James is sixteen and does not attend school. He continuously disobeys his parents and has been caught selling drugs from his parent's home on at least one occasion.

13. James MOST likely qualifies as a(n)
   A. incarcerated person
   B. person in need of supervision
   C. indemnified individual
   D. indigent prisoner

14. May James' parents hire an attorney to represent James?
   A. No, the attorney will represent James and his parents wholly
   B. No, James must be proven guilty before an attorney can be appointed
   C. No, there is no such "Attorney for Child" concept in New York State
   D. Yes

15. James sold cocaine from his parent's apartment to an acquaintance of his from his old school. The buyer of the drugs, Sam, died of an overdose. Sam's parents have sued James. How is a court case against James commenced?
   A. Sam's parents must file a PINS petition in Family Court.
   B. A subpoena must be served on James' parents.
   C. An indictment must be filed in the county where the commission of the crime occurred or, in this case, in the county where James' parents reside.
   D. Discovery demands should be fulfilled by both sides before an action can be commenced.

16. Proceedings for adoption from an authorized agency shall be calendared within _____ days of the filing of the petition to review said petition and determine if there is an adequate basis for approving the adoption.
   A. 20   B. 30   C. 45   D. 60

17. Assume the same facts as in Question 16. The court shall schedule the appearance of the adoptive parent(s) and the child before the court, for approval of the adoption within _____ days of the date of the review.
   A. 20   B. 30   C. 45   D. 60

18. Is there a time limit for proceedings involving custody or visitation?
   A. Yes, once a hearing or trial is commenced, it must proceed to conclusion within 90 days
   B. Yes, once a hearing or trial is commenced, it must proceed to conclusion within 120 days
   C. No, as each case must be determined by the specific fact pattern presented to the court
   D. No, unless there is a petition from either party to expedite the proceeding

19. Admissions of fact, fixing a date for fact-finding and dispositional hearings are most appropriately confined to a
   A. pre-trial conference
   B. subpoena conference
   C. disposition hearing
   D. engagement of counsel determination

20. Which of the following individuals is LEAST likely to be permitted to access the pleadings of a Family Court case?
   A. A child who is a party to a proceeding
   B. Parents who are legally responsible for the care of the child subject to a proceeding
   C. A reporter for the New York Ledger
   D. An authorized representative of the child protective agency involved in the proceeding

21. The general public or any person may be excluded from a Family Court courtroom only if the judge presiding in the courtroom determines, on a case-by-case basis such exclusion
   A. is warranted in that case
   B. would prejudice the rights of the child
   C. would prejudice the rights of the parents
   D. would bring negative press to either party's attorney

22. Which of the following two documents are provided by the Family Court to assist in filing an appeal?
   A. Request for Appellate Division Intervention Form; Notice of Appeal
   B. Subpoena Request Form; Notice of Appeal
   C. Request for Appellate Division Intervention Form; Order of Appeal
   D. Order of Appeal; Notice of Appeal

23. The _____ shall conduct preliminary conferences with any person seeking to have a juvenile delinquency petition filed, concerning the advisability of requesting that a juvenile delinquency petition be filed and in order to gather information needed for a determination of the suitability of the case for adjustment.
    A. Chief Judicial Administrator
    B. Probation Service
    C. Court Clerk
    D. Family Services

24. Can hearings be recorded?
    A. No
    B. Not unless all parties consent in writing at least 60 days prior to arraignment
    C. Not unless the court's clerk approves
    D. yes

25. John's hearing to determine whether he is willfully not paying child support is scheduled for Tuesday morning. On Monday night, John becomes extremely ill with food poisoning.
    Will John's hearing be adjourned?
    A. No, under no circumstances will a hearing for willful nonpayment be adjourned
    B. No, unless the court's clerk is able to communicate John's illness to the court within 24 hours of the hearing
    C. Yes, if the court bailiff consents to the adjournment
    D. Yes, the hearing may be adjourned for illness of a party or other good cause

KEY (CORRECT ANSWERS)

1. C
2. D
3. C
4. C
5. B

6. B
7. C
8. D
9. D
10. D

11. C
12. D
13. B
14. D
15. A

16. D
17. B
18. A
19. A
20. C

21. A
22. A
23. B
24. D
25. D

EXAMINATION SECTION
TEST 1

DIRECTIONS: Each question or incomplete statement is followed by several suggested answers or completions. Select the one that BEST answers the question or completes the statement. *PRINT THE LETTER OF THE CORRECT ANSWER IN THE SPACE AT THE RIGHT.*

1. The rules contained in the Civil Practice Law and Rules (CPLR) MAY be amended ONLY by the
    I. Appellate Divisions
    II. Judicial Conference
    III. Legislature
    IV. Court of Appeals
   The CORRECT answer is:

   A. I only   B. II only   C. I, IV   D. II, III

2. The procedure in civil judicial proceedings in all courts of the state is

   A. governed by the CPLR unless the procedure is regulated by an inconsistent statute
   B. governed by the CPLR when there is an inconsistent statute
   C. governed by the Civil Practice Act
   D. always governed by the CPLR

3. Which of the following statements is(are) CORRECT?
    I. Procedural requirements under the CPLR should be strictly construed.
    II. The words *special proceeding* include an action.
    III. Except where otherwise prescribed by law, procedure in special proceedings shall be the same as in actions.
    IV. If a court has obtained jurisdiction over the parties, a civil judicial proceeding can still be dismissed SOLELY because it is not brought in the proper form.
    V. Under the CPLR, the word *judgment* means only a final judgment.
   The CORRECT answer is:

   A. I, II, III, IV, V   B. I, II, III, IV
   C. I, II, IV, V   D. III only

4. Which of the following are CORRECT?
   The person prosecuting a civil action or proceeding may be called
    I. petitioner
    II. poor person
    III. plaintiff
    IV. respondent
    V. defendant
   The CORRECT answer is:

   A. I, II, III   B. II, III, V   C. IV, V   D. II, III

5. A special proceeding may BEST be described as

   A. an important civil judicial proceeding
   B. a civil judicial proceeding wherein prosecution in the form of a special proceeding is authorized
   C. all civil judicial proceedings which are not designated *actions* in the CPLR
   D. a civil judicial proceeding relating solely to election matters

6. A civil action is commenced by the service of a

   A. subpoena
   B. subpoena duces tecum
   C. summons
   D. complaint

7. Which of the following, if any, are necessary parties who MUST be joined in an action? Persons
   I. who ought to be parties if complete relief is to be accorded between the parties who are parties to the action
   II. who assert a right of joint relief arising out of the same transaction involved in the complaint where there is a common question of law or of fact
   III. designated by the court in an order to show cause
   IV. who, if not joined, might be inequitably affected by a judgment

   The CORRECT answer is:

   A. None of the above
   B. All of the above
   C. II, III
   D. I, IV

8. Which of the following statements is(are) INCORRECT?
   I. The difference between permissive joinder and necessary joinder is that permissive joinder means that parties may be joined in an action only when they consent.
   II. An action may continue without joinder of necessary parties but only by permission of the court when justice requires and when jurisdiction cannot be obtained over the necessary party except by his consent or appearance.
   III. When a person who should be a plaintiff refuses to join the action, he may be made a third-party defendant.
   IV. When a person who should be a plaintiff refuses to join the action as such, he may be made a defendant.
   V. An action may never continue without joinder of necessary parties.

   The CORRECT answer is:

   A. V *only*   B. I, II, IV   C. II, IV   D. I, III, V

9. In determining whether to permit an action to proceed without the joinder of a necessary party, the court should consider whether
   I. the guardian of an infant may be made a party
   II. jurisdiction may be obtained by substituted service
   III. the plaintiff has an effective remedy in case the action is dismissed on account of the nonjoinder
   IV. an effective judgment may be rendered in the absence of a person who is not joined

   The CORRECT answer is:

   A. I, II, III   B. II, III, IV   C. I, II   D. III, IV

10. Which of the following statements is (are) INCORRECT?
    I. Misjoinder of parties may be a ground for dismissal of an action.
    II. The court may order the addition or deletion of a party only on a motion by one of the parties.
    III. A guardian of an infant's property may be sued without joining the infant as a party.
    IV. An action may never be dismissed for nonjoinder of a necessary party.
    The CORRECT answer is:

    E. III only   F. I, II   G. I, II, III   H. I, II, III, IV

11. An action in which there is a common question of interest to many persons may be brought in the form of a(n)

    A. motion for leave to intervene
    B. successive third-party complaint
    C. class action
    D. interpleader action

12. Which of the following statements, if any, is(are) INCORRECT?
    I. The Attorney-General must be notified by the court when the constitutionality of a state statute is involved in the action.
    II. The Attorney-General may be permitted to intervene in the discretion of the court when public retirement benefits are at issue.
    III. A person shall be permitted to intervene as of right when the representation of that person's interest by the parties already in the action may be inadequate provided a timely motion is made.
    IV. A person shall be permitted to intervene in an action as of right at any time prior to final judgment.
    The CORRECT answer is:

    A. I, III   B. I only   C. II, III   D. II, IV

13. Which of the following statements, if any, is(are) INCORRECT?
    I. The stakeholder may be discharged of his liability for a liquidated claim by conceding the liability and paying the fund or the object of the claim into court.
    II. Interpleader is a procedure whereby a person who is called a stakeholder may be brought into an action in which there are adverse claimants to the same fund.
    III. Intervention is a procedure whereby a person who is called a stakeholder may be brought into an action in which there are adverse claimants to the same fund.
    IV. Intervention is a procedure by which a person not a party to an action enters that action for the purpose of protecting his rights.
    The CORRECT answer is:

    A. I, IV   B. II only   C. I only   D. II, III

14. John Doe has been held in contempt for his refusal to call off an illegal strike against his employer. Doe has been arrested and is lodged in the civil jail.
Doe may be kept in jail

    A. not more than three months
    B. not more than six months
    C. until he posts bail
    D. until he calls off the strike

15. In executing an order of civil arrest, the LEAST desirable place to make the arrest is

    A. the defendant's place of business
    B. in a public place
    C. on the street outside the defendant's home
    D. the defendant's home

16. An order of civil arrest has been issued for an Orthodox Jew.
On which of the following days is he immune from arrest?

    A. Only on Saturday
    B. Only on Sunday
    C. On both Saturday and Sunday
    D. Neither on Saturday nor on Sunday

17. Of the following persons, the one who is NOT immune from civil arrest is a(n)

    A. ordained clergyman
    B. maid who works at the French Ambassador's home
    C. fireman on duty
    D. marine on active duty

18. After an order of civil arrest has been signed, it

    A. may not be withdrawn without a court order
    B. must be executed within ten days
    C. must be filed in the county clerk's office
    D. may be withdrawn by the plaintiff's attorney anytime before it is executed

19. Even though the defendant is known to be in New York, the one of the following which need NOT be personally served upon him is a(n)

    A. order preliminarily enjoining the defendant
    B. order temporarily restraining the defendant
    C. subpoena duces tecum commanding defendant to deliver books
    D. summons

20. The provisional remedy of civil arrest is available in an action for

    A. trespass to a chattel
    B. ejectment
    C. specific performance of a contract to convey land located outside the state
    D. specific performance of a contract to convey land located in the state

KEY (CORRECT ANSWERS)

1. D
2. A
3. D
4. A
5. B

6. C
7. D
8. D
9. D
10. C

11. C
12. D
13. D
14. D
15. D

16. C
17. A
18. D
19. A
20. C

TEST 2

DIRECTIONS: Each question or incomplete statement is followed by several suggested answers or completions. Select the one that BEST answers the question or completes the statement. *PRINT THE LETTER OF THE CORRECT ANSWER IN THE SPACE AT THE RIGHT.*

1. The FIRST paper served in a civil action in the Supreme Court is a   1.___

   A. subpoena   B. injunction   C. summons   D. complaint

2. The books containing the decisions of the New York courts are known as   2.___

   A. framed issues   B. citations
   C. reports   D. references

3. The term applied to a person appointed to represent an infant in an action in the Supreme Court is: 3.___

   A. Testamentary guardian   B. Guardian ad litem
   C. Referee   D. Guardian of the person

4. The statute of limitations is a law limiting the   4.___

   A. sentence that may be imposed upon conviction for a particular crime
   B. courts in which an action may be brought
   C. amount of money that may be awarded in a civil action
   D. time within which criminal prosecution or civil action must be commenced

5. A guardian ad litem is a guardian for   5.___

   A. the purpose of conserving real property
   B. the purpose of representing a corporation
   C. a particular lawsuit
   D. all purposes

6. In an ex parte proceeding,   6.___

   A. special relief is sought by both parties in judge's chambers
   B. only one side is heard without notice to the other side
   C. each side is heard separately before the court on different days
   D. both sides are heard before a court without a jury

7. 29 N.Y.S. 2d 53 means, in part,   7.___

   A. 53rd volume   B. 29th page
   C. second volume   D. 2d series

8. When a court refers to *McKinney's,* it means the   8.___

   A. rules of evidence
   B. local ordinances
   C. consolidated laws of New York State
   D. federal rules

9. A poor person is a(n)

   A. infant whose father has less than $300 in property
   B. person who has been adjudicated an incompetent
   C. person who is unable to pay the costs, fees, and expenses necessary to prosecute or defend the action
   D. person who has less than $300 in real or personal property

10. Which of the following statements are CORRECT?
    I. A motion for the appointment of a guardian ad litem may be made at any stage of the action.
    II. The court may direct the appearance of an adult who is incapable of adequately prosecuting or defending his rights by a guardian ad litem even if that adult has not been judicially declared incompetent.
    III. An infant must always appear in an action by a guardian ad litem.
    IV. Where an infant is over 14 years of age, it is not necessary to serve a copy of a notice of motion for the appointment of a guardian ad litem on anyone other than the infant.
    V. A default judgment may never be entered against an infant or a person judicially declared to be an incompetent.
    VI. A controversy involving an adult incapable of adequately protecting his rights may be submitted to arbitration without a court order.

    The CORRECT answer is:

    A. I, IV, V   B. I, II, III   C. I, II, IV   D. I, II, VI

11. New York courts do NOT acquire jurisdiction over a nonresident under the *long-arm* statute when the cause of action arises out of

    A. the commission of a tort in New York
    B. solicitation of business within New York by the circulation of catalogues
    C. entering into a contract in New York
    D. possession of real property in New York

12. An article 78 proceeding may be brought against a public official or body

    A. to review capricious acts
    B. to enjoin such a body from proceeding where it is claimed that the action is unauthorized
    C. to compel the performance of a duty required by law
    D. for all of the above

13. A motion for summary judgment in lieu of a complaint is available in an action

    A. on account stated
    B. to recover payments pursuant to a separation agreement
    C. other than a matrimonial action if the moving papers establish a prima facie case and there is no real defense
    D. based upon a judgment

14. In which of the following provisional remedies, granted before a summons is served, must jurisdiction be acquired over the defendant or his property within a certain time limit or else the provisional remedy becomes void?
Attachment

    A. and arrest
    B. and lis pendens (notice of pendency)
    C. arrest, and receivership
    D. injunction, and lis pendens (notice of pendency)

15. The sheriff has properly delivered an income execution to D's employer. The employer has refused to honor the execution.
The plaintiff's lawyer should NOW serve

    A. motion papers on the employer to punish him for contempt
    B. a notice of petition and a petition to obtain a judgment against the employer
    C. motion papers on the employer, to obtain an order directing payment
    D. a subpoena upon the employer restraining him from paying D

16. An order of civil arrest has been signed against Doe in an action for fraud. The action has not yet been commenced.
The summons MUST be served

    A. within 48 hours after Doe is arrested
    B. within 30 days after the arrest order is signed or the arrest order will become void
    C. at the time the deputy sheriff arrests Doe
    D. at a time not specified by any of the foregoing

17. The date on which a summons is prepared in a civil action

    A. is the date upon which the statute of limitations stops running
    B. is the date from which the defendant measures his time in which to appear
    C. must be typed on the face of the summons
    D. has no legal significance

18. An attorney has delivered an execution to the sheriff's office.
A levy may thereafter be made under this execution within sixty days

    A. or else the execution becomes void and cannot be extended
    B. unless the period is extended (by a maximum of one sixty-day increment) in writing by the plaintiff's attorney
    C. unless the period is extended by court order
    D. unless the period is extended by successive sixty-day periods in writing by the plaintiff's attorney

19. John Doe, a judgment debtor, has personal property stored in a warehouse owned by X. X has issued to Doe a negotiable warehouse receipt for the property.
A PROPER way to levy upon this property is to

    A. go to the warehouse and seize the property
    B. seize the warehouse receipt from Doe
    C. go to the warehouse and leave the execution with X
    D. do none of the foregoing

20. A and B, two individuals, are partners in a finance company known as Ace Finance. A judgment has been entered against B for his negligence in driving his family automobile on a pleasure trip to Miami.
This judgment may be executed by levying upon

   A. B's desk in the office of Ace Finance
   B. B's interest in the partnership
   C. a bank account maintained in the name of Ace Finance
   D. B's Timex watch, worth $25.00

20.____

KEY (CORRECT ANSWERS)

1.	C	11.	B
2.	C	12.	D
3.	B	13.	D
4.	D	14.	B
5.	C	15.	B
6.	B	16.	C
7.	D	17.	D
8.	C	18.	D
9.	C	19.	B
10.	D	20.	B

TEST 3

DIRECTIONS: Each question or incomplete statement is followed by several suggested answers or completions. Select the one that BEST answers the question or completes the statement. *PRINT THE LETTER OF TEE CORRECT ANSWER IN THE SPACE AT THE RIGHT.*

1. Escheat is a legal term meaning that   1.____

   A. a fraud has been committed
   B. property has reverted to the state
   C. an agent's license has been revoked
   D. property under a trust deed may be reconveyed

2. A contract of sale passes   2.____

   A. the full fee simple title to the purchaser
   B. only an equitable title
   C. the legal title
   D. an estate for years

3. The instrument used to remove the lien of a trust deed from record is called a   3.____

   A. satisfaction
   B. release
   C. deed of reconveyance
   D. certificate of redemption

4. A power of attorney is terminated by   4.____

   A. an express revocation by the principal
   B. the death of the principal
   C. incapability of the principal to contract
   D. any of the above

5. For negotiating the sale of a business opportunity business without a license, a person may be prosecuted by a(n)   5.____

   A. jury
   B. judge of a superior court
   C. district attorney
   D. attorney general

6. A married woman is legally capable of contracting at the minimum age of   6.____

   A. seventeen   B. eighteen   C. twenty   D. twenty-one

7. In searching the records at the county recorder's office, you can usually distinguish a second trust deed from the first trust deed by the   7.____

   A. heading of the recorded documents
   B. information contained in the note
   C. recorder's declaration
   D. time and date of recordation

8. The MINIMUM time which must run after publication of a notice to creditors, under the provisions of the Uniform Commercial Code pertaining to bulk sales before consummation of the sale, is _____ days.   8.____

   A. 5   B. 10   C. 15   D. 20

9. To be valid, a bill of sale MUST be

   A. dated B. signed C. notarized D. witnessed

10. Property held in joint tenancy, upon the death of one of the tenants, passes to the

    A. landlord
    B. state
    C. county assessor
    D. surviving joint tenant

11. Alienation expresses a meaning MOST completely opposite to

    A. acquisition
    B. ad valorem
    C. acceleration
    D. amortization

12. Anything that is fastened or attached to real property permanently is considered to be _____ property.

    A. personal B. real C. private D. separate

13. The instrument used to secure a loan on personal property is called a

    A. bill of sale
    B. trust deed
    C. security agreement
    D. bill of exchange

14. A promissory note that provides for payment of interest only during the term of the note would be a(n) _____ note.

    A. installment
    B. straight
    C. amortized
    D. non-negotiable

15. Community property is property owned by

    A. churches
    B. husband and wife
    C. the municipality
    D. the community

16. The seller is sometimes called the

    A. vendee B. vendor C. lessee D. lessor

17. A contract based on an illegal consideration is

    A. valid B. void C. legal D. enforceable

18. A check that has been altered or raised by a person other than the maker is

    A. valid B. invalid C. cancelled D. dishonorable

19. A valid bill of sale MUST contain

    A. a date
    B. an acknowledgment
    C. the seller's signature
    D. a verification

20. A security agreement is USUALLY given in connection with

    A. real property
    B. agricultural property
    C. rentals
    D. personal property

21. Title to fixtures, shelves, counters, and merchandise is transferred or conveyed by

    A. deed
    B. bill of sale
    C. security agreement
    D. escrow

22. Involuntary alienation of an estate means:

    A. Estate cannot be transferred without the consent of the owner
    B. Aliens are forbidden to own estates in fee simple in the state
    C. Ownership of estates may be transferred by operation of law
    D. No one can be compelled to transfer title without his consent

23. When a broker receives a deposit on a business which he has listed, the money becomes the property of the

    A. seller
    B. broker
    C. escrow company
    D. prospective buyers

24. A financing statement may be released from the records by

    A. payment in full
    B. a reconveyance
    C. filing a release statement
    D. death of the mortgagor

25. The stock and fixtures that are to be transferred with the sale of a business are usually enumerated in a(n)

    A. contract of sale
    B. inventory
    C. deed
    D. appraisal

KEY (CORRECT ANSWERS)

1.	B		11.	A
2.	C		12.	B
3.	A		13.	C
4.	D		14.	B
5.	C		15.	B
6.	B		16.	B
7.	B		17.	B
8.	A		18.	B
9.	B		19.	C
10.	D		20.	D

21.	A
22.	C
23.	A
24.	A
25.	B

EXAMINATION SECTION
TEST 1

DIRECTIONS: Each question or incomplete statement is followed by several suggested answers or completions. Select the one that BEST answers the question or completes the statement. *PRINT THE LETTER OF THE CORRECT ANSWER IN THE SPACE AT THE RIGHT.*

1. Change of venue of trial of action pending in another court may be made in the Supreme Court upon motion of

    A. plaintiff
    B. defendant
    C. plaintiff's attorney
    D. defendant's attorney
    E. any party

2. Exceptions for size for each paper served or filed include all of the following EXCEPT:

    A. Summonses
    B. Subpoenas
    C. Complaints
    D. Notices of appearance
    E. Notes of issue and exhibits

3. The title of action shall include the names of all parties in each paper served or filed in a

    A. subpoena
    B. summons
    C. notice of appearance
    D. note of issue and exhibit
    E. all of the above

4. Papers to be served or filed MUST be *originals* rather than copies for

    A. orders
    B. affidavits
    C. exhibits
    D. all of the above
    E. none of the above

5. How long does the party upon whom a paper is served have to return the paper to the party serving it with a statement of particular objections?

    A. 12 hours
    B. 1 day
    C. 2 days
    D. 1 week
    E. 10 days

6. Who can serve papers?

    A. Any officer of the court
    B. The clerk of the court or the clerk of the county
    C. Any person of the age of 21 years or over
    D. Any person not a party of the age of 18 years or over
    E. Any person not a party of the age of 21 years or over

7. Service of papers upon an attorney can be made in several ways. Which method should be used ONLY if the others are not possible?

A. Mailing the paper to him
B. Leaving the paper at his office with a person in charge
C. Leaving the paper at his office in a conspicuous place
D. Leaving the paper at his residence with a person of suitable age and discretion
E. Depositing the paper, enclosed in a sealed wrapper directed to him, in his office letter drop

8. A subpoena to compel production of an original record where a certified copy is admissable in evidence shall be issued by

   A. the clerk of the county
   B. the Court
   C. the Attorney General
   D. the attorney of record for a party
   E. any of the above

9. An agreement relating to any matter in an action is NOT binding upon a party unless it

   A. is made between parties
   B. is in writing subscribed by him or his attorney
   C. is made between parties and their attorneys
   D. all of the above
   E. none of the above

10. Which instrument requires the attendance of a person to give testimony? A

    A. subpoena
    B. summons
    C. notice of appearance
    D. notice of motion
    E. summons and order

11. A motion to quash, fix conditions, or modify a subpoena shall be made

    A. in the court in which the subpoena is returnable
    B. to the person issuing it
    C. in the Supreme Court
    D. to an attorney of record for a party to an action
    E. in an administrative proceeding authorized by law to determine the matter

12. A subpoena *duces tecum* requires production of books

    A. *only*
    B. by *any* person
    C. by any person able to identify and testify respecting origin, purpose and custody
    D. by the person subpoenaed
    E. and payment of cost of reproduction and transportation

13. A subpoena duces tecum served upon a hospital requiring production of records relating to a patient must be served AT LEAST _____ hours before the time fixed for production.

    A. 24   B. 36   C. 48   D. 60   E. 72

14. Review of proceedings following the warrant of commitment issued for disobedience of a subpoena shall be held within _____ days.

    A. 3   B. 10   C. 20   D. 30   E. 90

15. A subpoenaed person failing to comply with a subpoena shall be liable for a penalty NOT exceeding 15._____

   A. $1.00   B. $20.00   C. $50.00   D. $100.00   E. $250.00

16. The certificate of an oath administered by an authorized officer of the armed forces of the United States must state 16._____

   A. the rank of the person taking the oath
   B. place where oath is taken
   C. command to which person taking the oath is attached
   D. serial number of the person taking the oath
   E. all of the above

17. Calendar rules shall be uniform within 17._____

   A. the state
   B. each county
   C. each judical division
   D. the city
   E. each city having population of one million or more inhabitants

18. The clerk shall enter the case upon the calendar as of the date of 18._____

   A. filing of the note of issue
   B. joinder of issue
   C. service of the summons
   D. return of service
   E. proof of service

19. All of the following are entitled to trial preference EXCEPT an action 19._____

   A. brought by or against the state
   B. where preference is provided by statute
   C. in which the interests of justice will be served by an early trial
   D. upon the application of a party at least 75 years old
   E. to recover pecuniary damages

20. Civil cases are generally tried in the order in which 20._____

   A. the clerk shall determine
   B. justice will be best served
   C. notes of issue have been filed
   D. the court directs
   E. joinder of issue has been filed

21. Unless the court otherwise orders, notice of a motion for preference is served by the party serving the note of issue 21._____

   A. along with the note of issue
   B. ten days after such service
   C. twenty four hours after such service
   D. 48 hours after such service
   E. at any time prior to trial

22. A case in the Supreme Court is deemed abandoned if it is struck from the calendar and NOT restored within

    A. 3 months
    B. 6 months
    C. 1 year
    D. 10 years
    E. 20 years

23. At what point is it admissable to establish if the cost of medical care in a medical malpractice action was replaced from any collateral source? It

    A. depends on the type of action
    B. depends on the amount involved
    C. depends on whether the indemnification was in whole or in part
    D. is admissable at the trier's discretion
    E. is always admissable

24. All of the following collateral sources shall be considered in any action for medical malpractice EXCEPT:

    A. Insurance
    B. Sources entitled by law to liens against recovery
    C. Social Security
    D. Worker's Compensation
    E. Employee benefit program

25. The sequence in which issues shall be tried are determined by

    A. the plaintiff's attorney
    B. the defendant's attorney
    C. motion
    D. the court
    E. stipulation of the parties

26. The judge is furnished with copies of each pleading by

    A. the party who filed the note of issue
    B. the clerk of the court
    C. the plaintiff's attorney
    D. the defendant's attorney
    E. both attorneys

27. The presiding judge may direct trial at a place other than the courthouse

    A. in the interest of justice
    B. at his discretion
    C. to effect an early trial
    D. upon stipulation of the parties
    E. if the action is brought by or against the state or a political subdivision

28. A motion for trial by a referee shall generally be made

    A. at the same time note of issue is filed
    B. within 10 days after note of issue is filed
    C. within 20 days after note of issue is filed
    D. within 30 days after note of issue is filed
    E. upon at least one day's notice before trial

29. Where increased damages are granted by statute

    A. decision shall be entered for the increased amount
    B. judgment shall be entered for the increased amount
    C. report shall be entered for the increased amount
    D. verdict shall specify the increased amount
    E. a referee shall report the specific amount

30. An action in which a party demands and sets forth facts which permit a judgment for a sum of money only is

    A. tried by witnesses   B. tried by examination
    C. tried by the court   D. determined by referee
    E. tried by a jury

31. A party may NOT withdraw a demand for trial by jury *without*

    A. the consent of the other parties
    B. serving upon each party the withdrawal
    C. filing a note of issue containing such withdrawal
    D. filing a written withdrawal with the clerk
    E. an oral withdrawal in open court

32. A party served with a note of issue NOT containing a demand for trial by jury has _____ day(s) after service to file a demand for jury trial.

    A. 1   B. 5   C. 10   D. 15   E. 20

33. The right to trial by jury shall be deemed waived by all parties if

    A. the note of issue did not contain a demand
    B. no note of issue is filed in the action
    C. no party demands trial by jury
    D. a party files a written waiver
    E. no undue prejudice to the rights of all parties would result

34. After service of the demand for trial by jury of *only* some of the issues a party has _____ day(s) to file a demand for trial by jury of any other issues in the action.

    A. 1   B. 5   C. 10   D. 15   E. 20

35. A party specifies the issues of an action which he wishes tried by jury by

    A. filing a written waiver with the clerk
    B. filing an oral waiver in open court
    C. stipulation prior to trial
    D. specifying those issues in his demand for trial by jury
    E. the court shall decide any issue not required to be tried by jury

36. A party who has demanded the trial of an issue of fact by a jury waives his right by

    A. failing to file a written waiver with the clerk
    B. failing to appear at the trial
    C. failing to give an oral waiver in open court
    D. all of the above
    E. none of the above

37. When does a waiver NOT withdraw a demand for trial by jury? When

    A. no note of issue is filed
    B. there is no consent of the other parties
    C. the party fails to appear at the trial
    D. the waiver was not filed within 15 days of service
    E. the note of issue does not contain an express waiver

38. A party is deemed to have waived the right to trial by jury of the issues of fact arising upon a claim

    A. by joining it with another claim with no right to trial by jury
    B. by joining it with another claim which is based on a separate transaction
    C. when an issue of fact arises upon a counter-claim
    D. by asserting it in an action with no right to trial by jury
    E. none of the above

39. The Appellate Division in each department may by rule provide that a party shall have demanded trial by jury by

    A. filing a note of issue
    B. filing a note of issue containing a demand for trial by jury
    C. serving upon all other parties such demand
    D. filing a note of issue not specifying the issues
    E. filing a note of issue not containing an express waiver of trial by jury

40. A court may relieve a party from the effect of failing to comply with rules for demanding or waiving trial by jury when

    A. no undue prejudice to the rights of another party would result
    B. a party is entitled by the constitution to trial by jury
    C. there has been improper service
    D. failure to comply is the result of a defect in the form of a paper
    E. the issue to be tried arises on motion or pursuant to a judgment

41. When it appears in the course of a trial by the court that the adverse party is entitled to a trial by jury of certain issues of fact, the court shall

    A. give the adverse party opportunity to demand jury trial
    B. order a jury trial
    C. order a joint trial
    D. order any actions consolidated
    E. adjourn until such issues are tried and judgment filed

42. In a civil trial, what is the MINIMUM number of jurors?

    A. 4   B. 6   C. 7   D. 9   E. 12

43. In a civil trial, how many alternate jurors are chosen?

    A. 0   B. 1   C. 2   D. 3   E. 4

7 (#1)

44. Additional jurors may be drawn   44._____
    A. at the court's discretion
    B. unless the right is specifically waived by a party
    C. when one or more of the regular jurors has reached the age of 75 years
    D. upon the request of a party
    E. as they are needed

45. Alternate jurors are drawn in the same manner as regular jurors EXCEPT that they are   45._____
    A. not drawn at the same time
    B. not drawn from the same source
    C. not required to have the same qualifications
    D. not subject to the same examinations and challenges
    E. none of the above

46. The treatment of alternate jurors differs from that of regular jurors in that they   46._____
    A. are not seated with them
    B. do not take the oath with them
    C. are not treated in the same manner
    D. are discharged before the final submission of the case
    E. are discharged after the final submission of the case

47. When an alternate juror replaces a regular juror that is unable to perform his duty, he 47._____
    A. must be first approved and sworn
    B. is treated as an active alternate juror
    C. is treated as if he had been seated as one of the regular jurors
    D. must have the same qualification as the replaced juror
    E. is sworn at the time of replacement or before the final submission of the case, whichever comes first

48. A judge shall be present at the examination of the jurors   48._____
    A. on application of any party
    B. unless appearance is waived
    C. unless parties stipulate to excuse him
    D. on stipulation of the parties
    E. upon motion of any party

49. An objection to the qualifications of a juror MUST be made by   49._____
    A. motion   B. challenge   C. demand
    D. waiver   E. objection

50. In a civil trial, how many peremptory challenges shall each party have?   50._____
    A. 1   B. 2   C. 3   D. 4   E. 5

KEY (CORRECT ANSWERS)

1. E	11. A	21. A	31. A	41. A
2. C	12. C	22. C	32. D	42. B
3. B	13. A	23. E	33. C	43. C
4. E	14. E	24. B	34. C	44. D
5. C	15. C	25. D	35. D	45. E
6. D	16. D	26. A	36. B	46. E
7. D	17. D	27. D	37. B	47. C
8. B	18. A	28. C	38. E	48. A
9. B	19. E	29. B	39. E	49. B
10. A	20. C	30. E	40. A	50. C

EXAMINATION SECTION
TEST 1

DIRECTIONS: Each question or incomplete statement is followed by several suggested answers or completions. Select the one that BEST answers the question or completes the statement. *PRINT THE LETTER OF THE CORRECT ANSWER IN THE SPACE AT THE RIGHT.*

1. How many peremptory challenges for alternate jurors shall each party have?

    A. The unused challenges allowed for regular jurors
    B. The unused challenges allowed for regular jurors plus one additional challenge
    C. One challenge for every two alternates
    D. One challenge for each alternate
    E. One challenge for all alternates

2. In order to disqualify a juror for relationship, any other unrelated party MUST raise the objection

    A. no later than 6 months after the verdict
    B. before the case is opened
    C. at the time of verdict
    D. before the final submission of the case
    E. during the pendency of the action

3. The court instructs the jury on the law as set forth in the requests

    A. before the jury retires
    B. after the jury is sworn
    C. before the close of the evidence
    D. at the close of the evidence
    E. after the arguments are completed

4. When the answers to interrogatories are consistent with each other, but one or more is inconsistent with the general verdict, the court shall

    A. direct the entry of judgment in accordance with the answers, notwithstanding the general verdict
    B. require the jury to further consider its answers
    C. require the jury to further consider its verdict
    D. order a new trial
    E. all of the above

5. All of the following are included in the clerk's entry when the jury renders a verdict EXCEPT the

    A. time and place of the verdict
    B. time and place of the trial
    C. names of jurors and witnesses
    D. the general verdict
    E. answers to written interrogatories

2 (#1)

6. A referee to inquire and report shall have power to

   A. determine the issues
   B. motion for trial
   C. expedite the disposition of the issues
   D. take affidavits
   E. make conclusions of law

7. The decision of the court shall state

   A. all the facts
   B. the facts it deems essential
   C. none of the facts
   D. only facts reported by referee to report
   E. facts of demand

8. How many days are allowed for the decision of the court after the cause or matter is finally submitted?

   A. 10   B. 30   C. 40   D. 60   E. 90

9. A motion for judgment must be granted as to any cause of action for medical malpractice based *solely* on lack of informed consent if

   A. the plaintiff moves for judgment
   B. it is in the interest of justice
   C. the defendant has failed to adduce expert medical testimony in support of the alleged qualitative insufficiency of the consent
   D. the plaintiff has failed to adduce expert medical testimony in support of the alleged qualitative insufficiency of the consent
   E. any party has failed to adduce expert medical testimony in support of the alleged qualitative insufficiency of the consent

10. The above motion is made

    A. at the end of the defendant's case
    B. at the end of the plaintiff's case
    C. after close of the evidence presented by an opposing party
    D. after the close of evidence
    E. at any time during the trial

11. The date from which interest is to be computed shall be

    A. filed with the note of issue
    B. stipulated
    C. fixed by the court
    D. fixed by the clerk of the court
    E. specified in the verdict, report or decision

12. The amount of interest shall be computed

    A. from the date the verdict was rendered
    B. to the date the verdict was rendered
    C. from the date the case was placed upon the calendar

D. to the date the case was placed upon the calendar
E. to the opening of the trial

13. The court may direct judgment upon a part of a cause of action 13.____

    A. upon motion of any party
    B. on its own iniative
    C. upon recitation of a default
    D. upon having ordered a severance
    E. only when judgment is interlocutory

14. Where judgment is set aside, the court may direct and enforce restitution in like manner 14.____
    as where a judgment is

    A. reversed on appeal   B. reviewed on appeal
    C. dismissed on appeal   D. was taken by default
    E. unmodified

15. Entry of judgment is deemed effected when 15.____

    A. the general verdict of a jury after a trial by jury is read
    B. signed by the presiding judge and filed by him
    C. entered by the clerk of the court
    D. signed by the clerk of the court
    E. signed by the clerk of the court and filed by him

16. When a party dies 16.____

    A. the verdict or decision is set aside
    B. no verdict or decision shall be rendered against him
    C. dismissal of an action is barred
    D. dismissal of an action is not barred
    E. judgment shall be made in the interest of justice

17. In addition to the usual content of the judgment-roll, in an action to recover a chattel, it 17.____
    also contains

    A. the required proof
    B. the sheriff's return
    C. the paper on which recovery was heard
    D. the affidavit and copy of the judgment
    E. each order involving the merits affecting the final judgment

18. The duration of the judgment lien on real property shall be measured from 18.____

    A. the docketing of the judgment
    B. when the judgment was entered
    C. filing of the final judgment
    D. the filing of certified copy of the order
    E. the filing of the judgment-roll

19. The cost of filing and mailing the satisfaction-piece is *ultimately* borne by the 19.____

    A. judgment creditor
    B. judgment debtor

C. person entitled to enforce judgment
D. the attorney of record for the judgment creditor
E. the attorney of record for the judgment debtor

20. The penalty for failing to execute and file the satisfaction-piece within the time allowed when the judgment is fully satisfied is

    A. $20.00   B. $50.00   C. $100.00   D. $250.00   E. $500.00

21. A money judgment may be enforced against any property UNLESS it

    A. could be assigned and transferred
    B. consists of a future right
    C. is vested
    D. is exempt from application
    E. is joint property of such persons against whom the judgment is entered

22. Where a judgment creditor has secured an order for payment of a debt owed to the judgment creditor, the judgment creditor's rights in the debt are _____ to the rights of any transferree of the debt.

    A. superior   B. equal   C. inferior
    D. separate   E. inapplicable

23. For what period of time may the court order an extension of the lien of a money judgment upon real property?

    A. No longer than 10 years
    B. For any time necessary
    C. No longer than the time during which the judgment creditor was stayed from enforcing the judgment
    D. For a period of one year renewable upon motion and notice
    E. For as long as justice requires

24. What percent of the earnings of the judgment debtor is EXEMPT from application to the satisfaction of a money judgment?

    A. 100   B. 90   C. 80   D. 75   E. 70

25. The exemption of a household from the application to the satisfaction of money judgments whose value exceeds $10,000.00 is

    A. void
    B. not void but the lien of a judgment attaches to 90% to the surplus
    C. not void if surplus interest is properly sold to another party
    D. not void but the lien of judgment attaches to the surplus
    E. not void for one year

26. In which court is the special proceeding commenced if no court in which a special proceeding is authorized by article could be commenced is in session?

    A. District   B. Municipal   C. Civil
    D. City   E. County

27. An information subpoena shall be returned with answers within _____ days after receipt.

    A. 5   B. 7   C. 10   D. 20   E. 30

28. What is required to compel a judgment debtor to appear for the taking of his disposition within one year after the conclusion of a previous examination of him with respect to the same judgment?

    A. A subpoena requiring attendance
    B. Failure of the witness to sign the deposition of the previous examination
    C. Leave of the court
    D. Motion of the judgment creditor, notice to the judgment debtor
    E. Court order

29. Within how many days after issuance must an execution be returned?

    A. 10   B. 15   C. 20   D. 30   E. 60

30. An interested person may commence a proceeding to determine adverse claims by serving a

    A. notice of petition
    B. notice of motion
    C. notice of action
    D. notice of protest
    E. presumptive notice

31. A petition for a writ of habeas corpus shall contain all of the following EXCEPT:

    A. The place of detention
    B. The cause of detention
    C. That a court or judge does not have exclusive jurisdiction to order the release
    D. A show cause order why the person detained has not been released
    E. The date and the court to whom every previous application for the writ has been made

32. If the person served with a writ of habeas corpus refuses to obey it

    A. a warrant of attachment shall be issued against him
    B. he may be compelled by the sheriff to obey
    C. he shall be brought to court and examined as in a criminal case
    D. a mandate shall be delivered to the person
    E. he forfeits to the person detained one thousand dollars to be recovered by an action in his name

33. The fact that a juror is in the employ of a party to the action shall constitute a ground for a

    A. challenge Propter Affectum
    B. challenge Propter Honoris Respectum
    C. principal challenge
    D. challenge for cause
    E. challenge to the favor

34. When the jury finds in favor of one or more parties it is a _____ verdict.

    A. special
    B. general
    C. adverse
    D. quotient
    E. open

35. If the court omits any issue of fact when requiring a special verdict, each party waives his right to trial by jury of the omitted issue UNLESS he demands its submission

    A. after the arguments are completed
    B. at the close of the evidence
    C. before the jury retires
    D. before the jury renders a verdict
    E. before the entry of the verdict

36. What type of verdict is required in medical malpractice actions?

    A. Itemized   B. Special   C. Quotient
    D. Unanimous   E. General

37. Any issue NOT required to be tried by a jury or referred to a referee is decided by

    A. stipulation   B. an advisory jury
    C. arbitration   D. opinion
    E. the court

38. In a medical malpractice action the decision of the court shall state the amount assigned to each element of _____ damages.

    A. special and general
    B. permanent and prospective
    C. actual
    D. compensatory and consequential
    E. compensatory and continuing

39. On motion of any party the court may order a new trial

    A. at the end of the plaintiff's case
    B. after the close of evidence
    C. at any time during the trial
    D. if motion is made within 15 days after the verdict
    E. if the verdict is contrary to the weight of evidence

40. A post trial motion for judgment and new trial shall be made before

    A. the appellate division
    B. the judge who presided at the trial
    C. any court
    D. any judge
    E. the court clerk

41. Within how many days after decision, verdict, or discharge, of the jury shall post trial motion be made?

    A. 10   B. 15   C. 20   D. 30   E. 45

42. Interest upon damage incurred after the earliest ascer-tainable date the cause of action existed is computed from

    A. the first date the cause of action existed
    B. the date fixed by the clerk of the court
    C. the date fixed by verdict, report, or decision

D. the date damage was incurred
E. a single reasonable intermediate date

43. Interest from verdict, report, or decision to judgment shall be computed by   43._____

    A. the clerk of the court
    B. the judge who presided at the trial
    C. the referee to report
    D. an advisory jury
    E. the court

44. The determination of the rights of the parties in an action is a(n)   44._____

    A. satisfaction-piece   B. decision
    C. verdict   D. opinion
    E. judgment

45. An action upon a money judgment entered in a court of the state may be maintained   45._____
    between the original parties to the judgment where

    A. five years have elapsed since the first docketing of the judgment
    B. the judgment was entered against the plaintiff by default for want of appearance
    C. the judgment was entered against the defendant for want of appearance and the summons was served by personal delivery
    D. the court in which the action is to be brought so orders on motion with such notice to such other persons as the court may direct
    E. all of the above

46. Judgment upon the decision of a court, or a referee to determine, shall be   46._____

    A. entered by referee to determine
    B. entered by the presiding judge
    C. entered by the court
    D. entered by the clerk
    E. an interlocutory judgment

47. A judgment may be entered in the name of an original party who is deceased when the   47._____
    party dies *before*

    A. entry of judgment and after a verdict
    B. an entered verdict
    C. verdict and after testimony
    D. verdict and after opening statements
    E. no event; it may not be entered

48. The _____ may require a mistake in the papers in the action of a judgment to be cured.   48._____

    A. county clerk
    B. appellate court
    C. clerk of the court
    D. Supreme Court clerk
    E. party whose right is affected

49. The county clerk makes an appropriate entry on his docket upon the filing of a certified copy of the order effecting the change in the case of a judgment of a court other than the

   A. appellate or circuit court
   B. city, county or supreme court
   C. municipal or civil court
   D. supreme, county or family court
   E. county or supreme court *only*

50. Within what period of time must the satisfaction-piece be executed after the entry of a judgment?

   A. 20 days
   B. 30 days
   C. 1 year
   D. 5 years
   E. 10 years

KEY (CORRECT ANSWERS)

1. D	11. E	21. D	31. D	41. B
2. A	12. B	22. A	32. A	42. D
3. E	13. D	23. C	33. E	43. A
4. E	14. A	24. B	34. B	44. E
5. A	15. E	25. D	35. C	45. D
6. C	16. B	26. E	36. A	46. D
7. B	17. B	27. B	37. E	47. A
8. D	18. E	28. C	38. A	48. B
9. D	19. B	29. E	39. C	49. D
10. B	20. C	30. A	40. B	50. E

EXAMINATION SECTION
TEST 1

DIRECTIONS: Each question or incomplete statement is followed by several suggested answers or completions. Select the one that BEST answers the question or completes the statement. *PRINT THE LETTER OF THE CORRECT ANSWER IN THE SPACE AT THE RIGHT.*

Questions 1-12.

DIRECTIONS: Questions 1 through 12 are based on the Criminal Procedure Law. Each question consists of two statements. Mark your answer.
- A. if only sentence I is correct
- B. if only sentence II is correct
- C. if sentences I and II are correct
- D. if neither sentence I nor II is correct

1. I. Except as otherwise provided in the Criminal Procedure Law, a prosecution for a misdemeanor must be commenced within three years after the commission thereof.
    II. Except as otherwise provided in the Criminal Procedure Law, a prosecution for a petty offense must be commenced within two years after the commission thereof.

2. I. A person may not be prosecuted twice for the same offense.
    II. A defendant may not be convicted of any offense upon the testimony of an accomplice unsupported by corroborative evidence tending to connect the defendant with the commission of such offense.

3. I. A defendant may testify in his own behalf, but his failure to do so is not a factor from which any inference unfavorable to him may be drawn.
    II. A child less than twelve years old may not testify under oath in a criminal proceeding in a court of law.

4. I. A person may be convicted of an offense solely upon evidence of a valid confession or admission made by him without additional proof that the offense charged has been committed.
    II. Evidence of a written or oral confession, admission, or other statement made by a defendant with respect to his participation or lack of participation in the offense charged may not be received in evidence against him in a criminal proceeding if such statement was involuntarily made.

5. I. A summons may be served by a police officer, or by a complainant at least eighteen years of age, or by any other person at least eighteen years old designated by the court.
    II. A summons may be served anywhere in the county of issuance or anywhere in an adjoining county in the state.

6. I. Any person may arrest another person for a felony anywhere in the state when the latter has in fact committed such felony.
    II. Any person may arrest another person for any offense other than a felony when the latter has in fact committed such offense in his presence, provided that the arrest is made only in the county in which such offense was committed.

7.   I. A search warrant must be executed not more than three days after the date and time of issuance and it must thereafter be returned to the court without unnecessary delay.
    II. No search warrant may be executed unless the police officer gives notice of his authority and purpose to the occupant of the premises or vehicle to be searched. In addition, the police officer must serve a copy of the warrant upon the occupant of said premises or vehicle.

8.   I. An appearance ticket may be issued by a police officer following an arrest without a warrant if the arrest was for a Class B misdemeanor but not if the arrest was for a Class A misdemeanor.
    II. An appearance ticket may, at the discretion of the police officer or other public servant authorized to issue appearance tickets, be served either personally or by registered or certified mail, return receipt requested.

9.   I. Under the *Youthful Offender Treatment* article of the Criminal Procedure Law (Article 720), *youth* means a person charged with a crime who was at least sixteen years old and less than nineteen years old at the time of his alleged commission of such crime.
    II. When an individual has been adjudged eligible for youthful offender treatment, he may be found guilty by reason of a preponderance of the evidence rather than guilty based upon proof beyond a reasonable doubt.

10.   I. A police officer may arrest a person without a warrant for any offense, other than for a petty offense, when he has reasonable cause to believe that such person has committed such offense, whether in his presence or otherwise.
    II. A police officer may arrest a person for a petty offense without a warrant when such offense was committed in the officer's presence, within the geographical area of such police officer's employment, and such arrest is made in the county where such offense was committed.

11.   I. A police officer may stop a person in a public place located within the geographical area of such officer's employment when he reasonably suspects that such person is committing, has committed or is about to commit either (a) a felony or (b) any misdemeanor as defined in the penal law, and may demand of him his name, address, occupation, the name and address of his employer, and an explanation of his conduct.
    II. Whenever a police officer stops a person in a public place for temporary questioning, he may search such person for a deadly weapon or any instrument, article or substance readily capable of causing serious physical injury and of a sort not ordinarily carried in public places by law-abiding persons.

12.   I. A defendant in any criminal action who is less than eighteen years old may refuse to permit himself to be fingerprinted unless accompanied by a parent or legal guardian.
    II. A police officer who is executing an arrest warrant need not have the warrant in his possession; if he has not, he must show it to the defendant upon request as soon after the arrest as possible.

Questions 13-24.

DIRECTIONS: Questions 13 through 24 are to be answered SOLELY on the basis of the Penal Law.

13. A person is guilty of grand larceny in the first degree when he steals property which

    A. consists of personal property valued at more than $1500
    B. is obtained by instilling in the victim a fear that that the victim's membership in a subversive organization will be revealed
    C. consists of goods valued in excess of $250
    D. is obtained by instilling in the victim a fear that an antique vase which he owns will be damaged

14. Using or threatening the immediate use of a dangerous instrument is an element of all of the following offenses EXCEPT _____ in the _____ degree.

    A. robbery; first
    B. burglary; first
    C. robbery; second
    D. burglary; second

15. Which of the following describes a person guilty of escape in the first degree?

    A. A person convicted of a felony escapes from a detention facility.
    B. A person just convicted of a misdemeanor escapes from a courtroom by impersonating a police officer.
    C. A person escapes from a police officer's custody by causing serious physical injury to the officer.
    D. After committing a felony, a person escapes from the scene of the crime by using or threatening the immediate use of a deadly weapon.

16. A person who wantonly and recklessly fires a rifle into a crowd of people without any specific intent to injure or kill would NOT be guilty of

    A. murder if death results
    B. assault in the first degree if serious physical injury results
    C. assault in the second degree if physical injury results
    D. reckless endangerment in the first degree if no injury results

17. Each of the following choices states an offense involving the forcible stealing of property, and certain additional facts.
    In which choice would the defendant be guilty of the offense stated, based SOLELY on the facts given in the choice? Robbery in the

    A. first degree - defendant robs a bank while carrying two sticks of dynamite, which cannot be seen under his jacket
    B. second degree - while defendant and his partner are fleeing from a store they have just robbed, the partner pushes a bystander to the ground, thereby causing a painful bruise to bystander's shoulder
    C. first degree - while robbing a bank, defendant threatens to kidnap and kill the manager's wife unless the manager gives him all the money in the vault
    D. second degree - defendant robs a jewelry store, while his partner waits in a getaway car parked around the corner

18. A person is ALWAYS guilty of a felony if he unlawfully possesses

    A. any loaded firearm in a vehicle
    B. any deadly weapon and is not a citizen of the United States
    C. any dagger or razor with intent to use the same unlawfully against another
    D. a shotgun in a building used for educational purposes

19. Knowing that Jones intends to rob a bank, Smith gives Jones a rifle to use during the robbery. However, the day before the robbery is supposed to occur, the police arrest Jones on an old charge, thereby preventing the robbery.
    Based on these facts, it would be CORRECT to state that Smith is

    A. *not guilty* of any crime
    B. *guilty* of conspiracy in the second degree and criminal facilitation in the second degree
    C. *guilty* of criminal facilitation in the second degree but is not guilty of conspiracy in the second degree
    D. *guilty* of conspiracy in the second degree but is not guilty of criminal facilitation in the second degree

20. Each of the following choices states an offense involving the death of a person, and certain additional facts.
    In which choice would the defendant NOT be guilty of the offense stated, based SOLELY on the facts given in the choice?

    A. Manslaughter in the second degree - when the defendant intentionally causes or aids another person to commit suicide
    B. Murder - when the defendant and two other persons attempt to commit escape in the second degree, and one of the participants causes the death of a person other than one of the participants
    C. Manslaughter in the first degree - when with intent to cause serious physical injury to another person, the defendant causes the death of a third person
    D. Murder - when the defendant engages in conduct which creates a grave risk of death of another person, and thereby causes the death of another person

21. Which of the following elements would raise the crime of custodial interference from the second degree to the first degree?

    A. The intent to hold a child permanently or for a protracted period
    B. Exposure of the person taken to a risk that his health will be materially impaired
    C. The taking of a child less than sixteen years old from his lawful custodian
    D. Enticement of an incompetent person from lawful custody

22. Which one of the following elements must ALWAYS be present for a person to be guilty of arson in the first degree?

    A. The presence in the building at the time of another person who is not a participant in the crime
    B. Intentional damage to a building caused by a fire
    C. Knowledge by the person that another person not a participant in the crime is present in the building
    D. Circumstances which render the presence in the building of another person not a participant in the crime a reasonable possibility

23. For which of the following crimes is it a necessary element that a person knowingly enter or remain unlawfully in a dwelling, as the word *dwelling* is defined in the Penal Law?

    A. Criminal trespass in the first and second degree
    B. Criminal trespass in the second degree and burglary in the first degree
    C. Criminal trespass in the first degree and burglary in the second degree
    D. Burglary in the first and second degree

24. Assume that the police stop a car in which three men are riding. Ward is the driver, and Jones and King are passengers. During a lawful search, the police find one-quarter ounce of morphine concealed in King's coat. Based SOLELY on these facts, it would be CORRECT to state that

    A. King, Jones, and Ward are all guilty of criminal possession of a dangerous drug
    B. a presumption of knowingly possessing the morphine applies to Ward but not to Jones
    C. King is guilty of criminal possession of a dangerous drug and Ward is guilty of conspiracy
    D. King is guilty of criminal possession of a dangerous drug but Ward and Jones are not

KEY (CORRECT ANSWERS)

1.	D	11.	D
2.	A	12.	B
3.	C	13.	D
4.	B	14.	C
5.	C	15.	A
6.	C	16.	C
7.	D	17.	B
8.	D	18.	A
9.	A	19.	A
10.	C	20.	D

21. B
22. A
23. B
24. D

TEST 2

DIRECTIONS: Each question or incomplete statement is followed by several suggested answers or completions. Select the one that BEST answers the question or completes the statement. *PRINT THE LETTER OF THE CORRECT ANSWER IN THE SPACE AT THE RIGHT.*

1. Which of the following statements is(are) CORRECT?
   The Criminal Procedure Law (CPL) applies to
   I. all criminal actions and proceedings commenced on or after September 1, 1971, and appeals and other post-judgment proceedings relating thereto.
   II. criminal actions and proceedings commenced before September 1, 1971 but pending thereafter
   III. appeals and other post-judgment proceedings commenced on or after September 1, 1971 which relate to criminal actions and proceedings commenced or concluded prior thereto, provided that, where application of CPL would not be feasible or would work injustice, the former Code of Criminal Procedure shall apply
   IV. criminal procedure matters occurring on or after September 1, 1971 which are not a part of any particular action or case
   The CORRECT answer is:

   A. All of the above
   B. I *only*
   C. I, II, III
   D. II, III, IV

2. Which of the following is hearsay?
   A(n)

   A. written statement by a person not present at the court hearing where the statement is submitted as proof of an occurrence
   B. oral statement in court by a witness of what he saw
   C. written statement of what he saw by a witness present in court
   D. re-enactment by a witness in court of what he saw

3. In a criminal case, a statement by a person not present in court is

   A. *acceptable* evidence if not objected to by the prosecutor
   B. *acceptable* evidence if not objected to by the defense lawyer
   C. *not acceptable* evidence except in certain well-settled circumstances
   D. *not acceptable* evidence under any circumstances

4. The rule on hearsay is founded on the belief that

   A. proving someone said an act occurred is not proof that the act did occur
   B. a person who has knowledge about a case should be willing to appear in court
   C. persons not present in court are likely to be unreliable witnesses
   D. permitting persons to testify without appearing in court will lead to a disrespect for law

5. One reason for the general rule that a witness in a criminal case MUST give his testimony in court is that

   A. a witness may be influenced by threats to make untrue statements
   B. the opposite side is then permitted to question him
   C. the court provides protection for a witness against unfair questioning
   D. the adversary system is designed to prevent a miscarriage of justice.

6. An appeal MAY be taken from a

   A. verdict
   B. judgment
   C. decision
   D. conviction

7. Jury trial commences

   A. with the selection of a jury
   B. when the defendant makes opening address
   C. when the first opening address is made
   D. when the first witness is sworn

8. Adjective criminal law is governed PRIMARILY by the

   A. Penal Law
   B. Civil Practice Law and Rules
   C. Criminal Procedure Law
   D. Code of Criminal Procedure

9. Which of the following contain(s) references included in the definition of *warrant of arrest*?
   - I. Process of local criminal court to produce defendant for arraignment
   - II. Produce defendant for arraignment upon filed accusatory instrument
   - III. Addressed to peace officer to produce defendant for arraignment
   - IV. Process of any criminal court requiring defendant to appear before it for arraignment on a prosecutor's information

   The CORRECT answer is:

   A. I, II, III, IV
   B. III *only*
   C. I, II, III
   D. I, II, IV

10. Superior courts have jurisdiction in the following areas:
    - I. Unlimited trial jurisdiction of all offenses
    - II. Exclusive trial jurisdiction of felonies
    - III. Concurrent trial jurisdiction of misdemeanors
    - IV. Preliminary jurisdiction of all offenses, exercised only through grand juries

    The CORRECT answer is:

    A. I *only*
    B. I, II
    C. I, II, III
    D. II, III, IV

11. Petty offense means

    A. all violations and traffic infractions
    B. some misdemeanors and all violations
    C. only conduct which is not a traffic infraction and is punishable by imprisonment for not more than 15 days
    D. a class B misdemeanor only

12. An offense committed near a boundary between two adjoining counties of this state may be prosecuted in either of such counties.
    The MAXIMUM distance from a county border is

    A. 1,000 feet   B. 1,000 yards   C. 500 feet   D. 500 yards

13. A felony is committed on the Hudson River south of the northern boundary of New York City.
    The county or counties having jurisdiction to try the case is(are)

    A. New York, Richmond, Bronx, Kings, and Queens Counties
    B. New York, Richmond, and Bronx Counties
    C. New York and Richmond Counties only
    D. New York County only

14. A crime is committed on a bus regularly carrying passengers from Nassau County to Manhattan by way of Queens. At the time of the occurrence, the bus is in Nassau on its way to its terminal point—Manhattan. The victim is a Queens resident. The alleged perpetrator is a resident of Manhattan.
    The county or counties having jurisdiction in this case is(are)

    A. Nassau or New York   B. Nassau or Queens
    C. Nassau, Queens, or Manhattan   D. Nassau only

15. Prosecution of a crime MUST be commenced within

    A. one year after commission, for all misdemeanors and petty offenses
    B. two years after commission, for all misdemeanors and petty offenses
    C. 5 years after commission, for all felonies
    D. 5 years after commission, for some felonies

16. A private person in making an arrest is limited as follows:

    A. For an offense, at any hour of day or night
    B. For a crime only, at any hour of any day or night
    C. For a felony only, at any hour of any day or night
    D. All of the above

17. An appearance ticket directs a specific person to appear in a criminal court in connection with the alleged commission of a designated offense.
    This appearance ticket may be issued only by a

    A. local criminal court judge
    B. local criminal court judge or police officer
    C. police officer or authorized public servant
    D. police officer, authorized public servant, or local criminal court judge

18. An arrest by a private person without a warrant can PROPERLY be made in which one of the following situations?

    A. There is reasonable cause to believe that the person being arrested committed a felony.
    B. The person arrested for a felony has in fact committed the felony.
    C. The person arrested for a misdemeanor has in fact committed the misdemeanor.
    D. The person arrested for any offense has in fact committed the offense.

19. A peace officer, outside the geographical area of his employment, has reasonable cause to believe that a felony was committed in his presence.
    In the circumstances,

    A. he may make an arrest, without restriction
    B. he may make an arrest only on the same authority as that of a private person
    C. he may make an arrest during the commission of the felony, immediately thereafter or during immediate flight
    D. none of the above

20. After making an arrest, a police officer must perform all required recording, fingerprinting, and other related duties.
    He MUST do so

    A. immediately
    B. without unnecessary delay
    C. within 24 hours
    D. within 8 hours

21. A police officer, acting without a warrant, may arrest a person

    A. only in the geographical area of his employment
    B. outside the geographical area of his employment only for a felony
    C. without restriction, for a petty offense committed anywhere in the state
    D. for a crime committed anywhere in the state

22. Summons is a process whose SOLE function is to

    A. commence a criminal action
    B. substitute for a warrant of arrest, where a warrant may not be issued
    C. produce defendant for arraignment upon a filed accusatory instrument
    D. inform defendant as to nature of the offenses charged

23. A summons may be served by

    A. any person without restriction
    B. any person at least 18 years old
    C. a police officer, without restriction
    D. a peace officer, without restriction

24. An arrest warrant is addressed to and can be executed by

    A. any adult person
    B. a police officer or classification of police officers
    C. a peace officer or classification of peace officers
    D. any person over the age of 18, not a party to the action

25. Which of the following would invalidate an acknowledgment?

    A. Failure to say deponent is known to notary
    B. Seal is missing
    C. Acts done on Sunday
    D. Affiant misspells his name

KEY (CORRECT ANSWERS)

1.	A	11.	A
2.	A	12.	D
3.	C	13.	A
4.	A	14.	A
5.	B	15.	D
6.	B	16.	A
7.	A	17.	C
8.	C	18.	B
9.	D	19.	C
10.	D	20.	B

21. D
22. C
23. C
24. B
25. A

TEST 3

DIRECTIONS: Each question or incomplete statement is followed by several suggested answers or completions. Select the one that BEST answers the question or completes the statement. *PRINT THE LETTER OF THE CORRECT ANSWER IN THE SPACE AT THE RIGHT.*

1. A warrant of arrest may be executed anywhere in the state

    A. without restriction, if it is issued by a city court
    B. in all cases, without restriction
    C. in all cases, provided it is appropriately endorsed by a local criminal court of the county where the arrest is to be made
    D. when issued by the city criminal court

2. A warrant of arrest may be executed on any day

    A. of the week, at any hour
    B. except Sunday, at any hour of the day; but on Sunday only between 9:00 A.M. and 6:00 P.M.
    C. including Sunday, provided it is so endorsed by the issuing court
    D. except Sunday

3. A police officer or court officer of a criminal court may stop a person, under specified circumstances, when he reasonably suspects that the person is committing, has committed, or is about to commit any felony

    A. or a Class A misdemeanor defined in the Penal Law
    B. or misdemeanor defined in the Penal Law
    C. or any misdemeanor only
    D. only

4. At a hearing on a felony complaint, defendant

    A. may testify in his own behalf within the discretion of the court, but he has a right to call witnesses
    B. has a right to testify in his own behalf, but he may call witnesses only within the discretion of the court
    C. has a right to testify in his own behalf and to call witnesses
    D. may testify in his own behalf, within the discretion of the court, and call witnesses in his behalf, within the discretion of the court

5. A grand jury, to be legally constituted, MUST consist of _____ members.

    A. not less than 16 and not more than 23
    B. not less than 12 and not more than 16
    C. not less than 12 and not more than 23
    D. at least 12

6. At a preliminary hearing on a felony complaint,
    I. the defendant must be present
    II. the defendant has a right to be present, but he may waive this right
    III. the defendant has a right to call witnesses in his behalf
    IV. all witnesses called may be cross-examined

The CORRECT answer is:

A. I, II   B. II, III   C. I, IV   D. II, IV

7. The number and term of grand juries empanelled for a court are determined generally by

    A. Supreme Court in the county, on application of the District Attorney showing the estimated need
    B. Rules of the court for which the grand jury is drawn
    C. Judicial Conference regulations
    D. Appellate Division rules

8. The quantum of proof required for a court to hold a defendant for grand jury action on a felony complaint is proof

    A. affording the court reasonable cause to believe
    B. sufficient for a reasonable man
    C. by a fair preponderance of the evidence
    D. beyond a reasonable doubt

9. The acting foreman of a grand jury is

    A. chosen by lot
    B. chosen by the court
    C. the second grand juror to be empanelled
    D. chosen by the grand jurors

10. When a grand jury requires legal advice, they may receive it

    A. only from the court, District Attorney, or an attorney designated by either
    B. either from the court or District Attorney, only
    C. only from the District Attorney
    D. only from the court

11. In all cases, when a motion is made for a change of venue, a(n)

    A. application for a stay, denied by a Supreme Court justice, may not thereafter be granted by a justice of the Appellate Division
    B. application for a stay, denied by a Supreme Court justice, may be reviewed and granted by a justice of the Appellate Division
    C. stay may be granted only by any Supreme Court justice in the judicial district
    D. stay may be granted by any superior court judge in the judicial district

12. Evidence of mental disease or defect as a trial defense excluding criminal responsibility is admissible

    A. only as to a defendant who has previously been examined under court order by two qualified psychiatrists
    B. provided the defendant has served and filed timely written notice of intention to rely thereon
    C. provided the People have served a demand on the defendant to give notice of this defense
    D. in all cases without restriction

13. On a defense of alibi,

    A. the People in all cases are entitled on trial to an adjournment not in excess of 3 days
    B. a court may receive testimony as in D below but on application must grant an adjournment of not less than 7 days
    C. a court may not receive testimony as in D below
    D. a court may receive testimony, in its discretion, from a witness who was not included in defendant's notice of alibi

14. Which of the following statements are CORRECT?
    I. The People, having the burden of proof, address the jury before defendant at all stages.
    II. A closing address to the jury by the prosecution is required.
    III. A closing address to the jury by both sides is discretionary.
    IV. An opening address to the jury by both sides is discretionary.
    V. The People in all cases must make an opening address to the jury.

    The CORRECT answer is:

    A. I, II, III
    B. II, III, IV
    C. I, II, IV
    D. I, II, V

15. In selecting a jury, the MAXIMUM total number of challenges to alternate jurors that may be exercised by BOTH parties is

    A. 16
    B. 8
    C. 4
    D. 2

16. A grand jury witness may be called only on request of the

    A. court, District Attorney, or grand jury
    B. court
    C. District Attorney or the grand jury
    D. grand jury

17. A prospective defendant in a grand jury proceeding who wishes the grand jury to hear a witness in his behalf is limited by the fact that

    A. the grand jury, in its discretion, may hear the witness if the defendant makes an oral or written request
    B. the grand jury must hear the witness if the defendant makes an oral or written request
    C. the grand jury must hear the witness only if the defendant makes a written request
    D. there may be no legal basis for such a request

18. When a charge has been dismissed by a grand jury following its consideration of the matter, which of the following is CORRECT?

    A. It may be resubmitted to successive grand juries by court order, without limitation.
    B. It may be resubmitted to a grand jury if a court so authorizes, but no further submission thereafter is permissible.
    C. Without court order, it may be considered by another grand jury, but not by the same grand jury.
    D. It may again be considered by the same grand jury, without court order.

19. An indictment MUST contain
    I. endorsement, *A True Bill,* signed by the district attorney
    II. applicable section number of the statute allegedly violated
    III. date or period when alleged conduct occurred
    IV. statement in each court that the grand jury accuses the defendant of a designated offense

    The CORRECT answer is:

    A. I, II, IV
    B. III, IV
    C. II, III, IV
    D. I, II, III, IV

20. With respect to an offense raised to higher grade by reason solely of a previous conviction, which of the following statements is CORRECT?

    A. Under no circumstances is a jury permitted to know of the previous conviction.
    B. The order of trial is in this instance substantially the same as in other cases, except for arraignment on a special information.
    C. Before any proceeding to establish defendant's identity and previous conviction, he must be advised of the privilege against self-incrimination.
    D. The defendant's conviction of the predicate case may be established at any time before the case goes to the jury.

21. The term *petty offense* includes

    A. no misdemeanors, some violations, all traffic infractions
    B. no misdemeanors, but all violations and traffic infractions
    C. some misdemeanors, all violations and traffic infractions
    D. all misdemeanors, violations, and traffic infractions

22. Conviction, as defined in CPL, means

    A. entry of guilty plea, or guilty verdict
    B. serving of sentence
    C. entry of final judgment
    D. imposition and entry of sentence

23. With regard to a non-jury trial, which of the following is CORRECT?

    A. Trial commences when both parties appear, are ready, and the court announces that the case is on trial. The court's determination as to guilt or innocence is properly termed a verdict.
    B. If there is no opening address, trial commences when the first witness is sworn, and the court's determination as to guilt or innocence is properly termed a verdict.
    C. An opening address, if made, commences the trial, and the court's determination of guilt or innocence is properly termed a decision.
    D. There must be an opening address to the court; this commences the trial; and the court's determination of guilt or innocence is properly termed a decision.

24. In relation to double jeopardy, a person may not be twice prosecuted for the same offense.
    Assuming the same offense, which of the following does NOT relate to double jeopardy under CPL?

A. Defendant is found not guilty after trial in one jurisdiction
B. An accusatory instrument is filed in a court of another country
C. An accusatory instrument is filed in a Federal court
D. An accusatory instrument is filed in a state other than New York

25. Which of the following is NOT applicable to a warrant of arrest?   25._____

    A. Its function is to produce defendant for arraignment.
    B. It commences a criminal action.
    C. It is issued only by a local criminal court.
    D. It is addressed to a police officer.

KEY (CORRECT ANSWERS)

1.	D	11.	A
2.	A	12.	B
3.	A	13.	D
4.	B	14.	D
5.	A	15.	A
6.	D	16.	C
7.	D	17.	A
8.	A	18.	B
9.	B	19.	B
10.	B	20.	B

21. B
22. A
23. B
24. B
25. B

EXAMINATION SECTION
TEST 1

DIRECTIONS: Each question or incomplete statement is followed by several suggested answers or completions. Select the one that BEST answers the question or completes the statement. *PRINT THE LETTER OF THE CORRECT ANSWER IN THE SPACE AT THE RIGHT.*

1. R forcibly stole property from Z.
   Which one of the following additional elements, if present, would MOST properly justify charging R with robbery in the first degree, rather than robbery in the third degree?
   R

   A. punched Z during the robbery, giving Z a black eye
   B. used a motor vehicle to escape from the robbery scene
   C. was aided by an accomplice when committing the robbery
   D. produced a knife and threatened to use it, but did not stab Z, when committing the robbery
   E. produced a gun and threatened to use it during the robbery. The gun was unloaded but Z did not know this.

   1.____

2. Patrolman P, having received information from a reliable third party that Z had committed a misdemeanor, arrests Z without a warrant and drives him to the lockup. As Z is being transferred from the patrol car to the lockup, he breaks away from P and runs into a crowd of persons. After a ten-minute foot chase, P reapprehends Z.
   Which one of the following BEST states the offense or offenses, if any, for which P may now properly arrest Z without a warrant?

   A. Only escape in the third degree
   B. Only escape in the second degree
   C. Only the misdemeanor for which he was originally arrested
   D. P may not properly arrest Z for any of the above offenses
   E. The misdemeanor for which he was originally arrested, and escape in the third degree

   2.____

3. A stolen car with three occupants is stopped after a high speed chase and the occupants are arrested. P, one of the occupants, has an unloaded, but operable, .32 caliber pistol tucked in his belt, and six .32 caliber rounds in his pocket. U, the second occupant, has an unloaded, but operable, .45 caliber pistol in his pants' pocket and has no bullets on his person. L, the driver, has neither a pistol nor any ammunition on his person. When the vehicle is searched, a loaded .38 caliber pistol is found under the right front seat. None of the occupants of the car has ever been convicted of a crime and none has a valid license for any of the weapons.
   Which one of the following BEST states which weapon or weapons each man may properly be charged with felonious possession of?

   A. P, U, and L may each properly be charged with felonious possession of only the .32 and the .38.
   B. P, U, and L may each properly be charged with felonious possession of the .32, the .38, and the .45.

   3.____

C. P may properly be charged only with felonious possession of the .32, and both U and L may not be properly charged with the felonious possession of any of the weapons.
D. P may properly be charged with felonious possession of only the .32, U may properly be charged only with the felonious possession of the .45, and L may not be properly charged with the felonious possession of any of the weapons.
E. P may properly be charged with felonious possession only of the .32 and the .38, U may properly be charged with felonious possession only of the .45 and the .38, and L may properly be charged with felonious possession only of the .38.

4. Following are three situations in which a police officer might possibly be justified in using deadly physical force upon another person:
   I. To prevent the escape of an unarmed person who was seen by the officer snatching a woman's purse
   II. To arrest an unarmed person observed by the officer committing arson
   III. To arrest an unarmed person when the officer reasonably believes that the person is likely to inflict serious physical injury to a third party unless apprehended without delay, under conditions that do not amount to imminent use of deadly physical force

Which one of the following choices lists ALL of the above cases in which a police officer is actually justified in using deadly physical force and NONE in which he is not?
He is

A. justified in I, II, and III
B. not justified in I, II, or III
C. justified in I and III, but not in II
D. justified in II but not in I and III
E. justified in II and III, but not in I

5. L lends R a pistol, believing that R intends to use the pistol to rob V. During the robbery, with which L had no further part, R kills V.
Which one of the following, if any, is the MOST serious crime with which L may properly be charged?

A. Conspiracy in the fourth degree
B. Criminal facilitation in the first degree
C. Criminal facilitation in the second degree
D. Criminal solicitation in the second degree
E. None of the above, since he may not properly be charged with any crime

6. Which one of the following is LEAST likely to be a degree-raising factor for the crime of assault?
That

A. a dangerous instrument was used
B. the assailant was over 18 years of age when the assault occurred
C. serious physical injury rather than ordinary physical injury was caused
D. physical injury was caused intentionally rather than recklessly
E. physical injury was inflicted in the course of the commission of an independent felony

7. R and S, while planning an armed robbery of an armored truck, study the route taken by the truck from a bank to a factory where payroll money is delivered every Thursday. A bartender hears their conversation and informs the police. Part of the plan involves staging an automobile accident along the route taken by the truck, and robbing the truck when the driver stops. On the day of the intended robbery, the route taken by the truck is altered so that it will not pass by the location where R and S have staged the accident; and R and S, both heavily armed, are arrested by police at the scene.
Which one of the following is the MOST serious crime with which R and S may properly be charged?

   A. Robbery in the first degree
   B. Conspiracy in the third degree
   C. Conspiracy in the second degree
   D. Attempted robbery in the first degree
   E. Attempted robbery in the second degree

8. The section of the State Penal Law dealing with murder has been modified in several respects. One such modification concerned an aspect of the *felony murder* doctrine of the law.
Which one of the following is both the MOST accurate statement as to how the felony murder doctrine was modified and also the APPARENT legislative intent therefor?

   A. Listing certain specific felonies, to clarify the meaning of the term *any felony* in the former statute
   B. Including all felonies under the felony murder doctrine, so that a fatality which occurs during the commission of any felony is punishable as murder
   C. Including all felonies in which a motor vehicle is used, either in committing the felony or in escaping from the scene, so that fatalities which occur in these cases are punishable as murder
   D. Excluding certain non-violent felonies from the felony murder doctrine, so that a fatality which is either accidental or which the perpetrator cannot reasonably foresee is not punishable as murder
   E. Adding the necessity of proving intent as an element of murder in non-violent felonies, so that a fatality in connection with a non-violent felony is not punishable as murder when intent cannot be proved

9. While on duty, P, a police officer, received from his superior a description of Z, who was involved in a robbery, and believed to be in P's area. The superior officer's information concerning Z's involvement in the robbery came from a reliable third party. P observes a person closely matching Z's description. When P approaches, the person starts to run, but is quickly apprehended and placed under arrest for robbery. While searching this person for weapons, P discovers a quantity of narcotics in his inside coat pocket and forthwith seizes the narcotics.
Which one of the following MOST properly evaluates both whether or not the seizure of the narcotics was proper in this case and also the BEST reason therefor?
The seizure was

   A. *proper*, but only because narcotics are contraband
   B. *proper*, since it was made incident to a lawful arrest
   C. *improper*, since P did not have an arrest warrant for Z
   D. *improper*, since P did not have probable cause for arrest
   E. *improper*, since the narcotics were unrelated to the crime for which the arrest was made

10. Following are three situations in which *Miranda* warnings were not given when the confessions made by the persons involved might possibly be admissible as evidence:
A person
   I. walks into a police station and volunteers a statement to the desk sergeant implicating himself in a robbery
   II. in prison for committing a certain crime, being questioned concerning his involvement in a second crime, confesses to the second crime
   III. arrested at the scene of a robbery attempt, being questioned concerning the crime, confesses to the crime

Which one of the following choices lists all of the above situations in which the confession is ADMISSIBLE and none in which it is NOT?
The confession is admissible in

- A. I, but not in II and III
- B. I and II, but not in III
- C. I, II, and III
- D. I and III, but not in II
- E. III, but not in I and II

KEY (CORRECT ANSWERS)

1. D	6. B
2. D	7. D
3. A	8. D
4. D	9. B
5. C	10. A

TEST 2

DIRECTIONS: Each question or incomplete statement is followed by several suggested answers or completions. Select the one that BEST answers the question or completes the statement. *PRINT THE LETTER OF THE CORRECT ANSWER IN THE SPACE AT THE RIGHT.*

1. According to the Criminal Procedure Law, the decision of the judge presiding in the court in which the crime is triable is final with respect to bail. An order denying bail is non-appealable and so any attack on such a denial of bail must be by other means.
   The *other means* is by resort to the prisoner's separate and different right to test the legality of his detention by a

   A. writ of coram nobis
   B. writ of habeas corpus
   C. writ of certiorari
   D. certificate of reasonable doubt

   1._____

2. X, intending to rob Y, points an unloaded revolver at him.
   The element which makes the assault involved here assault, second degree, is the fact that

   A. there is no intent to kill
   B. the revolver is unloaded
   C. the injury, if any were sustained, would be relatively light
   D. the intent is thus shown to be to secure property and not to inflict grave bodily harm

   2._____

3. One of the defenses available to one accused of crime is that of entrapment.
   The defense of entrapment is LEAST likely to be met with in _____ cases.

   A. narcotics   B. prostitution
   C. gambling   D. rape

   3._____

4. With respect to the review of convictions in state courts by the Supreme Court of the United States, the latter has stated that, so far as due process affects admissions before trial of the defendant, the accepted test of the admissibility of such admissions is their

   A. voluntariness   B. timeliness
   C. materiality   D. motivation

   4._____

5. A very important rule in the law of evidence is that known as the *best evidence rule.*
   This rule applies to

   A. documents   B. judicial notice
   C. eyewitness testimony   D. oral testimony

   5._____

6. The one of the following statements which is LEAST correct, according to the Criminal Procedure Law, is that a peace officer may arrest a person

   A. without warrant for a felony when he has reasonable cause for believing that a felony has been committed and that the person arrested committed it
   B. with a warrant at any hour of the day or night for any crime provided the arrest is made in the same county where the warrant was issued

   6._____

C. without a warrant when a felony has in fact been committed and he has reasonable cause for believing the person to be arrested to have committed it
D. at night with a warrant for a misdemeanor when directed by the issuing judge's endorsement upon the warrant

7. The one of the following statements concerning arrests by private persons which is INCORRECT is:

   A. A private person who has arrested another for the commission of a crime must deliver him to a peace officer
   B. A private person may arrest another for a crime committed or attempted in his presence
   C. A private person makes an arrest for a felony at his peril if he arrests the wrong person
   D. Except when making an arrest during the actual commission of a crime or on pursuit immediately after its commission, a private person before making an arrest, must inform the person to be arrested of the cause thereof, and require him to submit

8. A change in the Criminal Procedures Law in relation to filing complaints against a youthful offender so that he may be adjudged a wayward minor provides that a new class of individuals who may lay such an information before the judge is that of

   A. peace officers
   B. other persons standing in parental relation as being the next of kin
   C. principals or teachers of any school where such person is registered for attendance
   D. representatives of an incorporated society doing charitable or philanthropic work

9. Persons apprehended by Federal agents in conjunction with city police in many narcotics arrests are frequently tried under the State law in a State court.
   Of the following, the PRINCIPAL reason for this procedure is that

   A. more expeditious handling of the case is assured due to the unusually heavy caseload in the Federal courts in the city
   B. it is then not necessary to reveal the identity of the Federal agents involved in an arrest
   C. the penalties in the state courts are more certain and usually more drastic
   D. state courts are less severe with respect to the admissibility of certain kinds of evidence

10. It has been suggested that in reducing a confession to writing it is desirable to include several errors and to have the person making the confession make the corrections and sign or initial them.
    The one of the following which MOST supports this suggestion is that such corrections by the person making the confession

    A. helps to minimize the credibility of possible later denials concerning the material set forth in the confession
    B. is likely to encourage the investigator to continue his investigation on the corrected matter and thereby discourages a complete reliance on the confession itself

C. provides additional and new evidence which links the person making the confession to the crime charged
D. provides additional corroboration of facts which only the person making the confession would know about

KEY (CORRECT ANSWERS)

1. B
2. B
3. D
4. A
5. A

6. B
7. A
8. C
9. D
10. A

EXAMINATION SECTION

TEST 1

DIRECTIONS: Each question or incomplete statement is followed by several suggested answers or completions. Select the one that BEST answers the question or completes the statement. *PRINT THE LETTER OF THE CORRECT ANSWER IN THE SPACE AT THE RIGHT.*

1. Police Officer Jones, while on patrol, attempt to arrest a 15-year-old for Robbery 1st degree. The youth suddenly attacks the officer with a knife, slashing at Jones' face and hands. Officer Jones retreats until he can no longer back up. The youth continues to advance. Jones draws his revolver, orders the youth to stop, and fires one shot into the youth when he ignores the command.
Based on these facts, Officer Jones' action should legally be considered
   A. *justified*; a police officer may shoot to arrest any felon
   B. *unjustified*; Article 35 of the Penal Law prohibits deadly physical force
   C. *justified*; he was preventing the use of deadly physical force, and in this case the law does not contain any age restrictions
   D. *unjustified*; he should have called for assistance and subdued the youth without the use of deadly physical force

1.____

2. A conspiracy which is entered into in New York State, to engage in conduct in New Jersey, is punishable as a conspiracy in New York State if
   A. an overt act is committed in New York
   B. the conduct to be committed would be a crime in both states, and an overt act occurs
   C. the conduct to be committed would be a crime in New York
   D. the conduct to be committed would be a crime in New Jersey

2.____

3. Police Officer Smith has obtained an arrest warrant for Sam. The charge is issuing a bad check. When Smith tries to make the arrest, Sam punches him, causing Smith to suffer a concussion.
Sam has committed
   A. assault 1st   B. assault 2nd
   C. assault 3rd   D. reckless endangerment 1st

3.____

4. When a person engages in sexual conduct with an animal or a dead human body, he is guilty of
   A. sodomy   B. bestiality
   C. sexual misconduct   D. voyeurism

4.____

5. Jo and John get a divorce. She receives custody of the children. John, believing that Jo is not properly raising the children, fails to return them after a visit.
John would be found guilty of
   A. kidnapping
   B. custodial interference
   C. child abuse
   D. endangering the welfare of a minor

6. The MOST basic difference between unlawful imprisonment 1st and 2nd is:
   A. There is an affirmative defense to 2nd, but not 1st
   B. One is a felony and the other a misdemeanor
   C. One involves a serious risk, the other does not
   D. The age of the victim

7. The one of the following which is a factor in the affirmative defense to unlawful imprisonment but NOT in the affirmative defense to kidnapping is that the
   A. defendant is a relative of the victim
   B. defendant's sole purpose is to assume control over the victim
   C. victim is less than 16
   D. victim was not exposed to a serious risk

8. John, while armed with a deadly weapon (a switchblade knife), knowingly enters Smith's home at night. While inside, he steals the sum of $1,000 from a dresser drawer. He entered the house knowing that the money was there and intending to steal it.
John has committed
   A. burglary 1st and grand larceny 2nd
   B. burglary 1st and grand larceny 3rd
   C. criminal possession of a weapon and grand larceny
   D. criminal trespass 2nd, criminal possession of a weapon, and grand larceny 3rd

9. The crime of forgery in the 1st degree may be committed when, with intent to defraud, someone falsely makes, completes, or alters a written instrument which purports to be a
   A. codicil to a will
   B. postage stamp
   C. drug prescription
   D. deed to real property

10. Bob and Jane are married to each other. They have a quarrel, and Jane slaps Bob in the face. No injury is caused.
Because of these facts, which of the following statements is LEAST accurate?
   A. Jane committed the crime of harassment.
   B. If Bob wants to, he can institute a criminal court proceeding.
   C. If Bob wants to, he can institute a family court proceeding.
   D. Harassment of this kind is a family offense.

11. An offense committed on a bridge having terminals in different counties may be prosecuted in
    A. the county closest to the location of the offense
    B. any terminal county
    C. any county that borders the body of water over which the bridge passes
    D. no place

12. A petty offense committed in a city, town, or village, but within a specified distance of any other such political subdivision, may be prosecuted in either political subdivision.
    The distance specified is _____ yards.
    A. 100   B. 300   C. 500   D. 600

13. Barring exceptions, the criminal action for petty offenses must be commenced within _____ after its commission.
    A. 5 years   B. 2 years   C. 1 year   D. 6 months

14. Which of the following is a local criminal court accusatory instrument?
    A. Indictment
    B. Superior court information
    C. Appearance ticket
    D. Prosecutor's information

15. You arrest a man for a misdemeanor on a warrant addressed to you and properly endorsed, in a county other than the one in which the warrant is returnable or an adjoining county to it.
    You should FIRST
    A. bring him before a local criminal court of the county of arrest
    B. return him to the court in which the warrant was returnable
    C. ask the prisoner if he wants to go before a local criminal court in the county of arrest for bail or recognizance
    D. ask the prisoner to endorse the warrant

16. A robbery is committed in your jurisdiction by two males who make their getaway in a 2013 red Ford. This information is broadcast over the police radio. You spot a 2013 red Ford with two males and a female inside, within one mile of the robbery scene. You reasonably suspect that they might be the perpetrators.
    Based on these facts, you should
    A. call for assistance and then arrest the suspects
    B. make a note of the license number and then follow the suspects
    C. stop the car and question the occupants about their identity, residence, and what they are doing
    D. ignore the situation, since you do not have probable cause to make the arrest

17. Jane is a witness in a criminal action. The defendant has raised an alibi as proof of his innocence. Jane, while under oath, falsely swears that the alibi is true. Under these circumstances, she has committed
    A. falsely reporting an incident
    B. perjury 3rd degree
    C. perjury 2nd degree
    D. perjury 1st degree

18. Under Article 225 of the Penal Law, unlawful gambling is prohibited. Not all "gambling" activity, however, is unlawful.
Which of the following persons would properly be chargeable under Article 225?
   I. Connolly sells out-of-state lottery tickets in New York.
   II. George, on his 19th birthday, bet $50 on a baseball game.
   III. Henry and Jesse made a $50 bet on a paddleball game.
   IV. A wife sets up a social game of cards for money. It is a surprise birthday gift for her husband.
   The CORRECT answer is:
   A. I only   B. I, III   C. II, IV   D. III, IV

19. Under Article 265 of the Penal Law, the term "firearm" is a defined term. In addition, unlawful possession of a "firearm" is at least a Class A misdemeanor.
Which of the weapons listed below would support a charge of possession of a concealed weapon under Article 265?
   I. An unloaded muzzle-loading flintlock pistol with percussion cap
   II. A sawed-off shotgun 23 inches long
   III. A one-short derringer
   The CORRECT answer is:
   A. I only   B. I, II   C. I, III   D. II, III

20. An offense is committed on an airliner which flew from River County to Niagara Falls. Jurisdiction of the offense rests
   A. only in the county of termination of flight
   B. only in the county of origin of flight
   C. only in the county over which the plane was flying at the time of the offense
   D. in the county of origin, termination, or any county over which the plane few during the night

21. A man shoots his wife in Brook County intending to kill her. He puts her body into the trunk of his car and drives it to River County, where he expects to dispose of it. When he opens the trunk, he sees that she is still breathing and so he shoots her again, killing her.
Jurisdiction over the killing lies in
   A. River County only
   B. Brook County only
   C. both River and Brook Counties
   D. either River or Brook County

22. In which of the following situations does the law provide for a two-year statute of limitations?
   A. Stealing $2.00 from the person of another
   B. Burglary 3rd degree
   C. Stealing $25.00 from a dwelling
   D. Possession of gambling records 1st degree

23. An arrest warrant will have limited geographical jurisdiction for purposes of execution when it is issued by
    A. a district court
    B. a superior court judge sitting as a local criminal court
    C. the city criminal court
    D. a town court

    23.____

24. The following arrests have been made without a warrant:
    I. By a police officer, anywhere in the state, who had reasonable cause to believe the person committed petit larceny anywhere in the state
    II. By a civilian, for arson 3rd degree, anywhere in the state, who witnessed the person arrested commit the arson 3rd degree
    III. By a police officer, anywhere in the state, who had reasonable grounds to believe harassment was committed anywhere in the state
    Of the following, which is MOST accurate according to the Criminal Procedure Law?
    A. II and III were proper, but I was improper.
    B. I and III were proper, but II was improper.
    C. All were proper.
    D. I and II were proper, but III was improper.

    24.____

25. A New Jersey state trooper has pursued a fleeing criminal into New York State and arrested him there.
    Under what circumstances might he be able to return him to New Jersey after an appearance before a local criminal court in New York?
    A. The offense was a felony in New Jersey.
    B. The offense was at least a crime in New Jersey.
    C. The officer was in close pursuit immediately after the commission of the crime.
    D. The offense would have been a crime in New York as well as in New Jersey.

    25.____

KEY (CORRECT ANSWERS)

1.	C	11.	B
2.	B	12.	A
3.	B	13.	C
4.	C	14.	D
5.	B	15.	C
6.	C	16.	C
7.	C	17.	D
8.	C	18.	A
9.	B	19.	D
10.	A	20.	D

21. D
22. C
23. D
24. D
25. D

TEST 2

DIRECTIONS: Each question or incomplete statement is followed by several suggested answers or completions. Select the one that BEST answers the question or completes the statement. *PRINT THE LETTER OF THE CORRECT ANSWER IN THE SPACE AT THE RIGHT.*

1. Lisa, unable to resist her husband's plea, supplies him with sleeping pills so he can end his suffering from a painful disease. He takes the pill and dies. Lisa has committed
   A. aiding a suicide attempt
   B. murder
   C. manslaughter 1st
   D. manslaughter 2nd

   1.____

2. Tony had sexual intercourse with Beth. When she asked him for payment, Tony became annoyed and slapped her to the floor. He then took a broom handle and shoved it into her vagina, causing a physical injury. Tony has committed
   A. rape
   B. sodomy
   C. sexual misconduct
   D. aggravated sexual abuse

   2.____

3. Diane, age 17, believing that she is pregnant, seeks out her pharmacist boyfriend. He gives her pills to cause a miscarriage. She takes the pills, becomes ill, and is hospitalized. At the hospital, it is discovered that she is not pregnant.
   Her boyfriend has committed
   A. abortion 1st degree
   B. abortion 2nd degree
   C. attempted abortion 2nd
   D. attempted abortion 1st

   3.____

4. Sam is a world famous thief and shoplifter. The security chief in a local department store knows that Sam is in town. He places a large sign at each entrance to the store saying, "Sam, keep out." These signs are conspicuously displayed. Sam enters the store during business hours and steals merchandise valued at $200 from a counter.
   Based on these facts, the statement below which is INCORRECT is:
   A. Sam did not commit criminal trespass.
   B. Sam did not commit a felony.
   C. The statute of limitations for Sam's offense is 2 years.
   D. Sam committed grand larceny.

   4.____

5. Don and Carol are in the auto repair business. In order to assure that business will remain on the upswing, Don removes a manhole cover from a sewer in front of their premises. His objective is to cause vehicles to fall into the open hole damaging them and necessitating immediate repairs. He sees the risk that someone might get hurt. A car falls into the hole, and the driver suffers an injury when he strikes his head on his vehicle.
   Based on these facts, Don has committed
   A. assault 1st
   B. assault 2nd
   C. assault 3rd
   D. reckless endangerment

   5.____

125

6. Carol, celebrating the fact that she has just been appointed as the first female lion-cage supervisor, drinks to excess and becomes intoxicated. While in this condition, to see what the reaction will be, Carol frees her favorite lioness and allows it to enter the Sunday afternoon crowd at the zoo. The lioness kills a young child.
   Based on these facts, Carol has committed
   A. felony murder
   B. murder 2nd
   C. assault 1st
   D. criminally negligent homicide

7. A new tenant kin a previously occupied apartment finds a cable TV line that is still connected and which belonged to the former tenant. She hooks into it and uses it for 6 months. The cable TV company discovers what is happening and brings charges.
   The woman can be charged with
   A. grand larceny
   B. theft of services
   C. petit larceny
   D. unauthorized use

8. Cora knows of an appliance store with a faulty lock on the rear door. She waits until dark and then, when the store is closed, enters the store to steal an electronic game. Before she can take anything, she is frightened off by a passing police car. She runs from the store and is caught.
   She has committed
   A. burglary 3rd
   B. burglary 2nd
   C. criminal trespass 2nd
   D. attempted burglary 3rd

9. Fred is in the business of making usurious loans. He lends money to Maddy at a rate which exceeds 25% a year.
   Based on these facts, Fred has committed
   A. extortion
   B. criminal usury 2nd
   C. criminal usury 1st
   D. larceny

10. A public servant who, upon a threat to use or abuse his position as a public servant, extorts the sum of $100 from another, is guilty of
    A. grand larceny 1st
    B. grand larceny 2nd
    C. grand larceny 3rd
    D. extortion

11. Unlawful assembly requires AT LEAST _____ persons.
    A. 3   B. 4   C. 5   D. 7

12. A person who makes unreasonable noise and who intentionally causes annoyance at a lawfully assembled religious service (or recklessly creates a risk of such annoyance) or within a certain distance of said service, commits the offense known as "Disruption or Disturbance of a Religious Service."
    The distance referred to in the law is _____ feet.
    A. 1,000   B. 100   C. 250   D. 500

13. The offense below which would be a felony under the Penal Law is   13.____
    A. jostling
    B. accepting a monetary benefit not to prosecute after an auto accident
    C. possession of one stolen credit card
    D. maintaining a place for the unlawful use of narcotics

14. Which of the following sets of facts would give rise to the crime of arson?   14.____
    A. Burning someone's law furniture valued at $1,500
    B. Discarding a lit cigarette which ignites gasoline and burns down a rival's gasoline station
    C. Intentionally setting fire to another's mobile home
    D. Intentionally destroying forest land by fire

15. In which of the following situations does the law provide for a 5 year statute of limitations?   15.____
    A. Bribing a juror
    B. Theft of services
    C. Loitering 1st degree
    D. Criminal possession of stolen property 3rd degree

16. John, a police officer, observes Jack, his neighbor, in a compromising situation. John threatens to tell Jack's wife if Jack doesn't give John Jack's brand new lawnmower worth $300. Jack gives John the mower.   16.____
    John is guilty of
    A. grand larceny 1st   B. grand larceny 2nd
    C. grand larceny 3rd   D. robbery 3rd

17. You are a police officer and a female friend complains to you that she was unlawfully discriminated against by being excused from jury duty without being given a reason therefor.   17.____
    You should tell her
    A. to file a complaint with the local office of equal opportunity
    B. that you will investigate the matter
    C. that each side in a criminal trial is allowed a certain number of challenges for which no reason need be given
    D. to contact the U.S. Justice Department

18. Which of the following local criminal court accusatory instruments CANNOT be used to prosecute the offense named therein?   18.____
    A. Simplified information   B. Misdemeanor complaint
    C. Information   D. Felony complaint

19. You have applied for and received a search warrant for a building where you know stolen property is being concealed. You execute the warrant, conduct the search, and find the property. The owner of the premises is not present at the time that the property is seized and removed.   19.____
    Under these circumstances, you should
    A. leave a receipt for the property with anyone who is inside the building
    B. return with the property to headquarters and promptly notify the owner

4 (#2)

    C. return the property to court and give a receipt for the property to the judge who issued the warrant
    D. leave a receipt on the building owner's desk

20. Mr. Smith, who lives in South County, receives a subpoena from the District Attorney of North County directing Mr. Smith to appear in court as a witness in a criminal case being tried in North County, which adjoins South County. Mr. Smith does
    A. not have to appear because the trial is not in South County
    B. not have to appear since the subpoena, signed only by the D.A., is not legally sufficient
    C. have to appear because in this case the D.A.'s subpoena is lawfully issued
    D. not have to appear because there is insufficient information in the subpoena

Questions 21-15.

DIRECTIONS: Questions 21 through 25 are to be answered on the basis of the provisions of the Penal Law.

21. When considering the crime of "assault," which of the following will NOT be considered as a form of "aggravating factor" that could raise the degree?
    A. A deadly weapon was used.
    B. A dangerous instrument was used.
    C. The injury was inflicted through criminal negligence.
    D. Serious physical injury was inflicted.

22. Under the provisions of the N.Y.S. Penal Law, the situations in which deadly physical force can be used legally are:
    I. By a police officer to prevent the burglary of an occupied factory building at night
    II. By a civilian to arrest a person who has just attempted to kill another person
    III. By a police officer to arrest a person who has escaped from his custody after having been arrested for grand larceny of an automobile
    IV. By a civilian to prevent the commission of a robbery
The CORRECT answer is:
    A. I, II   B. I, IV   C. II, III, IV   D. III, IV

23. Assume that Leslie has committed a robbery.
Which of the following sets of circumstances would NOT justify a charge of robbery 1st degree?
    A. Leslie was armed with a deadly weapon.
    B. Leslie was assisted by Jack who was actually present.
    C. Leslie displayed a loaded pistol.
    D. Leslie displayed what appeared to be a pistol but it turned out to be an unloaded toy gun painted black.

24. A person who inflicts serious physical injury upon another through the criminally negligent operation of a motor vehicle should properly be charged with
    A. assault 3rd
    B. assault 2nd
    C. criminally negligent homicide
    D. none of the above

25. A person who causes the death of another through the reckless operation of a motor vehicle should properly be charged with
    A. criminally negligent homicide
    B. murder, but with an affirmative defense
    C. manslaughter 2nd
    D. manslaughter 1st

KEY (CORRECT ANSWERS)

1.	B	11.	B
2.	D	12.	B
3.	B	13.	C
4.	D	14.	C
5.	C	15.	A
6.	B	16.	C
7.	B	17.	C
8.	A	18.	D
9.	C	19.	D
10.	B	20.	C

21.	C
22.	B
23.	C
24.	A
25.	C

TEST 3

DIRECTIONS: Each question or incomplete statement is followed by several suggested answers or completions. Select the one that BEST answers the question or completes the statement. *PRINT THE LETTER OF THE CORRECT ANSWER IN THE SPACE AT THE RIGHT.*

1. A "juvenile offender" would include all of the following EXCEPT a   1.____
   A. 13-year-old who has committed a "depraved mind" murder
   B. 14-year-old who has committed a "felony murder" where the underlying felony is kidnapping 1st degree
   C. 15-year-old who has committed a "felony murder" where the underlying felony is kidnapping 2nd degree
   D. 13-year-old who has intentionally murdered a police officer in the performance of duty

2. A "deadly weapon" would include all of the following EXCEPT   2.____
   A. a loaded, working firearm
   B. a dagger
   C. metal knuckles
   D. an attack dog

3. Which one of the following defenses or affirmative defenses require action on the part of a public servant, or someone cooperating with a public servant?   3.____
   A. Justification   B. Duress   C. Infancy   D. Entrapment

4. In which of the following defenses or affirmative defenses is the burden of proof "beyond a reasonable doubt"?   4.____
   A. Justification
   B. Entrapment
   C. Mental disease or defect
   D. Duress

5. In which of the following situations may both police and private citizens use deadly physical force in order to effect an arrest?   5.____
   A. Burglary 1st
   B. Kidnapping
   C. Escape 1st
   D. Robbery 1st

6. The one of the following which would NOT amount to assault 1st degree is   6.____
   A. causing serious physical injury to another recklessly through a depraved indifference to human life which created a grave risk of death
   B. causing serious physical injury to a police officer while intentionally trying to prevent him from performing a lawful duty
   C. intentionally biting off an ear of another person
   D. intentionally causing serious physical injury to another by means of a dangerous knife known as a dirk

7. If a defendant at a criminal trial maintains that he did not actually commit the crime charged and, as a matter of fact, voluntarily withdrew from the criminal enterprise, while at the same time he made a substantial effort to convince the persons with whom he had been acting in concert also to withdraw, he would have raised the   7.____

A. defense of justification
B. defense of duress
C. affirmative defense of entrapment
D. affirmative defense of renunciation

8. For which of the following offenses would a person 14 or 15 years of age have the defense of infancy available to him?
   A. Robbery 1st degree
   B. Arson 1st degree
   C. Robbery 2nd degree when a gun was displayed
   D. Assault 1st degree where the serious injury was the result of a depraved indifference to human life, creating a grave risk of death

9. Leslie, knowing that Police Officer Smith is working in his official capacity as a police officer, intentionally causes serious physical injury to him by stabbing him with a dagger.
   Leslie has committed
   A. aggravated assault upon a police officer
   B. assault 1st
   C. assault 2nd
   D. reckless endangerment

10. Steve commits an abortional act upon Leslie, intending to cause a miscarriage. Unfortunately, both Leslie and her unborn child die as a result.
    The MOST appropriate charge against Steve is
    A. manslaughter 2nd
    B. abortion 2nd
    C. manslaughter 2nd and abortion 2nd
    D. manslaughter 1st and abortion 1st

11. The one of the following which would NOT amount to murder 2nd is
    A. the intentional killing of a police officer in the performance of duty by a 17-year-old
    B. intentionally causing or aiding another to commit suicide
    C. felony murder when the underlying felony is kidnapping 1st
    D. intent to cause serious physical injury, but causing the death of another

12. Which of the following would NOT necessarily be an example of murder?
    A. Intentionally causing the death of another
    B. Under circumstances evincing a depraved indifference to human life, recklessly engaging in conduct which creates a grave risk of death and which causes the death of another
    C. Causing the death of a non-participant during the course of and in furtherance of the commission of any degree of burglary
    D. Causing the death of a non-participant during the course of and in furtherance of the commission of any degree of rape

13. Which of the following situations would NOT result in manslaughter 2nd degree? 13.____
    A. Causing the death of a female as a result of an unjustifiable abortion
    B. Recklessly causing the death of another
    C. Intentionally causing the death of another through the operation of a vehicle
    D. Intentionally aiding another to commit suicide without the use of duress or deception

14. Concerning the homicide offense in the Penal Law, which of the following is LEAST correct? 14.____
    A. Homicide is not always a felony.
    B. It is not necessary for a person to be killed in order to have a homicide.
    C. Murder is always a Class A felony.
    D. Only the "intentional murder" has an affirmative defense attached to it.

15. Which of the following is LEAST correct concerning homicide? 15.____
    A. A person who is 17 at the time of murdering a police officer may under no circumstances be sentenced to death for that murder.
    B. Not all felonies may serve as the basis for a charge of felony murder.
    C. Acting under "extreme emotional disturbance" gives rise to the defense of mental disease or defect.
    D. Intentionally aiding another to commit suicide by the use of duress or deception is murder.

16. Which of the following offenses would NOT be an underlying offense for a charge of felony murder? 16.____
    A. Robbery 3rd degree
    B. Arson 2nd degree
    C. Escape 1st degree
    D. Sexual intercourse with an 11-year-old girl

17. Amy, pregnant for 30 weeks, submits to an abortional act at the hands of White. As a result of the abortional act, Amy dies, but the fetus survives. According to the Penal Law, which of the following is LEAST correct? 17.____
    A. White is guilty of manslaughter 1st degree.
    B. White is not guilty of abortion 1st degree.
    C. If Amy had survived too, she would be guilty of self-abortion 1st degree.
    D. White is guilty of attempted abortion 1st degree.

18. Which of the following is LEAST correct with respect to felony murder? 18.____
    A. The crime of burglary in any degree may be the underlying felony.
    B. Sexual abuse 1st, rape 1st, or sodomy 1st may be the underlying felony.
    C. Any degree of arson may be the underlying felony.
    D. Escape 1st degree, but not escape 2nd or 3rd may be the underlying felony.

19. A defendant who, as a result of mental disease or defect, lacks capacity to understand the proceedings against him or to assist him in his own defense is known as a(n)
    A. insane person
    B. incapacitated person
    C. seriously incapacitated person
    D. mental defective

20. For purposes of search warrant execution, they may NOT be executed without special endorsement between
    A. sunset and sunrise
    B. ½ hour after sunset to ½ hour before sunrise
    C. 5:00 P.M. and 9:00 A.M.
    D. 9:00 P.M. and 6:00 A.M.

21. Under the provisions of the C.P.L., printing would be required for an arrest for
    I. jostling
    II. leaving the scene of an accident
    III. fortune telling
    The CORRECT answer is:
    A. I, II
    B. I, III
    C. II, III
    D. III only

22. In which of the following instances do you NOT have to explain why the person is being placed under arrest?
    A. The arrest is made under authority of a warrant.
    B. The arrest is made for a felony.
    C. You are arresting a person immediately after the commission of an offense.
    D. The person you are about to arrest flees from the scene.

23. A 20-year-old female is on trial for prostitution allegedly committed when she was 19 years of age.
    According to the law, which of the following is LEAST accurate?
    A. Prostitution is a crime.
    B. Fingerprints must be taken of a person arrested for prostitution.
    C. The female involved may not be considered as a person in need of supervision.
    D. The female involved may be accorded youthful offender treatment.

24. A Grand Jury consists of not less than _____ nor more than _____ persons.
    A. 15; 24
    B. 16; 24
    C. 16; 23
    D. 12; 23

25. A trial jury in a local criminal court, excluding alternate jurors, consists of _____ jurors.
    A. 4
    B. 6
    C. 8
    D. 12

KEY (CORRECT ANSWERS)

1.	C	11.	D
2.	D	12.	D
3.	D	13.	C
4.	A	14.	D
5.	D	15.	C
6.	B	16.	D
7.	D	17.	C
8.	D	18.	D
9.	B	19.	B
10.	C	20.	D

21. B
22. D
23. D
24. C
25. B

TEST 4

DIRECTIONS: Each question or incomplete statement is followed by several suggested answers or completions. Select the one that BEST answers the question or completes the statement. *PRINT THE LETTER OF THE CORRECT ANSWER IN THE SPACE AT THE RIGHT.*

1. Justin commits an abortional act on Sandi, who believes she is pregnant. She is not pregnant. She dies as a result of the abortional act. Justin is guilty of
   A. manslaughter 1st and abortion 1st
   B. manslaughter 2nd and abortion 2nd
   C. manslaughter 2nd only
   D. criminally negligent homicide

   1.____

2. Rich and Don are committing a burglary of a dwelling. The owner comes home and surprises them. In his haste to flee from the premises, Don knocks the owner down a flight of stairs, accidentally causing his death.
   The MOST serious charge that could be lodged against both Rich and Don is
   A. burglary 1st degree
   B. manslaughter 1st degree
   C. murder
   D. criminally negligent homicide

   2.____

3. The facts below which BEST describe a rape 2nd degree are a _____ engaging in sexual intercourse with a _____.
   A. male age 21; female age 15
   B. female age 19; male 13
   C. male age 18; 13-year-old female
   D. male age 21; female who is 14

   3.____

4. A male soldier on furlough, age 20, engages in sexual intercourse with a 14-year-old female. The soldier is guilty of
   A. rape 3rd degree
   B. rape 2nd degree
   C. rape 1st degree
   D. sexual misconduct

   4.____

5. If an aunt abducts her infant nephew and then seeks ransom for the return of the child, it would be MOST CORRECT to state that
   A. she is guilty of kidnapping 1st degree
   B. she, being a relative, has an affirmative defense to kidnapping 1st degree
   C. she is guilty of kidnapping 2nd if the abduction was for 12 hours or less
   D. if the charge against her was kidnapping 2nd, she would have an affirmative defense

   5.____

6. Carl, knowing of Dixie's past as a prostitute, threatens to call Dusty, her current boyfriend, unless Dixie has sexual intercourse with him.
   According to the Penal Law, it would be MOST CORRECT to state that Carl has committed
   A. coercion 1st degree
   B. coercion 2nd degree
   C. attempted coercion 1st degree
   D. attempted coercion 2nd degree

   6.____

7. The LEAST accurate statement regarding the crime of criminal mischief is that criminal mischief
   A. has four degrees
   B. in the fourth degree may be committed intentionally (any amount) or recklessly (over $250)
   C. in the third degree, second degree, or first degree requires the culpable mental state of intentionally
   D. in the first degree may be committed by fire or explosive

8. John, because he was angry with Sam and Sue, walked into their printing shop and, having no right to do so, disarranged the files and records maintained thereat. It took Sam and Sue four hours to straighten out the files. John is guilty of criminal
   A. mischief in the 3rd degree
   B. mischief in the 2nd degree
   C. mischief in the 1st degree
   D. tampering in the 3rd degree

9. While supervising patrol, you are called to the scene of an arrest. The arresting officer has taken a male into custody for having broken into an enclosed motor truck trailer which was parked at a resting site in your jurisdiction. Nothing was stolen from the truck because it was empty. The arresting officer informs you that he advised the suspect of his rights, and the suspect blurted out, "I wouldn't have broken into it if I knew it was empty. I thought it had crates of watches in it." When searched, the suspect was found to have a dagger concealed upon his person. You advise the arresting officer regarding the law involved in this case.
   All of the following would be good advice, EXCEPT that the
   A. admission made by the suspect will be suppressed since a lawyer was not present
   B. trailer involved was a building for burglary purposes
   C. proper degree of burglary with which the suspect should be charged is burglary 2nd
   D. suspect should be charged with criminal possession of a weapon

10. Knowingly and unlawfully entering a dwelling with intent to commit a crime therein is
    A. burglary 2nd
    B. burglary 3rd, if the dwelling is not occupied
    C. burglary 1st
    D. burglary 1st, if the defendant is armed with a weapon

11. The MOST basic difference between "burglary" and "criminal trespass" is that
    A. burglary always requires a building and criminal trespass never does
    B. burglary requires an unlawful entry or remaining
    C. burglary requires an "intent" to commit a crime therein
    D. armed with a "deadly weapon" may be an aggravating factor in burglary, but not in criminal trespass

12. Which of the following would NOT be a sufficient aggravating factor to raise the degree of burglary?
    A. Being armed with a dangerous instrument
    B. Causing physical injury to a non-participant
    C. Threatening the immediate use of a deadly weapon
    D. Displaying what appears to be a firearm

13. Mark Greene knowingly and unlawfully enters an unoccupied building at night while armed with a dagger.
    He has committed
    A. burglary 1st
    B. burglary 2nd
    C. criminal trespass 1st
    D. criminal trespass 2nd

14. Sam, aware and knowing that he is unlawfully entering a dwelling, is guilty of
    A. burglary 1st
    B. burglary 2nd
    C. burglary 3rd
    D. criminal trespass 2nd

15. Jack and Sam knowingly and unlawfully enter an occupied dwelling at night. Jack is armed with a switchblade knife.
    According to the Penal Law, Jack and Sam are guilty of
    A. burglary 1st
    B. burglary 2nd
    C. burglary 3rd
    D. none of the above

16. With respect to the various degrees of larceny, which of the following statements is MOST INCORRECT?
    A. Larceny by extortion may be 1st degree, 2nd degree, or 3rd degree.
    B. Grand larceny 1st degree is always larceny by extortion.
    C. The value of the property is not always the determining factor in the degrees of larceny.
    D. The value of the property is only an important factor in grand larceny 2nd degree.

17. Sam is a police officer assigned to traffic law enforcement. He observes a motorist commit a moving violation, and when he "pulls him over", he demands $20.00 from the motorist under a threat to arrest him for a more serious offense if the motorist does not pay. The motorist, afraid of the consequences, gives Sam the $20.00.
    The CORRECT statement(s) regarding the above paragraph is(are):
    I. Sam committed grand larceny 1st
    II. Sam committed bribe receiving 2nd
    III. Sam may be convicted of both grand larceny and bribery
    IV. The motorist committed bribery 2nd
    The CORRECT answer is:
    A. I, II
    B. I, II, IV
    C. II, III
    D. III, IV

18. Rob, angry over the fact that his new car has been causing him a great deal of trouble, smashes the windshield of a car with a hammer. Rob thought it was his car, but it was not. It was someone else's car, exactly the same color and model.
Based on this set of facts, Rob has committed
   A. criminal mischief 4th
   B. criminal mischief 3rd
   C. criminal mischief 2nd
   D. none of the above

19. Andrea, intending to burn Marc's house to the ground, sets fire to it at 2:00 A.M., believing that Marc is asleep in an upstairs bedroom. Fortunately for Marc, at about 1:55 A.M., he took his dog for a walk and was not in the house at the time.
Based on these facts, Andrea has committed arson
   A. 1st
   B. 2nd
   C. 3rd
   D. 4th

20. On July 4, Jack is standing on a street corner with a supply of newly purchased cherry bombs. He sees an old car being driven by and, intending to damage the car, he throws a cherry bomb into it. The cherry bomb explodes and breaks the windshield of the car. It never even dawned on Jack that the driver might also be injured, and he was surprised and sorry that the driver was permanently blinded.
Based on the above facts, Jack is guilt of arson
   A. 1st and assault 1st
   B. 2nd and attempted assault
   C. 1st and assault 3rd
   D. 4th and assault 3rd

21. According to the Penal Law, which of the following statements is LEAST accurate?
   A. Criminal possession of forgery devices is a felony.
   B. It is not always necessary to prove criminal intent in order to convict a person of criminal possession of forgery devices.
   C. In order to convict for criminal simulation, the prosecution must always prove intent to defraud.
   D. In order to convict for unlawfully using slugs 1st degree, the prosecution must prove that the value of the slugs exceeded $250.00.

22. Which of the following would NOT amount to forgery 1st degree? Forging
   A. an issue of U.S. money
   B. an issue of U.S. Government bonds
   C. of corporate securities
   D. of a drug prescription

23. The factor that separates bribery 1st degree from bribery 2nd degree is
   A. the nature of the benefit
   B. the dollar value of the benefit
   C. whether or not a public servant is involved
   D. whether or not a Class A drug felony is involved

24. According to the Penal Law, criminal usury is committed when a person knowingly and unlawfully charges interest at a rate which exceeds _____% per year.
    A. 25 B. 15 C. 10 D. 6

25. In which of the following instances would the offense of refusing to aid a peace officer or police officer occur?
    I. A uniformed police officer orders a civilian to assist him in making an arrest, and the civilian unreasonably refuses to do so.
    II. An identified police officer in civilian clothes commands a passing female to assist him in preventing the commission of an offense, but the female unreasonably refuses to do so.
    III. A uniformed police officer orders a passing civilian to assist him in rescuing three children who have fallen through ice on a frozen lake. The civilian unreasonably refuses to do so.
    The CORRECT answer is:
    A. I only B. I, II C. I, III D. II, III

KEY (CORRECT ANSWERS)

1.	B		11.	C
2.	C		12.	A
3.	C		13.	C
4.	D		14.	D
5.	A		15.	D
6.	D		16.	D
7.	D		17.	B
8.	D		18.	D
9.	A		19.	C
10.	A		20.	C

21. D
22. D
23. D
24. A
25. B

EXAMINATION SECTION
TEST 1

DIRECTIONS: Each question or incomplete statement is followed by several suggested answers or completions. Select the one that BEST answers the question or completes the statement. *PRINT THE LETTER OF THE CORRECT ANSWER IN THE SPACE AT THE RIGHT.*

1. Which one of the following statements is LEAST accurate according to Article 8 of the F.C.A.? 1.____

    A. The proceedings under this article are civil proceedings.
    B. The Family Court does NOT have exclusive jurisdiction over all family offense proceedings.
    C. The phrase "criminal complaint" includes an "information."
    D. If the family offense proceeding begins in the Family Court, it must be terminated there as a civil matter.

2. The one of the following offenses which is NOT considered to be a "family offense" is 2.____

    A. disorderly conduct
    B. attempted assault
    C. menacing or reckless endangerment
    D. incest

3. A criminal complaint alleging a true family offense which starts in the criminal court and is not withdrawn or dismissed for legal insufficiency may still be transferred to the Family Court within _____ hours. 3.____

    A. 12　　　　B. 24　　　　C. 48　　　　D. 72

4. According to Article 10 of the F.C.A., an "abused child" is a child whose parents, etc. permit certain conditions harmful to the child to take place, and the child is less than 4.____

    A. 14　　　　B. 15　　　　C. 16　　　　D. 18

5. According to the F.C.A., a "neglected child" is a child less than _____ years of age whose physical, mental, or emotional condition has been impaired in a certain way. 5.____

    A. 14　　　　B. 15　　　　C. 16　　　　D. 18

6. Which one of the following statements is LEAST correct according to the Family Court Act in Article 10? 6.____

    A. A child's "custodian" may include any person continually or at regular intervals found in the same household as the child when the conduct of such person causes or contributes to the abuse or neglect of the child.
    B. A police officer, when the circumstances are proper, may make an emergency removal of a child, without court order and without consent of parents.
    C. If a police officer as in B above acts in good faith in the removal of a child, he shall have immunity from any liability, civil or criminal.
    D. The authority for emergency removal as in B above is limited to police officers.

141

7. People who may originate a proceeding to determine abuse or neglect are
   I. any person at the court's direction
   II. a child protective agency
   III. a police officer
   The CORRECT answer is:

   A. I, II
   B. I, II, III
   C. I, III
   D. II, III

8. When a police officer takes a child under the age of 16 into custody, the thing he must do *immediately* according to the F.C.A. is to

   A. notify the parent or other person legally responsible for his care or the person with whom he is domiciled that he has been taken into custody
   B. release the child to the custody of his parent or other person legally responsible for his care upon the written promise, without security, of the person to whose custody the child is released that he will produce the child before the Family Court
   C. forthwith, and without a police station stopover, bring the child before the Family Court
   D. forthwith deliver the child to a place certified by the State Division for Youth as a juvenile detention facility for the reception of children

9. The one of the following which is NOT required to be alleged in a petition to have someone declared a "juvenile delinquent" is that the

   A. respondent did an act, which if done by an adult, would constitute a crime and specifying the act and the time and place of its commission
   B. respondent was a person under 16 years of age at the time of the alleged act
   C. respondent requires supervision, treatment, or confinement
   D. offense involved either physical injury to the victim or the use of a dangerous weapon

10. The required quantum of evidence in a fact finding hearing concerning juvenile delinquency proceedings shall be

    A. a preponderance of the evidence
    B. beyond a reasonable doubt
    C. probable cause
    D. reasonable cause to believe

11. An "adjournment in contemplation of dismissal" may NOT be granted when a J.D. is found to have committed a

    A. Class A felony
    B. "designated felony act"
    C. felony involving physical force
    D. robbery where a senior citizen is the victim

12. Where a child has been found to have committed a "designated Class A felony act" and the court determines that "restrictive placement" is necessary, the respondent shall be "placed" with the Division for Youth for an initial period of _____(s).

    A. 10
    B. 5
    C. 3
    D. 2

13. When the order for restrictive placement is made in connection with a youth found to have committed a "designated felony act" other than a "designated Class A felony act," the respondent shall be "placed" with the Division for Youth for an initial period of _____ (s).

    A. 10 B. 5 C. 3 D. 2

14. A 15-year-old boy has been arrested and charged with J.D. He is currently living with his 20-year-old sister. His parents reside in a city 500 miles away. You have tried to notify them but have been unsuccessful.
    Your NEXT step should be to

    A. continue trying to notify parents
    B. take him to a secure facility and question him further
    C. release him on recognizance to his 20-year-old sister
    D. advise him of his rights and question him to get the facts

15. According to the F.C.A., a private person may take a person under 16 into custody in cases in which he may arrest for a crime under 140.30 of the C.P.L. The private person may then
    I. take the child to the child's home
    II. take the child to a Family Court
    III. deliver the child to a police officer or a peace officer
    The CORRECT answer is:

    A. I, II, III   B. I, III
    C. II, III   D. III *only*

16. Under the provisions of the Family Court Act, in which of the following arrests of a juvenile delinquent must fingerprints be taken?

    A. John, age 11, commits robbery 1st degree
    B. Linda, age 12, commits robbery 2nd degree
    C. Robert, age 13, commits robbery 3rd degree
    D. Jane, age 14, commits burglary 3rd degree

17. If a juvenile delinquent is taken into custody and is charged with a crime which is NOT a "designated felony," and is to be issued a Family Court Appearance Ticket, the return date of such Appearance Ticket shall be no later than _____ after its issuance.

    A. 72 hours B. 5 days C. 10 days D. 14 days

18. According to the provisions of the Family Court Act in Article 8, which of the following offenses is NOT a "family offense" even if it occurs between members of the same family or household?

    A. harassment   B. menacing
    C. assault 1st degree   D. assault 2nd degree
    E. disorderly conduct

19. According to Section 822 of the Family Court Act, only certain persons are authorized to originate family offense proceedings. With respect to who may so originate, which of the following statements is INCORRECT?

    A. Any person in the relation to the respondent of spouse, parent, child, or member of the same family or household
    B. A duly authorized agency, association, society, or institution
    C. Any peace officer or police officer
    D. A person on the court's own motion

20. Under the provisions of the Family Court Act in Section 158, if a person is taken into protective custody as a material witness, the total period of protective custody may NOT exceed _____ days.

    A. 7   B. 14   C. 21   D. 35   E. 42

KEY (CORRECT ANSWERS)

1.	D	11.	B
2.	D	12.	B
3.	D	13.	C
4.	D	14.	A
5.	D	15.	A
6.	D	16.	A
7.	A	17.	D
8.	A	18.	C
9.	D	19.	C
10.	B	20.	E

TEST 2

DIRECTIONS: Each question consists of a statement. You are to indicate whether the statement is TRUE (T) or FALSE (F). *PRINT THE LETTER OF THE CORRECT ANSWER IN THE SPACE AT THE RIGHT.*

1. An adjudication as a J.D. does NOT operate as a forfeiture of any right or privilege to hold public office EXCEPT where it involves a "designated felony act" involving serious physical injury to a senior citizen. 1.____

2. Family offense proceedings are civil proceedings whose objective is to provide practical help to family members. 2.____

3. The Family Court and the Criminal Courts have concurrent jurisdiction over most "family offenses." (HAD-ARM) 3.____

4. An arrest is NOT a requirement for bringing a HAD-ARM offense before the Family Court, but it is in order to bring the offense before the Criminal Court. 4.____

5. The general rule is that when a choice of either the Criminal Court or Family Court is made, and 72 hours go by, the choice of court becomes a final choice. 5.____

6. A police officer may originate a family offense proceeding under Article 8. 6.____

7. A "certificate of warrant" issued by the clerk of the Family Court expires 90 days from the date of issue, but can be renewed from time to time by the clerk of the court. 7.____

8. The presentation of a valid certificate of warrant to a police officer authorizes him to arrest the respondent named therein. 8.____

9. At a fact-finding hearing under Article 8, only evidence which is competent, material, and relevant may be admitted. 9.____

10. Findings at an Article 8 fact-finding hearing must be based on proof beyond a reasonable doubt. 10.____

11. Evidence at a "dispositional" hearing under Article 8 must be relevant and material. 11.____

12. The age of an "abused" child under Article 10 is less than 18. 12.____

13. The age of a "neglected" child under Article 10 is less than 16. 13.____

14. An "abandoned" child under Article 10 is within the definition of a "neglected" child. 14.____

15. Notwithstanding the fact that a Criminal Court may be exercising jurisdiction over the facts giving rise to "abuse" or "neglect," the Family Court has jurisdiction over proceedings brought under Article 10 for the protection of the child. 15.____

16. If the Family Court concludes that the processes of the Family Court are *inappropriate,* the matter may be transferred to the Criminal Court. 16.____

17. A police officer may make an emergency removal of an abused or neglected child when there is reason to believe the child is in imminent danger to life or health. 17.____

18. The above emergency removal may be made over the objections of parents and without court order. 18.___

19. A police officer may originate proceedings under Article 10. 19.___

20. In an Article 10 fact-finding hearing, any adjudication that the child is abused or neglected must be based on a preponderance of the evidence. 20.___

KEY (CORRECT ANSWERS)

1.	F	11.	T
2.	T	12.	T
3.	T	13.	F
4.	F	14.	T
5.	T	15.	T
6.	T	16.	T
7.	T	17.	T
8.	T	18.	T
9.	T	19.	F
10.	F	20.	T

EXAMINATION SECTION
TEST 1

DIRECTIONS: Each question or incomplete statement is followed by several suggested answers or completions. Select the one that BEST answers the question or completes the statement. *PRINT THE LETTER OF THE CORRECT ANSWER IN THE SPACE AT THE RIGHT.*

1. Jon and Nicole moved with their daughter, Ella, to France in 2012. Shortly thereafter, Jon filed for divorce from Nicole. After years of court hearings in France, Jon and Nicole reached a child custody determination and final order for Ella. Jon and Nicole, separately, moved to New York. Will the French child custody be recognized by New York Courts?
   A. No, under any circumstances
   B. No, unless the French authorities consent to the recognition
   C. No, unless the American authorities consent to the recognition
   D. Likely yes

2. Assuming that a child custody determination is made in Richmond County, what is the effect of the order in Nassau County?
   A. The issues discussed in the order will need to be re-heard before a Nassau County judge in order to take effect.
   B. The order will not take effect unless the Richmond County Court consents.
   C. The order will have the same effect in Nassau County as it had in Richmond County.
   D. The order is null and void if any of the parties identified in the order move to another Nassau County, or any other county outside of where the original order is adjudicated.

3. Which of the following is MOST likely to be heard first on the court calendar concerning a child custody determination?
   A. Allocation of time between each parent
   B. The exercise of jurisdiction over the proceeding
   C. Child support payment determination
   D. Alimony payment determination

4. Which of the following is a proper way to serve notice to an individual living outside of New York State?
   A. A form of mail that requests a receipt
   B. Leaving the notice on the respondent's doorstep, without confirming the address of the respondent
   C. Asking another adult to leave the notice on the respondent's doorstep or mailbox, without confirming the address of the respondent
   D. Calling the respondent on the telephone and apprising him or her of the proceedings

Questions 5-7.

DIRECTIONS: Questions 5 through 7 are to be answered on the basis of the following fact pattern.

Mark and Luci are embattled in a bitter child custody battle over their son. Although Mark works in New York, he lives in Connecticut while Luci lives in New York. The child custody proceedings take place in New York.

5. When the issue of jurisdiction comes up during the proceedings, Luci's attorney argues that New York is proper because
    A. New York is where the mother of the child lives
    B. Mark has consented to jurisdiction because he maintains a job in New York
    C. Luci has not waived jurisdiction and, therefore, Connecticut is not the proper venue
    D. Neither New York nor Connecticut can exercise jurisdiction over the matter

6. Assuming the same facts as above, which of the following is the LEAST convincing argument that Mark availed himself of jurisdiction in New York?
    A. Mark attended the child custody hearings in New York.
    B. Mark works in New York.
    C. Mark has significant contacts in New York.
    D. The hearing began in New York.

7. Who may participate in the communications between the New York and Connecticut courts regarding the existence of jurisdiction?
    A. The bailiff
    B. The child at the center of the child custody determination
    C. The clerk of the Court
    D. The plaintiff and respondent

8. Which of the following may a New York court request of a court of another state?
    A. Hold an evidentiary hearing
    B. Order all parties to appear in a court of the other states' choosing
    C. Order the child to appear before the court without counsel or parents
    D. Order that all depositions relating to the case be held at a specified time

9. Jane has been deployed pursuant to her service in the armed forces. Prior to her deployment, she had sole physical custody of her daughter, Jolene. Jane's ex-husband and Jolene's father, Tom, has requested that the child custody order be modified on account of Jane's deployment. Tom's petition will likely be
    A. denied outright, given that an active deployment is not a reasonable reason to modify a court order
    B. heard but denied, given Jolene's age and maturity

C. heard and granted, if there is clear and convincing evidence a modification is in the best interests of the child
D. heard and granted, if Jolene wants to live with Tom full time on a go forward basis

10. Which of the following permits grants jurisdiction to a New York court to make the initial child custody determination?
    A. New York is the home state of the child on the date the proceeding commences.
    B. New York was the home state of the child at least six months prior to the date the proceeding commences.
    C. A court of another state does not have jurisdiction or denies to exercise jurisdiction over the proceeding.
    D. All of the above

Questions 11-13.

DIRECTIONS: Questions 11 through 13 are to be answered on the basis of the following fact pattern.

Jamal and Candace separated shortly after the birth of their son, Daniel. Jamal moved to Pennsylvania while Candace remained in New York. While Jamal lived in Pennsylvania, he and Candace agreed to have Daniel spend an equal amount of time with each parent and did not reach a child custody determination in a court of law. Recently, Jamal moved to Ohio. Candace would like to move the courts for a final child custody order.

11. Which court has continuing jurisdiction over the matter?
    A. New York Court
    B. Ohio Court
    C. Pennsylvania Court
    D. No courts, given that the matter has not yet been filed in any court

12. Which court is the MOST likely to deny jurisdiction?
    A. Pennsylvania
    B. Ohio
    C. New York
    D. A state cannot deny the exercise of jurisdiction

13. Assume that Candace files a petition for a child custody determination in a New York court. New York is presumed to have _____, continuing jurisdiction over the child custody determination.
    A. existential   B. exclusive   C. enormous   D. indefinite

14. Before a child custody determination can be made, which of the following must be made available to the parties?
    A. Notice only
    B. Notice and an opportunity to be heard
    C. An opportunity to be heard
    D. An opportunity to submit documentary evidence

15. Before a child custody order can be modified, a court must determine which of the following?
    A. Whether both parents still live within the state
    B. Whether the child lives within the state
    C. Whether a proceeding to enforce the determination has commenced in another state
    D. Whether each party has retained adequate counsel

16. Which party can raise the issue of an inconvenient forum in a motion?
    A. The child or the child's attorney
    B. The court upon its own motion
    C. By either party
    D. All of the above

17. Which of the following is NOT a relevant factor in determining whether it is appropriate for a court of another state to exercise jurisdiction?
    A. Relative financial circumstances of the parties
    B. An agreement of the parties as to which state should assume jurisdiction
    C. The age of the child
    D. The length of time the child has resided outside this state

18. May a court order the person who has physical custody to appear in person with the child?
    A. Yes, if they are in the state
    B. No, unless they work in the state
    C. No, unless the child consents to the appearance
    D. No

19. A visitation schedule made by the court of another state may be
    A. enforced by way of a temporary order by a New York Court
    B. cancelled by a New York Court
    C. deemed non-existent by a New York Court
    D. nullified by a New York Court

20. Who must be served with the petition and order?
    A. Any person who has physical custody of the child
    B. Any person who resides with the child
    C. Any person who maintains a substantive connection with the child
    D. Anyone who has legal custody of the child

21. Which of the following must be included in a warrant to take physical custody of a child?
    A. Recite the facts upon which a conclusion of imminent serious physical harm or removal from the jurisdiction is based
    B. Provide for the placement of the child pending final relief
    C. Direct law enforcement officers to take physical custody of the child immediately
    D. All of the above

22. May a child custody order be appealed?
    A. No
    B. No, unless both parties stipulate to the possibility of filing an appeal before the hearing commences
    C. No, unless there is an error of law or fact
    D. Yes

23. When will a respondent be assessed direct expenses and costs incurred by the prosecutor?
    A. When he or she volunteers to pay
    B. When he or she is the party responsible for the suit
    C. When he or she is the aggressive party
    D. When he is or she is not the prevailing party

24. In certain circumstances, a prosecutor may take any lawful action to do which of the following?
    A. Locate a child
    B. Obtain the return of a child
    C. Enforce a child custody determination
    D. All of the above

25. Which of the following is NOT a circumstance that would allow a prosecutor to take the lawful action in Question 24?
    A. An existing child custody determination
    B. A request to do so from a pending child custody proceeding
    C. A written request from one or both of the parents
    D. A reasonable belief that a criminal statute has been violated

KEY (CORRECT ANSWERS)

1.	D	11.	D
2.	C	12.	A
3.	B	13.	B
4.	A	14.	B
5.	B	15.	C
6.	A	16.	D
7.	D	17.	C
8.	A	18.	A
9.	C	19.	A
10.	D	20.	A

21.	D
22.	D
23.	D
24.	D
25.	C

EXAMINATION SECTION
TEST 1

DIRECTIONS: Each question or incomplete statement is followed by several suggested answers or completions. Select the one that BEST answers the question or completes the statement. *PRINT THE LETTER OF THE CORRECT ANSWER IN THE SPACE AT THE RIGHT.*

1. A putative father is generally defined as
   A. a man who claims or is alleged to be the father of a child whom is not married to the child's mother at the time of birth
   B. a man who is the father of the child but does not sign the birth certificate
   C. a man who is the alleged father of the child based on the fact that he is married to the child's mother at the time of the child's birth
   D. the child's presumptive father at law

   1.____

2. Which of the following people are entitled to notice to proceedings?
   A. Person identified as the father in a sworn written statement by the mother
   B. Any person recorded on the birth certificate as the child's father
   C. Any person adjudicated by the court as the child's father
   D. All of the above

   2.____

3. James is listed as the father on Bella's birth certificate, but has been twice convicted of rape in the second degree. Bella is the result of rape.
   Is James entitled to receive notice of Bella's guardianship hearing?
   A. Yes, because he is the legal father
   B. Yes, because he signed the birth certificate as the father
   C. Yes, unless Bella's mother objects to James receiving notice
   D. No

   3.____

4. A surrender for adoption executed by a parent, parents or guardian who is in foster care shall be executed only before a judge of the _____ court.
   A. surrogates   B. family   C. civil   D. probate

   4.____

5. Bill and Joel are both possible fathers to Diana's newborn baby. Diana only invited Bill to the hospital and he subsequently signed the birth certificate. After the birth, however, Bill lost contact with Diana. Joel has taken care of the baby since the child's birth.
   Who is the presumed father of Diana's baby?
   A. Bill
   B. Joel
   C. Whomever Diana designates as the father
   D. Whichever man Diana names in a sworn written statement as the father

   5.____

6. Which of the following is NOT listed as finding of legislative intent?
   A. Is it desirable for children to grow up with a normal family life in a permanent home
   B. It is generally desirable for the child to remain with or be returned to the birth parent because the child's need for a normal family life will usually best be met in the home of its birth parent, and that parents are entitled to bring up their own children unless the best interests of the child would be thereby endangered
   C. It is desirable for the child to live in one residence until the age of majority with both parents
   D. The state's first obligation is to help the family with services to prevent its break-up or to reunite if the child has already left home

7. The term "child" shall mean a person under the age of _____ years.
   A. sixteen   B. eighteen   C. twenty-one   D. twenty-five

Questions 8-9.

DIRECTIONS: Questions 8 and 9 are to be answered on the basis of the following passage from the New York Social Services Law.

"Permanently neglected child" shall mean a child who is in the care of an authorized agency and whose parent or custodian has failed for a period of either at least _____ or fifteen out of the most recent twenty-two months following the date such child came into the care of an authorized agency substantially and continuously or repeatedly to maintain contact with or plan for the future of the child, although physically and financially able to do so, notwithstanding the agency's diligent efforts to encourage and strengthen the parental relationship when such efforts will not be detrimental to the best interests of the child."

8. Please fill in the blank.
   A. one year   B. two years   C. three years   D. four years

9. The New York City agency tasked with ensuring the welfare of children and their families is called
   A. State of Children's Welfare Agency
   B. Administration for Children's Services
   C. Department of Child Welfare
   D. Agency of Family Services and Children's Needs

10. Rachel was placed in the home of her adoptive parents last July. What date is used to record the placement?
    A. The date of the adoption agreement will be recorded in a bound volume maintained by the agency along with the names of the adoptive parents
    B. The date the child moves into the home of the adoptive parents
    C. The date the child agrees to move into the home of the adoptive parents
    D. The date the adoptive parents agree to adopt a child

11. Surrenders must be written and can be either _____.
    A. jurisdictional or extra-territorial
    B. judicial or extra-judicial
    C. judicial or ex-parte
    B. jurisdictional or extra-judicial

12. In cases where a surrender is not executed and acknowledged before a judge, the authorized agency to which the child was surrendered shall file an application for approval in which court?
    A. The court in which the adoption proceeding is expected to be filed or, if not known, the family or surrogates court in the county in which the agency has its principal office
    B. The family or surrogates court in the county where the child was born
    C. The family or surrogates court in the county where the child was raised for the first eighteen months of life
    D. The court in which the adoption proceeding was already filed

13. Which of the following is NOT required to be stated in the affidavit accompanying the surrender?
    A. Date, time, and place where the surrender was executed and acknowledged
    B. A written statement that the parent was provided with ha copy of the surrender
    C. A statement that the parent executed and acknowledged the surrender
    D. A statement that the child executed and acknowledged the surrender

14. Katie is fifteen years old. Before Katie can be committed to the guardianship and custody of foster care, which of the following is MOST likely to occur at a court proceeding?
    A. The child care agency will likely provide proof of the likelihood the child will be adopted.
    B. The court may, in its discretion, consider Katie's wishes in determining who would be promoted by the commitment or guardianship
    C. The child's parents' wishes will be a strong consideration and the court will author a separate opinion on the matter
    D. The potential adoptive parents will be deposed so that a sworn, written statement can accompany Katie's permanent file with the court

Questions 15-16.

DIRECTIONS: Questions 15 and 16 are to be answered on the basis of the following passage.

The date of the child's entry into foster care is the earlier of __1__ days after the date on which the child was removed from the home or the date the child was found by a court to be an abused or neglected child pursuant to Article 10 of the __2__ Act.

15. Fill in the number of days for Blank #1.
    A. 20   B. 30   C. 60   D. 80

16. Fill in the name of the act for Blank #2.
    A. Family Court
    B. Child Welfare
    C. Emancipated Child
    D. Surrogates

17. Carol and Tom want to sign the surrender to terminate their parental rights of their child, but cannot afford an attorney.
    May they request the court to appoint a lawyer on their behalf free of charge?
    A. No, because Carol and Tom must pay for their own attorney
    B. No, because Carol and Tom are initiating the proceeding
    C. No, because Carol and Tom do not need an attorney to execute a surrender
    D. Yes

18. What rights does a parent forfeit in a surrender, unless different terms are specifically agreed to?
    A. The right to visit the child
    B. The right to write to or otherwise learn about the child
    C. The right to speak to the child
    D. All of the above

19. Where will the surrender be recorded?
    In the office of the county clerk where the
    A. surrender is executed
    B. child was born
    C. biological parents reside
    D. adoptive parents reside

20. Can the executed surrender which places a child in the custody of an authorized agency also be used to commit the same child to the custody of the child's maternal grandparents?
    A. Yes, because they are in the same bloodline
    B. Yes, because a surrender operates to place the child anywhere the child is safe
    C. No, because the surrender is deemed to only apply to the commitment to the authorized agency; any other document is not deemed a surrender
    D. No, because the surrender cannot be re-executed or re-signed after the authorized agency signs the document

21. May the court disapprove a surrender?
    A. No, once executed the court cannot nullify the document
    B. No, because the court does not have the authority to disapprove a surrender
    C. Yes, and if the court does so the surrender is deemed resigned
    D. Yes, and if the court does so the surrender is deemed nullified

22. The _____ is a state level legal option for unmarried males to document through a notary public any female they engage in intercourse, for the purpose of retaining parental rights for any child they may father.
    A. pool of potential fathers
    B. putative father registry
    C. unmarried father registry
    D. putative biological dad registry

5 (#1)

23. What is the purpose of a permanency hearing? 23._____
    A. To determine in which county a child should reside
    B. To determine the best interests of the child and develop a permanent plan for the placement of the child
    C. To develop a plan to determine the best interests of the child in three-year increments
    D. To schedule parties to testify on behalf of the child

24. When must the first permanency hearing be scheduled relative to when the place in the custody of the authorized agency, and thereafter how often must they continue thereafter? 24._____
    _____ months after the child is placed and every _____ thereafter.
    A. 8; 6 months   B. 6; month   C. 9; 5 months   D. 10; 2 months

25. Which of the following are possible options for disposition of the child after the fact-finding hearing? 25._____
    A. Releasing the child to the parents or guardian with supervision from the child protective agency
    B. Placing the child in foster care for a period of time
    C. Suspended judgment
    D. All of the above

KEY (CORRECT ANSWERS)

1.	A		11.	B
2.	D		12.	A
3.	D		13.	D
4.	B		14.	B
5.	A		15.	C
6.	C		16.	A
7.	B		17.	D
8.	A		18.	D
9.	B		19.	A
10.	A		20.	C

21. D
22. B
23. B
24. A
25. D

EXAMINATION SECTION
TEST 1

DIRECTIONS: Each question or incomplete statement is followed by several suggested answers or completions. Select the one that BEST answers the question or completes the statement. *PRINT THE LETTER OF THE CORRECT ANSWER IN THE SPACE AT THE RIGHT.*

1. Gary owns an apartment in downtown Brooklyn. Gary resides in Watkins Glen and rents the apartment in Brooklyn. His tenant moved out of the Brooklyn apartment about two weeks ago. Since then, he has received e-mails from friends in Brooklyn that a transient individual, Sean, has been sleeping in the apartment by breaking in the back window.
   Does a landlord-tenant relationship exist between Gary and Sean?
   A. Yes, because Gary owns the apartment
   B. Yes, because Sean is the rightful tenant of the apartment
   C. No, because Sean has not been in possession of the apartment for thirty consecutive days
   D. No, because Sean has not informed Gary that he wants to be Gary's tenant

2. If a landlord/tenant relationship exists and the grounds are met for a special proceeding to take place, the landlord must give the tenant _____ day notice of the special proceeding.
   A. ten B. fifteen C. twenty D. twenty-five

3. A real property proceedings may be brought by which of the following party(ies)?
   A. A landlord
   B. A person forcibly put or kept out
   C. The lessee of the premises, entitled to possession
   D. All of the above

4. A special proceeding to recover real property can be initiated in which of the following venues?
   A. County court
   B. District court
   C. Justice court
   D. Each of the above, and a court of civil jurisdiction in a city

5. How does James start a special proceeding to recover real property from his tenant, Marisol?
   A. James should file a complaint in civil court.
   B. James should file a notice of petition and petition to commence the action.
   C. James must arrange for the service of a subpoena upon Marisol.
   D. James should attempt to evict Marisol himself once Marisol stops paying rent.

Questions 6-8.

DIRECTIONS: Questions 6 through 8 are to be answered on the basis of the following fact pattern.

Jeremy wants to buy property in an up-and-coming neighborhood of Suffolk County. He enlists his friend and former co-worker, Danielle, to help him find a suitable house at a bargain. Danielle is a native of the area in which Jeremy wants to buy. Jeremy buys a home and asks Danielle to act as the landlord.

6. Danielle advertised the house for rent online. She subsequently rented the home to a man who used the house as the center of an illegal gambling ring. Danielle knows that the home is being used for that purpose, but does not inform Jeremy.
What is Danielle obligated to do given her knowledge of the activities happening at the house?
   A. Danielle has a duty to vacate the premises.
   B. Danielle, as the landlord, must make an application of removal of the tenant.
   C. Danielle is obligated to evict the tenants using brute force.
   D. Danielle is obligated to inform the local court of the activities taking place at the home.

7. Is Jeremy responsible for knowing how the rented property is being used?
   A. No, because Jeremy is not the landlord
   B. No, because Jeremy does not live near the property and has no way of knowing that the property is being used for illegal purposes
   C. Yes, because Jeremy can visit or drive by the property and clearly see it is used for illegal gambling purposes
   D. Yes, because Jeremy is the owner of the property

8. If Danielle does not bring an action to remove the tenants from the property, who is eligible to do so as if he/she is the owner of the property?
   A. Local law enforcement agency   B. Danielle's neighbors
   C. Jeremy's neighbors   D. The State of New York

9. After a final judgment for the landlord, the court shall issue a(n) _____ direct to the sheriff of the county or marshal of the city in which the property is situated, describing the property and commanding the officer to remove all persons.
   A. indictment   B. subpoena   C. warrant   D. summons

10. Court marshals appear at Bethany's apartment to execute the warrant for her eviction.
How much notice must the marshals provide Bethany?
_____ hours, excluding weekends and holidays.
   A. 24   B. 36   C. 72   D. 86

11. What effect does the warrant for an eviction have on the relationship between the landlord and tenant according to the New York Real Property Actions and Proceedings Law?
    The warrant _____ the landlord-tenant relationship.
    A. solidifies   B. redeems   C. rescinds   D. cancels

12. Jason was served with a notice of petition for removal from his landlord, Eric. Jason has never been late on his rent, but has not paid Eric since his lease expired two months ago.
    May Jason respond to Eric's petition and, if so, how?
    A. No, Jason must vacate the premises immediately.
    B. Jason can respond, but only after he has vacated the premises.
    C. Jason can respond directly to Eric and record the conversation so that it can be preserved and presented to the court at a later date.
    D. Yes, Jason can prepare and file an answer to Eric's petition.

13. Assume the same facts as in Question 12. After Eric filed a notice of petition, the court decided it needs more information before moving on in the proceedings. In lieu of a notice of petition, the court may require which of the following?
    A. Order to show cause
    B. Specific description of the noise complaints or other grounds for eviction
    C. Payment receipts
    D. Formal complaint and deposition testimony

Questions 14-17.

DIRECTIONS: Questions 14 through 17 are to be answered on the basis of the following facts.

Dawn did not keep a copy of the lease her tenant, Mike, signed. Mike does not have a copy of the lease either. Mike maintains that the lease term has not expired, while Dawn says the lease ended a month ago.

14. At trial, the lease term is considered a
    A. fact in dispute
    B. triable issue of fact
    C. respondent's contention
    D. contentious fact

15. The apartment that Mike rents in Manhattan is in a building with eight other rental units. The court that hears the dispute between Dawn and Mike must first and foremost have
    A. contacts with Mike and Dawn
    B. jurisdiction
    C. res ipsa
    D. pro se litigant allowance

16. During the summary proceeding, the court's preliminary asks if there is any undisputed amount of rent owed. Assuming that Mike agrees that he is already behind one month of rent and Dawn agrees, who will the court direct Mike to deliver that rent payment to?
    A. The court for safekeeping
    B. An escrow account established by Mike, but put in Dawn's name
    C. An escrow account which names the County Clerk as the legal owner
    D. Directly to Dawn

17. The amount in dispute between Mike and Dawn is $5,000. Mike wants to countersue Dawn for $3,000; however, Mike refuses to deposit the disputed amount of money to the court. Mike has not paid any portion of the $5,000. Upon application, what actions can Dawn ask the court to take?
    A. Dismiss without prejudice Mike's counterclaims and defenses and grant judgment for Dawn
    B. Imprison Mike for non-payment of rent
    C. Garnish Mike's paychecks for the back payment of rent, and other arrears
    D. Restrict Mike's counterclaims as to only those relating to monetary damages

18. The term "constructive eviction" is defined as a(n)
    A. circumstance where the landlord does something or provides or, in the adverse, does not do something or fails to provide, that renders the property uninhabitable
    B. circumstance where the tenant deems the property uninhabitable and informs the landlord of the condition
    C. eviction notice that was served upon a tenant with a material defect
    D. illegitimate eviction, such as evicting the wrong occupant or eviction executed prior to proper service upon the tenant

19. If a stipulation is made between the parties in a special proceeding, other than a stipulation solely to adjourn or stay the proceeding, and either the petitioner or the respondent is not represented by counsel, the court shall
    A. fully describe the terms of the stipulation to that party
    B. accept the stipulation and record the stipulation in a deposition hearing
    C. reject the stipulation unless expressly consented to by both parties in writing
    D. continue with the hearing

20. An "undertenant" is also considered a(n)
    A. subtenant   B. overtenant   C. lessor   D. assignor

21. Upon proper proof of the existence of a condition that constructively evict the tenant from a portion of the premises that is likely to become dangerous to life, health or safety, the court before which the case is pending may _____ proceedings to dispossess the tenant for non-payment of rent.
    A. adjourn   B. joinder   C. stay   D. rectify

22. If service is mailed to the respondent for the notice of petition, service is deemed complete after which of the following events?
    A. Filing of the notice
    B. Filing the proof of service
    C. Commencement of the action
    D. Start of trial

Questions 23-25.

DIRECTIONS: Questions 23 through 25 are to be answered on the basis of the following passage.

In a proceeding to recover the possession of premises in the City of New York occupied for dwelling purposes upon the ground that the occupant is holding over and continuing in possession of the premises after the expiration of his term and without permission of the landlord may stay the issuance of a warrant and also stay an execution to collect the costs of proceeding for a period of not more than __1__ months, if it appears that the premises are used __2__ purposes; that the application is made in good faith; that the applicant cannot within the neighborhood secure suitable premises similar to those occupied by him and that he made __3__ efforts to secure such other premises, or that by reason of other facts it would occasion extreme hardship to him or his family if the stay were not granted.

23. Please fill in the number of months for Blank #1.
    A. one   B. two   C. six   D. eight

24. Please fill in the correct word for Blank #2.
    A. illegal   B. dwelling   C. illicit   D. residential

25. Please fill in the correct phrase for Blank #3.
    A. due and reasonable
    B. fair and reasonable
    C. reasonable and due
    D. reasonable and fair

KEY (CORRECT ANSWERS)

1.	C		11.	D
2.	A		12.	D
3.	D		13.	A
4.	D		14.	B
5.	B		15.	B
6.	B		16.	D
7.	D		17.	A
8.	A		18.	A
9.	C		19.	A
10.	C		20.	A

21. C
22. B
23. C
24. B
25. A

EXAMINATION SECTION
TEST 1

DIRECTIONS: Each question or incomplete statement is followed by several suggested answers or completions. Select the one that BEST answers the question or completes the statement. *PRINT THE LETTER OF THE CORRECT ANSWER IN THE SPACE AT THE RIGHT.*

Questions 1-4.

DIRECTIONS: Questions 1 through 4 are to be answered on the basis of the following passage.

Those engaged in the exercise of First Amendment rights by pickets, marches, parades, and open-air assemblies are not exempted from obeying valid local traffic ordinances. In a recent pronouncement, Mr. Justice Baxter, speaking for the Supreme Court, wrote:

The rights of free speech and assembly, while fundamental to our democratic society, still do not mean that everyone with opinions or beliefs to express may address a group at any public place and at any time. The constitutional guarantee of liberty implies the existence of an organized society maintaining public order, without which liberty itself would be lost in the excesses of anarchy. The control of travel on the streets is a clear example of governmental responsibility to insure this necessary order. A restriction in that relation, designed to promote the public convenience in the interest of all, and not susceptible to abuses of discriminatory application, cannot be disregarded by the attempted exercise of some civil rights which, in other circumstances, would be entitled to protection. One would not be justified in ignoring the familiar red light because this was thought to be a means of social protest. Governmental authorities have the duty and responsibility to keep their streets open and available for movement. A group of demonstrators could not insist upon the right to cordon off a street, or entrance to a public or private building, and allow no one to pass who did not agree to listen to their exhortations.

1. Which of the following statements BEST reflects Mr. Justice Baxter's view of the relationship between liberty and public order?

    A. Public order cannot exist without liberty.
    B. Liberty cannot exist without public order.
    C. The existence of liberty undermines the existence of public order.
    D. The maintenance of public order insures the existence of liberty.

2. According to the above passage, local traffic ordinances result from

    A. governmental limitations on individual liberty
    B. governmental responsibility to insure public order
    C. majority rule as determined by democratic procedures
    D. restrictions on expression of dissent

3. The foregoing passage suggests that government would be acting IMPROPERLY if a local traffic ordinance

    A. was enforced in a discriminatory manner
    B. resulted in public inconvenience

1._____

2._____

3._____

C. violated the right of free speech and assembly
D. was not essential to public order

4. Of the following, the MOST appropriate title for the above passage is:

   A. THE RIGHTS OF FREE SPEECH AND ASSEMBLY
   B. ENFORCEMENT OF LOCAL TRAFFIC ORDINANCES
   C. FIRST AMENDMENT RIGHTS AND LOCAL TRAFFIC ORDINANCES
   D. LIBERTY AND ANARCHY

Questions 5-8.

DIRECTIONS: Questions 5 through 8 are to be answered on the basis of the following passage.

On November 8, 1976, the Supreme Court refused to block the payment of Medicaid funds for elective abortions. The Court's action means that a new Federal statute that bars the use of Federal funds for abortions unless abortion is necessary to save the life of the mother will not go into effect for many months, if at all.

A Federal District Court in Brooklyn ruled the following month that the statute was unconstitutional and ordered that Federal reimbursement for the costs of abortions continue on the same basis as reimbursements for the costs of pregnancy and childbirth-related services.

Technically, what the Court did today was to deny a request by Senator Howard Ramsdell and others for a stay blocking enforcement of the District Court order pending appeal. The Court's action was a victory for New York City. The City's Health and Hospitals Corporation initiated one of the two lawsuits challenging the new statute that led to the District Court's decision. The Corporation also opposed the request for a Supreme Court stay of that decision, telling the Court in a memorandum that a stay would subject the Corporation to a grave and irreparable injury."

5. According to the above passage, it would be CORRECT to state that the Health and Hospitals Corporation

   A. joined Senator Ramsdell in his request for a stay
   B. opposed the statute which limited reimbursement for the cost of abortions
   C. claimed that it would experience a loss if the District Court order was enforced
   D. appealed the District Court decision

6. The above passage indicates that the Supreme Court acted in DIRECT response to

   A. a lawsuit initiated by the Health and Hospitals Corporation
   B. a ruling by a Federal District Court
   C. a request for a stay
   D. the passage of a new Federal statute

7. According to the above passage, it would be CORRECT to state that the Supreme Court

   A. blocked enforcement of the District Court order
   B. refused a request for a stay to block enforcement of the Federal statute
   C. ruled that the new Federal statute was unconstitutional
   D. permitted payment of Federal funds for abortion to continue

8. Following are three statements concerning abortion that might be correct:
   I. Abortion costs are no longer to be Federally reimbursed on the same basis as those for pregnancy and childbirth
   II. Federal funds have not been available for abortions except to save the life of the mother
   III. Medicaid has paid for elective abortions in the past

   According to the passage given above, which of the following CORRECTLY classifies the above statements into those that are true and those that are not true?

   A. I is true, but II and III are not.
   B. I and III are true, but II is not.
   C. I and II are true, but III is not.
   D. III is true, but I and II are not.

9. A legal memorandum will often include the following six sections:
   I. Conclusions
   II. Issues
   III. Analysis
   IV. Facts
   V. Unknowns
   VI. Counter-analysis

   Which of the following choices lists these sections in the sequence that is generally MOST appropriate for a legal memorandum?

   A. III, VI, IV, V, II, I
   B. IV, II, III, VI, I, V
   C. V, II, IV, III, VI, I
   D. II, IV, V, III, I, VI

Questions 10-13.

DIRECTIONS: Questions 10 through 13 consist of two sentences each. The sentences deal with the use of court opinions and cases in the writing of legal memoranda. Select answer
A. if only sentence I is correct
B. if only sentence II is correct
C. if both sentences are correct
D. if neither sentence is correct

10. I. State the issues in the case as narrowly and precisely as possible.
    II. Quote frequently and at great length from the court opinions.

11. I. Describe briefly the issues in the case that are not related to your problem.
    II. Do not mention discrepancies between the facts of the case and the facts of your problem.

12. I. Do not refer to the holding or ruling in the case if it is harmful to your client.
    II. If the holding or ruling in the case is beneficial to your client, try to show that the facts of your problem are analogous to the facts of the case.

13. I. After stating your position concerning the issues and facts, present the opposite viewpoint as effectively as you can.
    II. Avoid stating your own opinions or conclusions concerning the applicability of the case.

13._____

14. Column V lists four publications in the legal field. Column W contains descriptions of basic subject matter of legal publications.
Select the one of the following choices which BEST matches the publications in Column V with the subject matter in Column W.

14._____

Column V	Column W
I. Harvard Law Review	1. Law
II. Supreme Court Reporter	2. Commentary on law
III. McKinney's Consolidated Laws of New York	3. Combination of law and commentary
IV. The Criminal Law Reporter	

A. I-3; II-1; III-2; IV-3
B. I-2; II-3; III-2; IV-3
C. I-2; II-1; III-3; IV-3
D. I-2; II-3; III-3; IV-1

15. Tickler systems are used in many legal offices for scheduling and calendar control. Of the following, the LEAST common use of a tickler system is to

15._____

A. keep papers filed in such a way that they may easily be retrieved
B. arrange for the appearance of witnesses when they will be needed
C. remind lawyers when certain papers are due
D. arrange for the gathering of certain types of evidence

KEY (CORRECT ANSWERS)

1. B
2. B
3. A
4. C
5. B

6. C
7. D
8. D
9. B
10. A

11. D
12. B
13. A
14. C
15. A

TEST 2

DIRECTIONS: Each question or incomplete statement is followed by several suggested answers or completions. Select the one that BEST answers the question or completes the statement. *PRINT THE LETTER OF THE CORRECT ANSWER IN THE SPACE AT THE RIGHT.*

1. Studying the legislative history of a statute by reading the transcript of the hearings that were held on that subject is useful to the legal researcher PRIMARILY because it

   A. is informative of the manner in which laws are enacted
   B. helps him to understand the intent of the statute
   C. provides leads to statutes on the same subject
   D. clarifies the meaning of other statutes

2. Following are three statements concerning legal research that might be correct:
   I. The researcher may begin with a particular premise and, in researching it, may discover an entirely new approach to the problem
   II. When the researcher has located a relevant statute, it is not necessary to read court opinions interpreting or applying this statute
   III. A statute which is related to, but not the same as, the point being researched may have notes which will refer the researcher to more relevant cases

   Which of the following ACCURATELY classifies the above statements into those which are correct and those which are not?

   A. II and III are correct, but I is not.
   B. I and III are correct, but II is not.
   C. I and II are correct, but III is not.
   D. I, II, and III are all correct.

3. Of the following, the FIRST action a legal researcher should take in order to locate the laws relevant to a case is to

   A. search the index of a law book
   B. read statutes on similar subjects to discover pertinent annotations
   C. read a legal digest to become familiar with the law on the subject
   D. prepare a list of descriptive words applicable to the facts of the case

4. Which of the following is the BEST source for a legal researcher to consult in order to find historical data, cross-references, and case excerpts on cases, statutes, and regulations?

   A. Annotations   B. Digests
   C. Hornbooks   D. Casebooks

Questions 5-8.

DIRECTIONS: Each of Questions 5 through 8 contains two sentences concerning criminal law. Some of the sentences contain errors in English grammar or usage. A sentence does not contain an error simply because it could be written in a different manner. For each question, choose answer
   A. if only sentence I is correct
   B. if only sentence II is correct
   C. if both sentences are correct
   D. if neither sentence is correct

5. I. Limiting the term *property* to tangible property, in the criminal mischief setting, accords with prior case law holding that only tangible property came within the purview of the offense of malicious mischief.
   II. Thus, a person who intentionally destroys the property of another, but under an honest belief that he has title to such property, cannot be convicted of criminal mischief under the Revised Penal Law.

6. I. Very early in it's history, New York enacted statutes from time to time punishing, either as a felony or as a misdemeanor, malicious injuries to various kinds of property: piers, booms, dams, bridges, etc.
   II. The application of the statute is necessarily restricted to trespassory takings with larcenous intent: namely with intent permanently or virtually permanently to *appropriate* property or *deprive* the owner of its use.

7. I. Since the former Penal Law did not define the instruments of forgery in a general fashion, its crime of forgery was held to be narrower than the common law offense in this respect and to embrace only those instruments explicitly specified in the substantive provisions.
   II. After entering the barn through an open door for the purpose of stealing, it was closed by the defendants.

8. I. The use of fire or explosives to destroy tangible property is proscribed by the criminal mischief provisions of the Revised Penal Law.
   II. The defendant's taking of a taxicab for the immediate purpose of affecting his escape did not constitute grand larceny

Questions 9-13.

DIRECTIONS: Questions 9 through 13 are to be answered SOLELY on the basis of the following passage.

The law is quite clear that evidence obtained in violation of Section 605 of the Federal Communications Act is not admissible in federal court. However, the law as to the admissibility of evidence in state court is far from clear. Had the Supreme Court of the United States made the wiretap exclusionary rule applicable to the states, such confusion would not exist.

In the case of Alton v. Texas, the Supreme Court was called upon to determine whether wiretapping by state and local officers came within the proscription of the federal statute and, if so, whether Section 605 required the same remedies for its vindication in state courts. In answer to the first question, Mr. Justice Minton, speaking for the court, flatly stated that Section 605 made it a federal crime for anyone to intercept telephone messages and divulge what he learned. The court went on to say that a state officer who testified in state court concerning the existence, contents, substance, purport, effect or meaning of an intercepted conversation violated the federal law and committed a criminal act. In regard to the second question, however, the Supreme Court felt constrained by due regard for federal-state relations to answer in the negative. Mr. Justice Minton stated that the court would not presume, in the absence of a clear manifestation of congressional intent, that Congress intended to supersede state rules of evidence.

Because the Supreme Court refused to apply the exclusionary rule to wiretap evidence that was being used in state courts, the states respectively made this decision for themselves. According to hearings held before a congressional committee in 1975, six states authorize wiretapping by statute, 33 states impose total bans on wiretapping, and 11 states have no definite statute on the subject. For examples of extremes, a statute in Pennsylvania will be compared with a statute in New York.

The Pennsylvania statute provides that no communications by telephone or telegraph can be intercepted without permission of both parties. It also specifically prohibits such interception by public officials and provides that evidence obtained cannot be used in court.

The lawmakers in New York, recognizing the need for legal wiretapping, authorized wiretapping by statute. A New York law authorizes the issuance of an ex parte order upon oath or affirmation for limited wiretapping. The aim of the New York law is to allow court-ordered wiretapping and to encourage the testimony of state officers concerning such wiretapping in court. The New York law was found to be constitutional by the New York State Supreme Court in 1975. Other states, including Oregon, Maryland, Nevada, and Massachusetts, enacted similar laws which authorize court-ordered wiretapping.

To add to this legal disarray, the vast majority of the states, including New Jersey and New York, permit wiretapping evidence to be received in court even though obtained in violation of the state laws and of Section 605 of the Federal act. However, some states such as Rhode Island have enacted statutory exclusionary rules which provide that illegally procured wiretap evidence is incompetent in civil as well as criminal actions.

9. According to the above passage, a state officer who testifies in New York State court concerning the contents of a conversation he overheard through a court-ordered wiretap is in violation of _____ law.

   A. state law but not federal
   B. federal law but not state
   C. federal law and state
   D. neither federal nor state

10. According to the above passage, which of the following statements concerning states statutes on wiretapping is CORRECT?

    A. The number of states that impose total bans on wiretapping is three times as great as the number of states with no definite statute on wiretapping.
    B. The number of states having no definite statute on wiretapping is more than twice the number of states authorizing wiretapping.
    C. The number of states which authorize wiretapping by statute and the number of states having no definite statute on wiretapping exceed the number of states imposing total bans on wiretapping.
    D. More states authorize wiretapping by statute than impose total bans on wiretapping.

11. Following are three statements concerning wiretapping that might be valid:
    I. In Pennsylvania, only public officials may legally intercept telephone communications
    II. In Rhode Island, evidence obtained through an illegal wiretap is incompetent in criminal, but not civil, actions
    III. Neither Massachusetts nor Pennsylvania authorizes wiretapping by public officials

    According to the above passage, which of the following CORRECTLY classifies these statements into those that are valid and those that are not?

    A. I is valid, but II and III are not.
    B. II is valid, but I and III are not.
    C. II and III are valid, but I is not.
    D. None of the statements is valid.

12. According to the foregoing passage, evidence obtained in violation of Section 605 of the Federal Communications Act is inadmissible in

    A. federal court but not in any state courts
    B. federal court and all state courts
    C. all state courts but not in federal court
    D. federal court and some state courts

13. In regard to state rules of evidence, Mr. Justice Minton expressed the Court's opinion that Congress

    A. intended to supersede state rules of evidence, as manifested by Section 605 of the Federal Communications Act
    B. assumed that federal statutes would govern state rules of evidence in all wiretap cases
    C. left unclear whether it intended to supersede state rules of evidence
    D. precluded itself from superseding state rules of evidence through its regard for federal-state relations

14. You begin to ask follow-up questions of a witness who has given a statement. The witness starts to digress before answering an important question satisfactorily.
    In this situation, the BEST of the following steps is to

    A. guide the interview by suggesting answers to questions as they are asked
    B. ask questions which can be answered only with a simple *yes* or *no*
    C. construct questions as precisely as possible
    D. tell the witness to keep his answers brief

15. During an interview with a client, you have occasion to refer to a matter which is described in the legal profession by a technical term.
    Of the following, it would generally be MOST appropriate for you to

    A. discuss the underlying legal concept in detail
    B. avoid the subject since it is too complicated
    C. ask the client if he is familiar with the technical term
    D. describe the matter in everyday language

KEY (CORRECT ANSWERS)

1. B
2. B
3. D
4. A
5. C

6. B
7. A
8. A
9. B
10. A

11. D
12. D
13. C
14. C
15. D

EXAMINATION SECTION
TEST 1

DIRECTIONS: Each question or incomplete statement is followed by several suggested answers or completions. Select the one that BEST answers the question or completes the statement. *PRINT THE LETTER OF THE CORRECT ANSWER IN THE SPACE AT THE RIGHT.*

Questions 1-50.

DIRECTIONS: Each of Questions 1 through 50 consists of a word in capital letters followed by four suggested meanings of the word. For each question, choose the word or phrase which means MOST NEARLY the same as the word in capital letters.

1. ABUT
   A. abandon   B. assist   C. border on   D. renounce

2. ABSCOND
   A. draw in   B. give up
   C. refrain from   D. deal off

3. BEQUEATH
   A. deaden   B. hand down   C. make sad   D. scold

4. BOGUS
   A. sad   B. false   C. shocking   D. stolen

5. CALAMITY
   A. disaster   B. female   C. insanity   D. patriot

6. COMPULSORY
   A. binding   B. ordinary   C. protected   D. ruling

7. CONSIGN
   A. agree with   B. benefit
   C. commit   D. drive down

8. DEBILITY
   A. failure   B. legality
   C. quality   D. weakness

9. DEFRAUD
   A. cheat   B. deny
   C. reveal   D. tie

10. DEPOSITION
   A. absence   B. publication
   C. removal   D. testimony

11. DOMICILE
   A. anger   B. dwelling
   C. tame   D. willing

1.____
2.____
3.____
4.____
5.____
6.____
7.____
8.____
9.____
10.____
11.____

12. HEARSAY
    A. selfish   B. serious   C. rumor   D. unlikely
13. HOMOGENEOUS
    A. human   B. racial   C. similar   D. unwise
14. ILLICIT
    A. understood   B. uneven   C. unkind   D. unlawful
15. LEDGER
    A. book of accounts   B. editor
    C. periodical   D. shelf
16. NARRATIVE
    A. gossip   B. natural   C. negative   D. story
17. PLAUSIBLE
    A. reasonable   B. respectful   C. responsible   D. rightful
18. RECIPIENT
    A. absentee   B. receiver   C. speaker   D. substitute
19. SUBSTANTIATE
    A. appear for   B. arrange
    C. confirm   D. combine
20. SURMISE
    A. aim   B. break   C. guess   D. order
21. ALTER EGO
    A. business partner   B. confidential friend
    C. guide   D. subconscious conflict
22. FOURTH ESTATE
    A. the aristocracy   B. the clergy
    C. the judiciary   D. the newspapers
23. IMPEACH
    A. accuse   B. find guilty
    C. remove   D. try
24. PROPENSITY
    A. dislike   B. helpfulness
    C. inclination   D. supervision
25. SPLENETIC
    A. charming   B. peevish   C. shining   D. sluggish
26. SUBORN
    A. bribe someone to commit perjury
    B. demote someone several levels in rank
    C. deride
    D. substitute

27. TALISMAN
    A. charm
    B. juror
    C. prayer shawl
    D. native

28. VITREOUS
    A. corroding
    B. glassy
    C. nourishing
    D. sticky

29. WRY
    A. comic
    B. grained
    C. resilient
    D. twisted

30. SIGNATORY
    A. lawyer who draws up a legal document
    B. document that must be signed by a judge
    C. person who signs a document
    D. true copy of a signature

31. RETAINER
    A. fee paid to a lawyer for his services
    B. document held by a third party
    C. court decision to send a prisoner back to custody pending trial
    D. legal requirement to keep certain types of files

32. BEQUEATH
    A. to receive assistance from a charitable organization
    B. to give personal property by will to another
    C. to transfer real property from one person to another
    D. to receive an inheritance upon the death of a relative

33. RATIFY
    A. approve and sanction
    B. forego
    C. produce evidence
    D. summarize

34. CODICIL
    A. document introduced in evidence in a civil action
    B. subsection of a law
    C. type of legal action that can be brought by a plaintiff
    D. supplement or an addition to a will

35. ALIAS
    A. assumed name
    B. in favor of
    C. against
    D. a writ

36. PROXY
    A. a phony document in a real estate transaction
    B. an opinion by a judge of a civil court
    C. a document containing appointment of an agent
    D. a summons in a lawsuit

37. ALLEGED
    A. innocent
    B. asserted
    C. guilty
    D. called upon

38. EXECUTE
    A. to complete a legal document by signing it
    B. to set requirements
    C. to render services to a duly elected executive of a municipality
    D. to initiate legal action such as a lawsuit

39. NOTARY PUBLIC
    A. lawyer who is running for public office
    B. judge who hears minor cases
    C. public officer, one of whose functions is to administer oaths
    D. lawyer who gives free legal services to persons unable to pay

40. WAIVE
    A. to disturb a calm state of affairs
    B. to knowingly renounce a right or claim
    C. to pardon someone for a minor fault
    D. to purposely mislead a person during an investigation

41. ARRAIGN
    A. to prevent an escape
    B. to defend a prisoner
    C. to verify a document
    D. to accuse in a court of law

42. VOLUNTARY
    A. by free choice   B. necessary
    C. important   D. by design

43. INJUNCTION
    A. act of prohibiting   B. process of inserting
    C. means of arbitrating   D. freedom of action

44. AMICABLE
    A. compelled   B. friendly
    C. unimportant   D. insignificant

45. CLOSED SHOP
    A. one that employs only members of a union
    B. one that employs union members and unaffiliated employees
    C. one that employs only employees with previous experience
    D. one that employs skilled and unskilled workers

46. ABDUCT
    A. lead   B. kidnap   C. sudden   D. worthless

47. BIAS
    A. ability   B. envy   C. prejudice   D. privilege

48. COERCE
    A. cancel   B. force   C. rescind   D. rugged

49. CONDONE
  A. combine   B. pardon   C. revive   D. spice

50. CONSISTENCY
  A. bravery
  C. strain
  B. readiness
  D. uniformity

KEY (CORRECT ANSWERS)

1. C	11. B	21. B	31. A	41. D
2. D	12. C	22. D	32. B	42. A
3. B	13. C	23. A	33. A	43. A
4. B	14. D	24. C	34. D	44. B
5. A	15. A	25. B	35. A	45. A
6. A	16. D	26. A	36. C	46. B
7. C	17. A	27. A	37. B	47. C
8. D	18. B	28. B	38. A	48. B
9. A	19. C	29. D	39. C	49. B
10. D	20. C	30. C	40. B	50. D

TEST 2

DIRECTIONS: Each question or incomplete statement is followed by several suggested answers or completions. Select the one that BEST answers the question or completes the statement. *PRINT THE LETTER OF THE CORRECT ANSWER IN THE SPACE AT THE RIGHT.*

1. In the sentence, *The prisoner was fractious when brought to the station house*, the word *fractious* means MOST NEARLY 1.___
    A. penitent
    B. talkative
    C. irascible
    D. broken-hearted

2. In the sentence, *The judge was implacable when the attorney pleaded for leniency*, the word *implacable* means MOST NEARLY 2.___
    A. inexorable
    B. disinterested
    C. inattentive
    D. indifferent

3. In the sentence, *The court ordered the mendacious statements stricken from the record*, the word *mendacious* means MOST NEARLY 3.___
    A. begging
    B. lying
    C. threatening
    D. lengthy

4. In the sentence, *The district attorney spoke in a strident voice*, the word *strident* means MOST NEARLY 4.___
    A. loud
    B. harsh-sounding
    C. sing-song
    D. low

5. In the sentence, *The speaker had a predilection for long sentences*, the word *predilection* means MOST NEARLY 5.___
    A. aversion
    B. talent
    C. propensity
    D. diffidence

6. A person who has an uncontrollable desire to steal without need is called a 6.___
    A. dipsomaniac
    B. kleptomaniac
    C. monomaniac
    D. pyromaniac

7. In the sentence, *Malice was immanent in all his remarks*, the word *immanent* means MOST NEARLY 7.___
    A. elevated
    B. inherent
    C. threatening
    D. foreign

8. In the sentence, *The extant copies of the document were found in the safe*, the word *extant* means MOST NEARLY 8.___
    A. existing
    B. original
    C. forged
    D. duplicate

9. In the sentence, *The recruit was more complaisant after the captain spoke to him*, the word *complaisant* means MOST NEARLY 9.___
    A. calm
    B. affable
    C. irritable
    D. confident

10. In the sentence, *The man was captured under highly creditable circumstances*, the word *creditable* means MOST NEARLY

    A. doubtful
    B. believable
    C. praiseworthy
    D. unexpected

11. In the sentence, *His superior officers were more sagacious than he*, the word *sagacious* means MOST NEARLY

    A. shrewd
    B. obtuse
    C. absurd
    D. verbose

12. In the sentence, *He spoke with impunity*, the word *impunity* means MOST NEARLY

    A. rashness
    B. caution
    C. without fear
    D. immunity

13. In the sentence, *The new officer displayed unusual temerity during the emergency*, the word *temerity* means MOST NEARLY

    A. fear
    B. rashness
    C. calmness
    D. anxiety

14. In the sentence, *The portions of food were parsimoniously served*, the word *parsimoniously* means MOST NEARLY

    A. stingily
    B. piously
    C. elaborately
    D. generously

15. In the sentence, *Generally the speaker's remarks were sententious*, the word *sententious* means MOST NEARLY

    A. verbose
    B. witty
    C. argumentative
    D. pithy

Questions 16-20.

DIRECTIONS: Next to the number which corresponds with the number of each item in Column I, place the letter preceding the adjective in Column II which BEST describes the persons in Column I.

COLUMN I		COLUMN II
16. Talkative woman	A.	abstemious
17. Person on a reducing diet	B.	pompous
18. Scholarly professor	C.	erudite
19. Man who seldom speaks	D.	benevolent
20. Charitable person	E.	docile
	F.	loquacious
	G.	indefatigable
	H.	taciturn

Questions 21-25.

DIRECTIONS: Next to the number which corresponds with the number preceding each profession in Column I, place the letter preceding the word in Column II which BEST explains the subject matter of that profession.

COLUMN I	COLUMN II
21. Geologist	A. animals
22. Oculist	B. eyes
23. Podiatrist	C. feet
24. Palmist	D. fortune-telling
25. Zoologist	E. language
	F. rocks
	G. stamps
	H. woman

21._
22._
23._
24._
25._

Questions 26-30.

DIRECTIONS: Next to the number corresponding to the number of each of the words in Column I, place the letter preceding the word in Column II that is MOST NEARLY OPPOSITE to it in meaning.

COLUMN I	COLUMN II
26. comely	A. beautiful
27. eminent	B. cowardly
28. frugal	C. kind
29. gullible	D. sedate
30. valiant	E. shrewd
	F. ugly
	G. unknown
	H. wasteful

26._
27._
28._
29._
30._

KEY (CORRECT ANSWERS)

1. C	11. A	21. F
2. A	12. D	22. B
3. B	13. B	23. C
4. B	14. A	24. D
5. C	15. D	25. A
6. B	16. F	26. F
7. B	17. A	27. G
8. A	18. C	28. H
9. B	19. H	29. E
10. C	20. D	30. B

SUPERVISION, ADMINISTRATION, MANAGEMENT AND ORGANIZATION
EXAMINATION SECTION
TEST 1

DIRECTIONS: Each question or incomplete statement is followed by several suggested answers or completions. Select the one that BEST answers the question or completes the statement. *PRINT THE LETTER OF THE CORRECT ANSWER IN THE SPACE AT THE RIGHT.*

1. The one of the following situations in which you as a supervisor of a group of clerks would probably be able to function MOST effectively from the viewpoint of departmental efficiency is where you are responsible DIRECTLY to
   A. a single supervisor having sole jurisdiction over you
   B. two or three supervisors having coordinate jurisdiction over you
   C. four or five supervisors having coordinate jurisdiction over you
   D. all individuals of higher rank than you in the department

2. Suppose that it is necessary to order one of the clerks under your supervision to stay overtime a few hours one evening. The work to be done is not especially difficult. It is the custom in your office to make such assignments by rotation. The particular clerk whose turn it is to work overtime requests to be excused that evening, but offers to work the next time that overtime is necessary. Hitherto, this clerk has always been very cooperative.
   Of the following, the BEST action for you to take is to
   A. grant the clerk's request, but require her to work overtime two additional nights to compensate for this concession
   B. inform the clerk that you are compelled to refuse any request for special consideration
   C. grant the clerk's request if another clerk is willing to substitute for her
   D. refuse the clerk's request outright because granting her request may encourage her to evade other responsibilities

3. When asked to comment upon the efficiency of Miss Jones, a clerk, her supervisor said, "Since she rarely makes an error, I consider her very efficient."
   Of the following, the MOST valid assumption underlying this supervisor's comment is that
   A. speed and accuracy should be considered separately in evaluating a clerk's efficiency
   B. the most accurate clerks are not necessarily the most efficient
   C. accuracy and competency are directly related
   D. accuracy is largely dependent upon the intelligence of a clerk

4. The one of the following which is the MOST accurate statement of one of the functions of a supervisor is to
   A. select scientifically the person best fitted for the specific job to be done
   B. train the clerks assigned to you in the best methods of doing the work of your office
   C. fit the job to be done to the clerks who are available
   D. assign a clerk only to those tasks for which she has the necessary experience

5. Assume that you, an experienced supervisor, are given a newly appointed clerk to assist you in performing a certain task. The new clerk presents a method of doing the task which is different from your method but which is obviously better and easy to adopt.
   Of the following you, the supervisor, should
   A. take the suggestion and try it out, even though it was offered by someone less experienced
   B. reject the idea, even though it appears an improvement, as it very likely would not work out
   C. send the new clerk away and get someone else to assist who will be more in accord with your ideas
   D. report him to the head of the office and ask that the new clerk be instructed to do things your way

6. As a supervisor, you should realize that the one of the following general abilities of a junior clerk which is probably LEAST susceptible to improvement by practice and training is
   A. intelligence
   B. speed of typing
   C. knowledge of office procedures
   D. accuracy of filing

7. As a supervisor, when training an employee, you should NOT
   A. correct errors as he makes them
   B. give him too much material to absorb at one time
   C. have him try the operation until he can do it perfectly
   D. treat any foolish question seriously

8. If a supervisor cannot check readily all the work in her unit, she should
   A. hold up the work until she can personally check it
   B. refuse to take additional work
   C. work overtime until she can personally finish it
   D. delegate part of the work to a qualified subordinate

9. The one of the following over which a unit supervisor has the LEAST control is
   A. the quality of the work done in his unit
   B. the nature of the work handled in his unit
   C. the morale of workers in his unit
   D. increasing efficiency of his unit

10. Suppose that you have received a note from an important official in your department commending the work of a unit of clerks under your supervision. Of the following, the BEST action for you to take is to
    A. withhold the note for possible use at a time when the morale of the unit appears to be declining
    B. show the note only to the better members of your staff as a reward for their good work
    C. show the note only to the poorer members of your staff as a stimulus for better work
    D. post the note conspicuously so that it can be seen by all members of your staff

10.____

11. If you find that one of your subordinates is becoming apathetic towards his work, you should
    A. prefer charges against him
    B. change the type of work
    C. request his transfer
    D. advise him to take a medical examination to check his health

11.____

12. Suppose that a new clerk has been assigned to the unit which you supervise. To give this clerk a brief picture of the functioning of your unit in the entire department would be
    A. *commendable*, because she will probably be able to perform her work with more understanding
    B. *undesirable*, because such action will probably serve only to confuse her
    C. *commendable*, because, if transferred, she would probably be able to work efficiently without additional training
    D. *undesirable*, because in-service training has been demonstrated to be less efficient than on-the-job training

12.____

13. Written instructions to a subordinate are of value because they
    A. can be kept up-to-date
    B. encourage initiative
    C. make a job seem easier
    D. are an aid in training

13.____

14. Suppose that you have assigned a task to a clerk under your supervision and have given appropriate instructions. After a reasonable period, you check her work and find that one specific aspect of her work is consistently incorrect. Of the following, the BEST action for you to take is to
    A. determine whether the clerk has correctly understood instructions concerning the aspect of the work not being done correctly
    B. assign the task to a more competent clerk
    C. wait for the clerk to commit a more flagrant error before taking up the matter with her
    D. indicate to the clerk that you are dissatisfied with her work and wait to see whether she is sufficiently intelligent to correct her own mistakes

14.____

15. If you wanted to check on the accuracy of the filing in your unit, you would
    A. check all the files thoroughly at regular intervals
    B. watch the clerks while they are filing
    C. glance through filed papers at random
    D. inspect thoroughly a small section of the files selected at random

16. In making job assignments to his subordinates, a supervisor should follow the principle that each individual generally is capable of
    A. performing one type of work well and less capable of performing other types well
    B. learning to perform a wide variety of different types of work
    C. performing best the type of work in which he has had least experience
    D. learning to perform any type of work in which he is given training

17. Of the following, the information that is generally considered MOST essential in a departmental organization survey chart is the
    A. detailed operations of the department
    B. lines of authority
    C. relations of the department to other departments
    D. names of the employees of the department

18. Suppose you are the supervisor in charge of a large unit in which all of the clerical staff perform similar tasks.
    In evaluating the relative accuracy of the clerks, the clerk who should be considered to be the LEAST accurate is the one
    A. whose errors result in the greatest financial loss
    B. whose errors cost the most to locate
    C. who makes the greatest percentage of errors in his work
    D. who makes the greatest number of errors in the unit

19. Aside from requirements imposed by authority, the frequency with which reports are submitted or the length of the interval which they cover should depend PRINCIPALLY on the
    A. availability of the data to be included in the reports
    B. amount of time required to prepare the reports
    C. extent of the variations in the data with the passage of time
    D. degree of comprehensiveness required in the reports

20. A serious error has been discovered by a critical superior in work carried on under your supervision.
    It is BEST to explain the situation and prevent its recurrence by
    A. claiming that you are not responsible because you do not check the work personally
    B. accepting the complaint and reporting the name of the employee responsible for the error
    C. assuring him that you hope it will not occur again
    D. assuring him that you will find out how it occurred, so that you can have the work checked with greater care in the future

21. A serious procedural problem develops in your office.
 In your solution of this problem, the very FIRST step to take is to
    A. select the personnel to help you
    B. analyze your problem
    C. devise the one best method of research
    D. develop an outline of your report

22. Your office staff consists of eight clerks, stenographers, and typists, cramped in a long narrow room. The room is very difficult to ventilate properly, and, as in so many other offices, the disagreement over the method of ventilation is marked. Two cliques are developing and the friction is carrying over into the work of the office.
 Of the following, the BEST way to proceed is to
    A. call your staff together, have the matter fully discussed giving each person an opportunity to be heard, and put the matter to a vote; then enforce the method of ventilation which has the most votes
    B. call your staff together and have the matter fully discussed. If a compromise arrangement is agreed upon, put it into effect. Otherwise, on the basis of all the facts at your disposal, make a decision as to how best to ventilate the room and enforce your decision
    C. speak to the employees individually, make a decision as to how to ventilate the room, and then enforce your decision
    D. study the layout of the office, make a decision as to how best to ventilate the room, and then enforce your decision

23. An organization consisting of six levels of authority, where eight persons are assigned to each supervisor on each level, would consist of APPROXIMATELY _____ persons.
    A. 50   B. 500   C. 5,000   D. 50,000

24. The one of the following which is considered by political scientists to be a GOOD principle of municipal government is
    A. concentration of authority and responsibility
    B. the long ballot
    C. low salaries and a narrow range in salaries
    D. short terms for elected city officials

25. Of the following, the statement concerning the organization of a department which is TRUE is:
    A. In general, no one employee should have active and constant supervision over more than ten persons.
    B. It is basically unwise to have a supervisor with only three subordinates.
    C. It is desirable that there be no personal contact between the rank and file employee and the supervisor once removed from him.
    D. There should be no more than four levels of authority between the top administrative office in a department and the rank and file employees.

26. Assuming that Dictaphones are not available, of the following, the situation in which it would be MOST desirable to establish a central stenographic unit is one in which the unit would serve
    A. ten correspondence clerks assigned to full-time positions answering correspondence of a large government department
    B. seven members of a government commission heading a large department
    C. seven heads of bureaus in a government department consisting of 250 employees
    D. fifty investigators in a large department

26._____

27. You are assigned to review the procedures in an office in order to recommend improvements to the commissioner directly. You go into an office performing seen routine operations in the processing of one type of office form.
    The question you should FIRST ask yourself in your study of any one of these operations is:
    A. Can it be simplified?
    B. Is it necessary?
    C. Is it performed in proper order or should its position in the procedure be changed?
    D. Is the equipment for doing it satisfactory?

27._____

28. You are assigned in charge of a clerical bureau performing a single operation. All five of your subordinates do exactly the same work. A fine spirit of cooperation has developed and the employees help each other and pool their completed work so that the work of any one employee is indistinguishable. Your office is very busy and all five clerks are doing a full day's work. However, reports come back to you from other offices that they are finding as much as 1% error in the work of your bureau. This is too high a percentage of error.
    Of the following, the BEST procedure for you to follow is to
    A. check all the work yourself
    B. have a sample of the work of each clerk checked by another clerk
    C. have all work done in your office checked by one of your clerks
    D. identify the work of each clerk in some way

28._____

29. You are put in charge of a small office. In order to cover the office during the lunch hour, you assign Employee A to remain in the office between the hours of 12 and 1 P.M. On your return to the office at 12:25 P.M., you note that no one is in the office and that the phone is ringing. You are forced to postpone your 12:30 P.M. luncheon appointment, and to remain in the office until 12:50 P.M. when Employee A returns to the office.
    The BEST of the following actions is:
    A. Ask Employee why he left the office
    B. Bring charges against Employee A for insubordination and neglect of duty
    C. Ignore the matter in your conversation with Employee A so as not to embarrass him
    D. Make a note to rate Employee A low on his service rating

29._____

30. You are assigned in charge of a large division. It had been the practice in that division for the employees to slip out for breakfast about 10:00 A.M. You had been successful in stopping this practice and for one week no one had gone out for breakfast. One day a stenographer comes over to you at 10:30 A.M. appearing to be ill. She states that she doesn't feel well and that she would like to go out for a cup of tea. She asks your permission to leave the office for a few minutes.
You should
    A. telephone and have a cup of tea delivered to her
    B. permit her to go out
    C. refuse her permission to go out inasmuch as this would be setting a bad example
    D. tell her she can leave for an early lunch hour

31. The following four remarks from a supervisor to a subordinate deal with different situations. One remark, however, implies a basically POOR supervisory practice.
Select this remark as your answer.
    A. "I've called the staff together primarily because I am displeased with the work which one of you is doing. John, don't you think you should be ashamed that you are spoiling the good work of the office?"
    B. "James, you have been with us for six months now. In general, I'm satisfied with your work. However, don't you think you could be more neat in your appearance? I also want you to try to be more accurate in your work."
    C. "Joe, when I assigned this job to you, I did it because it requires special care and I think you're one of our best men in this type of work, but here is a slip-up you've made that we should be especially careful to watch out for in the future."
    D. "Tim, first I'd like to tell you that, effective tomorrow, you are to be my assistant and will receive an increase in salary. Although I recommended you for this position because I felt that you are the best man for the job, there are some things about your work which could stand a bit of improvement. For instance, your manner with regard to visitors is not so polite as it could be."

32. Of the following, the BEST type of floor surface for an office is
    A. concrete   B. hardwood   C. linoleum   D. parquet

33. The GENERALLY accepted unit for the measurement of illumination at a desk or work bench is the
    A. ampere   B. foot-candle   C. volt   D. watt

34. The one of the following who is MOST closely allied with "scientific management" is
    A. Mosher   B. Probst   C. Taylor   D. White

35. Eliminating slack in work assignments is
    A. speed-up
    B. time study
    C. motion study
    D. efficient management

36. "Time studies" examine and measure
    A. past performance
    B. present performance
    C. long-run effect
    D. influence of change

37. The maximum number of subordinates who can be effectively supervised by one supervisor is BEST considered as
    A. determined by the law of "span of control"
    B. determined by the law of "span of attention"
    C. determined by the type of work supervised
    D. fixed at not more than six

38. In the theory and practice of public administration, the one of the following which is LEAST generally regarded as a staff function is
    A. budgeting
    B. firefighting
    C. purchasing
    D. research and information

39. Suppose you are part of an administrative structure in which the executive head has regularly reporting directly to him seventeen subordinates. To some of the subordinates there regularly report directly three employees, to others four employees, and to the remaining subordinates five employees.
    Called upon to make a suggestion concerning this organization, you would question FIRST the desirability of
    A. so large a variation among the number of employees regularly reporting directly to subordinates
    B. having so large a number of subordinates regularly reporting directly to the administrative head
    C. so small a variation among the number of employees regularly reporting directly to subordinates
    D. the hierarchical arrangement

40. Administration is the center but not necessarily the source of all ideas for procedural improvement.
    The MOST significant implication that this principle bears for the administrative officer is that
    A. before procedural improvements are introduced, they should be approved by a majority of the staff
    B. it is the unique function of the administrative officer to derive and introduce procedural improvements
    C. the administrative office should derive ideas and suggestions for procedural improvement from all possible sources, introducing any that promise to be effective
    D. the administrative officer should view employee grievances as the chief source of procedural improvements

41. The merit system should not end with the appointment of a candidate. In any worthy public service system there should be no dead-end jobs. If the best citizen is to be attracted to public service, there must be provided encouragement and incentive to enable such a career employee to progress in the service.
The one of the following which is the MOST accurate statement on the basis of the above statement is that
    A. merit system selection has replaced political appointment in many governmental units
    B. lack of opportunities for advancement in government employment will discourage the better qualified from applying
    C. employees who want to progress in the public service should avoid simple assignments
    D. most dead-end jobs have been eliminated from the public service

41._____

42. Frequently the importance of keeping office records is not appreciated until information which is badly needed cannot be found. Office records must be kept in convenient and legible form, and must be filed where they may be found quickly. Many clerks are required for this work in large offices and fixed standards of accomplishment often can and must be utilized to get the desired results without loss of time.
The one of the following which is the MOST accurate statement on the basis of the above statement is:
    A. In setting up a filing system, the system to be used is secondary to the purpose it is to serve.
    B. Office records to be valuable must be kept in duplicate.
    C. The application of work standards to certain clerical functions frequently leads to greater efficiency.
    D. The keeping of office records becomes increasingly important as the business transacted by an office grows.

42._____

43. The difference between the average worker and the expert in any occupation is to a large degree a matter of training, yet the difference in their output is enormous. Despite this fact, there are many offices which do not have any organized system of training.
The MOST accurate of the following statements on the basis of the above statement is that
    A. job training, to be valuable, should be a continuous process
    B. most clerks have the same general intelligence but differ only in the amount of training they have received
    C. skill in an occupation can be acquired as a result of instruction by others
    D. employees with similar training will produce similar quality and quantity of work

43._____

44. Sometimes the term "clerical work" is used synonymously with the term "office work" to indicate that the work is clerical work, whether done by a clerk in a place called "the office," by the foreman in the shop, or by an investigator in the field. The essential feature is the work itself, not who does it or where it is done. If it is clerical work in one place, it is clerical work everywhere.

44._____

Of the following, the LEAST DIRECT implication of the above statement is that
A. many jobs have clerical aspects
B. some clerical work is done in offices
C. the term "clerical work" is used in place of the term "office work" to emphasize the nature of the work done rather than by whom it is done
D. clerks are not called upon to perform other than clerical work

45. Scheduling work within a unit involves the knowledge of how long the component parts of the routine take, and the precedence which certain routines should take over others. Usually, the important functions should be attended to on a schedule, and less important work can be handled as fill-in.
The one of the following which is the VALID statement on the basis of the above statement is that
A. only employees engaged in routine assignments should have their work scheduled
B. the work of an employee should be so scheduled that occasional absences will not upset his routine
C. a proper scheduling of work takes the importance of the various functions of a unit into consideration
D. if office work is not properly scheduled, important functions will be neglected

45._____

46. A filing system is unquestionably an effective tool for the systematic executive, and it use in office practice is indispensable, but a casual examination of almost any filing drawer in any office will show that hundreds of letters and papers which have no value whatever are being preserved.
The LEAST accurate of the following statements on the basis of the above statement is that
A. it is generally considered to be good office practice to destroy letters or papers which are of no value
B. many files are cluttered with useless paper
C. a filing system is a valuable aid in effective office management
D. every office executive should personally make a thorough examination of the files at regular intervals

46._____

47. As a supervisor, you may receive requests for information which you know should not be divulged.
Of the following replies you may give to such a request received over the telephone, the BEST one is:
A. "I regret to advise you that it is the policy of the department not to give out this information over the telephone."
B. "If you hold on a moment, I'll have you connected with the chief of the division."
C. "I am sorry that I cannot help you, but we are not permitted to give out any information regarding such matters."
D. "I am sorry but I know nothing regarding this matter."

47._____

48. Training promotes cooperation and teamwork, and results in lowered unit costs of operation.
The one of the following which is the MOST valid implication of the above statement is that
   A. training is of most value to new employees
   B. training is a factor in increasing efficiency and morale
   C. the actual cost of training employees may be small
   D. training is unnecessary in offices where personnel costs cannot be reduced

49. A government employee should understand how his particular duties contribute to the achievement of the objectives of his department.
This statement means MOST NEARLY that
   A. an employee who understands the functions of his department will perform his work efficiently
   B. all employees contribute equally in carrying out the objectives of their department
   C. an employee should realize the significance of his work in relation to the aims of his department
   D. all employees should be able to assist in setting up the objectives of a department

50. Many office managers have a tendency to overuse form letters and are prone to print form letters for every occasion, regardless of the number of copies of these letters which is needed.
On the basis of this statement, it is MOST logical to state that the determination of the need for a form letter should depend upon the
   A. length of the period during which the form letter may be used
   B. number of form letters presently being used in the office
   C. frequency with which the form letter may be used
   D. number of typists who may use the form letter

KEY (CORRECT ANSWERS)

1. A	11. B	21. B	31. A	41. B
2. C	12. A	22. B	32. C	42. C
3. C	13. D	23. A	33. B	43. C
4. B	14. A	24. A	34. C	44. D
5. A	15. D	25. D	35. D	45. C
6. A	16. B	26. D	36. B	46. D
7. B	17. B	27. B	37. C	47. C
8. D	18. C	28. D	38. B	48. B
9. B	19. C	29. A	39. B	49. C
10. D	20. D	30. B	40. C	50. C

TEST 2

DIRECTIONS: Each question or incomplete statement is followed by several suggested answers or completions. Select the one that BEST answers the question or completes the statement. *PRINT THE LETTER OF THE CORRECT ANSWER IN THE SPACE AT THE RIGHT.*

1. Your bureau is assigned an important task.
   Of the following, the function that you, as an administrative officer, can LEAST reasonably be expected to perform under these circumstances is the
   A. division of the large job into individual tasks
   B. establishment of "production lines" within the bureau
   C. performance personally of a substantial share of all the work
   D. checkup to see that the work has been well done

2. Suppose that you have broken a complex job into its smaller components before making assignments to the employees under your jurisdiction.
   Of the following, the LEAST advisable procedure to follow from that point is to
   A. give each employee a picture of the importance of his work for the success of the total job
   B. establish a definite line of work flow and responsibility
   C. post a written memorandum of the best method for performing each job
   D. teach a number of alternative methods for doing each job

3. As an administrative officer, you are requested to draw up an organization chart of the whole department.
   Of the following, the MOST important characteristic of such a chart is that it will
   A. include all details of the organization which distinguish it from any other
   B. be a schematic representation of purely administrative functions within the department
   C. present a modification of the actual departmental organization in light of principles of scientific management
   D. present an accurate picture of the lines of authority and responsibility

4. Of the following, the MOST important principle in respect to delegation of authority that should guide you in your work as supervisor in charge of a bureau is that you should
   A. delegate as much authority as you effectively can
   B. make certain that all administrative details clear through your desk
   C. have all decisions confirmed by you
   D. discourage the practice of consulting you on matters of basic policy

5. Of the following, the LEAST valid criterion to be applied in evaluating the organization of the department in which you are employed as a supervisor is:
   A. Is authority for making decisions centralized?
   B. Is authority for formulating policy centralized?
   C. Is authority granted commensurate with the responsibility involved?
   D. Is each position and its relation to other positions from the standpoint of responsibility clearly defined?

6. Functional centralization is the bringing together of employees doing the same kind of work and performing similar tasks.
   Of the following, the one which is NOT an important advantage flowing from the introduction of functional centralization in a large city department is that
   A. inter-bureau communication and traffic are reduced
   B. standardized work procedures are introduced more easily
   C. evaluation of employee performances is facilitated
   D. inequalities in working conditions are reduced

7. As a supervisor, you find that a probationary employee under your supervision is consistently below a reasonable standard of performance for the job he is assigned to do.
   Of the following, the MOST appropriate action for you to take FIRST is to
   A. give him an easier job to do
   B. advise him to transfer to another department
   C. recommend to your superior that he be discouraged at the end of his probationary period
   D. determine whether the cause for his below-standard performance can be readily remedied

8. Certain administrative functions, such as those concerned with budgetary and personnel selection activities, have been delegated to central agencies separated from the operating departments.
   Of the following, the PRINCIPAL reason for such separation is that
   A. a central agency is generally better able to secure funds for performing these functions
   B. decentralization increases executive control
   C. greater economy, efficiency, and uniformity can be obtained by establishing central staff of experts to perform these functions
   D. the problems involved in performing these functions vary significantly from one operating department to another

9. The one of the following which is LEAST valid as a guiding principle for you, in your work as supervisor, in building team spirit and teamwork in your bureau is that you should attempt to
   A. convince the personnel of the bureau that public administration is a worthwhile endeavor
   B. lead every employee to visualize the integration of his own individual function with the program of the whole bureau
   C. develop a favorable public attitude toward the work of the bureau
   D. maintain impartiality by convenient delegation of authority in controversial matters

10. Of the following, the LEAST desirable procedure for the competent supervisor to follow is to
    A. organize his work before taking responsibility for helping others with theirs
    B. avoid schedules and routines when he is busy
    C. be flexible in planning and carrying out his responsibilities
    D. secure the support of his staff in organizing the total job of the unit

11. The responsibility for making judgment about staff members which is inherent in the supervisor's position may arouse hostilities toward the supervisor.
Of the following, the BEST suggestion to the supervisor for handling this responsibility is for the supervisor to avoid
    A. individual criticism by taking up problems directly through group meetings
    B. any personal feeling or action that would imply that the supervisor has any power over the staff
    C. making critical judgments without accompanying them with reassurance to the staff member concerned

12. To carry out MOST effectively his responsibility for holding to a standard of quantity and quality, the supervisor should
    A. demand much more from himself than he does from his staff
    B. provide a clearly defined statement of what is expected of the staff
    C. teach the staff to assume responsible attitudes
    D. help the staff out when they get into unavoidable difficulties

13. The supervisor should inspire confidence and respect.
This objective is MOST likely to be attained by the supervisor if he endeavors always to
    A. know the answers to the workers' questions
    B. be fair and just
    C. know what is going on in the office
    D. behave like a supervisor

14. Two chief reasons for the centralization of office functions are to eliminate costly duplication and to bring about greater coordination.
The MOST direct implication of this statement is that
    A. greater coordination of office work will result in centralization of office functions
    B. where there is no centralization of office functions, there can be no coordination of work
    C. centralization of office functions may reduce duplication of work
    D. decentralization of office functions may be a result of costly duplication

15. The efficient administrative assistant arranges a definite schedule of the regular work of his division, but assigns the occasional and emergency tasks when they arise to the employees available at the time to handle these tasks.
The management procedure described in this statement is desirable MAINLY because it
    A. relieves the administrative assistant of the responsibility of supervising the work of his staff
    B. enables more of the staff to become experienced in handling different types of problems
    C. enables the administrative assistant to anticipate problems which may arise
    D. provides for consideration of current work load when making special assignments

16. Well-organized training courses for office employees are regarded by most administrators as a fundamental and essential part of a well-balanced personnel program.
    Such training of clerical employees results LEAST directly in
    A. providing a reservoir of trained employees who can carry on the duties of other clerks during the absence of these clerks
    B. reducing the individual differences in the innate ability of clerical employees to perform complex duties
    C. bringing about a standardization throughout the department of operational methods found to be highly effective in one of its units
    D. preparing clerical employees for promotion to more responsible positions

17. The average typing speed of a typist is not necessarily a true indication of her efficiency.
    Of the following, the BEST justification for this statement is that
    A. the typist may not maintain her maximum typing speed at all times
    B. a rapid typist will ordinarily type more letters than a slow one
    C. a typist's assignments usually include other operations in addition to actual typing
    D. typing speed has no significant relationship to the difficulty of material being typed

18. Although the use of labor-saving machinery and the simplification of procedures tend to decrease unit clerical labor costs, there is, nevertheless, a contrary tendency in the overall cost of office work. This contrary tendency, evidenced by the increase in size of the office staffs, has developed from the increasingly extensive use of systems of analysis and methods of research.
    Of the following, the MOST accurate statement on the basis of the above statement is that
    A. the tendency for the overall costs of office work to increase is bringing about a counter-tendency to decrease unit costs of office work
    B. office machines are of little value in reducing the unit costs of the work of offices in which the overall costs are increasing
    C. The increasing use of systems of analysis and methods of research is bringing about a condition which will necessitate a curtailment of the use of these techniques in the office
    D. expanded office functions tend to offset savings resulting from increased efficiency in office management

19. The most successful supervisor wins his victories through preventive rather than through curative action.
    The one of the following which is the MOST accurate statement on the basis of this statement is that
    A. success in supervision may be measured more accurately in terms of errors corrected than in terms of errors prevented
    B. anticipating problems makes for better supervision than waiting until these problems arise

C. difficulties that cannot be prevented by the supervisor cannot be overcome
D. the solution of problems in supervision is best achieved by scientific methods

20. Assume that you have been requested to design an office form which is to be duplicated by the mimeograph process.
In planning the layout of the various items appearing on the form, it is LEAST important for you to know the
   A. amount of information which the form is to contain
   B. purpose for which the form will be used
   C. size of the form
   D. number of copies of the form which are required

20.____

21. The supervisor is responsible for the accuracy of the work performed by her subordinates.
Of the following procedures which she might adopt to insure the accurate copying of long reports from rough draft originals, the MOST effective one is to
   A. examine the rough draft for errors in grammar, punctuation, and spelling before assigning it to a typist to copy
   B. glance through each typed report before it leaves her bureau to detect any obvious errors made by the typist
   C. have another employee read the rough draft original to the typist who typed the report, and have the typist make whatever corrections are necessary
   D. rotate assignments involving the typing of long reports equally among all the typists in the unit

21.____

22. The total number of errors made during the month, or other period studied, indicates, in a general way, whether the work has been performed with reasonable accuracy. However, this is not in itself a true measure, but must be considered in relation to the total volume of work produced.
On the basis of this statement, the accuracy of work performed is MOST truly measured by the
   A. total number of errors made during a specified period
   B. comparison of the number of errors made and the quantity of work produced during a specified period
   C. average amount of work produced by the unit during each month or other designated period of time
   D. none of the above answers

22.____

23. In the course of your duties, you receive a letter which, you believe, should be called to the attention of your supervisor.
Of the following, the BEST reason for attaching previous correspondence to this letter before giving it to your supervisor is that
   A. there is less danger, if such a procedure is followed, of misplacing important letters
   B. this letter can probably be better understood in the light of previous correspondence

23.____

C. your supervisor is probably in a better position to understand the letter than you
D. this letter will have to be filed eventually so there is no additional work involved

24. Suppose that you are requested to transmit to the stenographers in your bureau an order curtailing certain privileges that they have been enjoying. You anticipate that your staff may resent curtailment of such privileges.
Of the following, the BEST action for you to take is to
   A. impress upon your staff that an order is an order and must be obeyed
   B. attempt to explain to your staff the probable reasons for curtailing their privileges
   C. excuse the curtailment of privileges by saying that the welfare of the staff was evidently not considered
   D. warn your staff that violation of an order may be considered sufficient cause for immediate dismissal

24.____

25. Suppose that a stenographer recently appointed to your bureau submits a memorandum suggesting a change in office procedure that has been tried before and has been found unsuccessful.
Of the following, the BEST action for you to take is to
   A. send the stenographer a note acknowledging receipt of the suggestion, but do not attempt to carry out the suggestion
   B. point out that suggestions should come from her supervisor, who has a better knowledge of the problems of the office
   C. try out the suggested change a second time, lest the stenographer lose interest in her work
   D. call the stenographer in, explain that the change if not practicable, and compliment her for her interest and alertness

25.____

26. Suppose that you are assistant to one of the important administrators in your department. You receive a note from the head of department asking your supervisor to assist with a pressing problem that has arisen by making an immediate recommendation. Your supervisor is out of town on official business for a few days and cannot be reached. The head of department, evidently, is not aware of his absence.
Of the following, the BEST action for you to take is to
   A. send the note back to the head of department without comment so as not to incriminate your supervisor
   B. forward the note to one of the administrators in another division of the department
   C. wait until your supervisor returns and bring the note to his attention immediately
   D. get in touch with the head of department immediately and inform him that your supervisor is out of town

26.____

27. One of your duties may be to estimate the budget of your unit for the next fiscal year. Suppose that you expect no important changes in the work of your unit during the next year.

27.____

Of the following, the MOST appropriate basis for estimating next year's budget is the
- A. average budget of your unit for the last five years
- B. budget of your unit for the current year plus fifty percent to allow for possible expansion
- C. average current budget of units in your department
- D. budget of your unit for the current fiscal year

28. As a supervisor, you should realize that the work of a stenographer ordinarily requires a higher level of intelligence than the work of a typist CHIEFLY because
    - A. the salary range of stenographers is, in most government and business offices, lower than the salary range of typists
    - B. greater accuracy and skill is ordinarily required of a typist
    - C. the stenographer must understand what is being dictated to enable her to write it out in shorthand
    - D. typists are required to do more technical and specialized work

29. Suppose that you are acting as assistant to an important administrator in your department.
    Of the following, the BEST reason for keeping a separate "pending" file of letters to which answers are expected very soon is that
    - A. important correspondence should be placed in a separate, readily accessible file
    - B. a periodic check of the "pending" file will indicate the possible need for follow-up letters
    - C. correspondence is never final, so provision should be made for keeping files open
    - D. there is seldom sufficient room in the permanent files to permit filing all letters

30. For a busy executive in a government department, the services of an assistant are valuable and almost indispensable.
    Of the following, the CHIEF value of an assistant PROBABLY lies in her
    - A. ability to assume responsibility for making major decisions
    - B. familiarity with the general purpose and functions of civil service
    - C. special education
    - D. familiarity with the work and detail involved in the duties of the executive whom she assists

31. The supervisor should set a good example.
    Of the following, the CHIEF implication of the above statement is that the supervisor should
    - A. behave as he expects his workers to behave
    - B. know as much about the worker as his workers do
    - C. keep his workers informed of what he is doing
    - D. keep ahead of his workers

32. Of the following, the LEAST desirable procedure for the competent supervisor to follow is to
    A. organize his work before taking responsibility for helping others with theirs
    B. avoid schedules and routines when he is busy
    C. be flexible in planning and carrying out his responsibilities
    D. secure the support of his staff in organizing the total job of the unit

33. Evaluation helps the worker by increasing his security.
    Of the following, the BEST justification for this statement is that
    A. security and growth depend upon knowledge by the worker of the agency's evaluation
    B. knowledge of his evaluation by agency and supervisor will stimulate the worker to better performance
    C. evaluation enables the supervisor and worker to determine the reasons for the worker's strengths and weaknesses
    D. the supervisor and worker together can usually recognize and deal with any worker's insecurity

34. Systematizing for efficiency means MOST NEARLY
    A. performing an assignment despite all interruptions
    B. leaving difficult assignments until the next day
    C. having a definite time schedule for certain daily duties
    D. trying to do as little work as possible

35. The CHIEF reason for an employee training program is to
    A. increase the efficiency of the employee's work
    B. train the employee for promotion examinations
    C. to meet and talk with each new employee
    D. to give the supervisor an opportunity to reprimand the employee for his lack of knowledge

36. A supervisor may encourage his subordinates to make suggestions by
    A. keeping a record of the number of suggestions an employee makes
    B. providing a suggestion box
    C. outlining a list of possible suggestions
    D. giving credit to a subordinate whose suggestion has been accepted and used

37. The statement that accuracy is of greater importation than speed means MOST NEARLY that
    A. slower work increases employment
    B. fast workers may be inferior workers
    C. there are many varieties of work to do in an office
    D. the slow worker is the most efficient person

38. To print tabular material is always much more expensive than to print straight text.
It follows MOST NEARLY that
    A. the more columns and subdivisions there are in a table, the more expensive is the printing
    B. the omission of the number and title from a table reduces printing costs
    C. it is always desirable to only print straight text
    D. do not print tabular material as it is too expensive

38.____

39. If you were required to give service ratings to employees under your supervision, you should consider as MOST important, during the current period, the
    A. personal characteristics and salary and grade of an employee
    B. length of service and the volume of work performed
    C. previous service rating given him
    D. personal characteristics and the quality of work of an employee

39.____

40. If a representative committee of employees in a large department is to meet with an administrative officer for the purpose of improving staff relations and of handling grievances, it is BEST that these meetings be held
    A. at regular intervals
    B. whenever requested b an aggrieved employee
    C. whenever the need arises
    D. at the discretion of the administrative officer

40.____

41. In order to be best able to teach a newly appointed employee who must learn to do a type of work which is unfamiliar to him, his supervisor should realize that during this first stage in the learning process the subordinate is GENERALLY characterized by
    A. acute consciousness of self
    B. acute consciousness of subject matter, with little interest in persons or personalities
    C. inertness or passive acceptance of assigned role
    D. understanding of problems without understanding of the means of solving them

41.____

42. The MOST accurate of the following principles of education and learning for a supervisor to keep in mind when planning a training program for the assistant supervisors under her supervision is that
    A. assistant supervisors, like all other individuals, vary in the rate at which they learn new material and in the degree to which they can retain what they do learn
    B. experienced assistant supervisors who have the same basic college education and agency experience will be able to learn new material at approximately the same rate of speed
    C. the speed with which assistant supervisors can learn new material after the age of forty is half as rapid as at ages twenty to thirty
    D. with regard to any specific task, it is easier and takes less time to break an experienced assistant supervisor of old, unsatisfactory work habits than it is to teach him new, acceptable ones

42.____

43. A supervisor has been transferred from supervision of one group of units to another group of units in the same center. She spends the first three weeks in her new assignment in getting acquainted with her new subordinates, their caseload problems and their work. In this process, she notices that some of the cash records and forms which are submitted to her by two of the assistant supervisors are carelessly or improperly prepared.
The BEST of the following actions for the supervisor to take in this situation is to
   A. carefully check the work submitted by these assistant supervisors during an additional three weeks before taking any more positive action
   B. confer with these offending workers and show each one where her work needs improvement and how to go about achieving it
   C. institute an in-service training program specifically designed to solve such a problem and instruct the entire subordinate staff in proper work methods
   D. make a note of these errors for documentary use in preparing the annual service rating reports and advise the workers involved to prepare their work more carefully

43.____

44. A supervisor, who was promoted to this position a year ago, has supervised a certain assistant supervisor for this one year. The work of the assistant supervisor has been very poor because he has done a minimum of work, refused to take sufficient responsibility, been difficult to handle, and required very close supervision. Apparently due to the increasing insistence by his supervisor that he improve the caliber of his work, the assistant supervisor tenders his resignation, stating that the demands of the job are too much for him. The opinion of the previous supervisor, who had supervised this assistant supervisor for two years, agrees substantially with that of the new supervisor. Under such circumstances, the BEST of the following actions the supervisor can take, in general, is to
   A. recommend that the resignation be accepted and that he be rehired should he later apply when he feels able to do the job
   B. recommend that the resignation be accepted and that he not be rehired should he later so apply
   C. refuse to accept the resignation but try to persuade the assistant supervisor to accept psychiatric help
   D. refuse to accept the resignation, promising the assistant supervisor that he will be less closely supervised in the future since he is now so experienced

44.____

45. Rumors have arisen to the effect that one of the staff investigators under your supervision has been attending classes at a local university during afternoon hours when he is supposed to be making field visits.
The BEST of the following ways for you to approach this problem is to
   A. disregard the rumors since, like most rumors, they probably have no actual foundation in fact
   B. have a discreet investigation made in order to determine the actual facts prior to taking any other action

45.____

C. inform the investigator that you know what he has been doing and that such behavior is overt dereliction of duty and is punishable by dismissal
D. review the investigator's work record, spot check his cases, and take no further action unless the quality of his work is below average for the unit

46. A supervisor must consider many factors in evaluating a worker whom he has supervised for a considerable time.
In evaluating the capacity of such a worker to use independent judgment, the one of the following to which the supervisor should generally give MOST consideration is the worker's
    A. capacity to establish good relationships with people (clients, colleagues)
    B. educational background
    C. emotional stability
    D. the quality and judgment shown by the worker in previous work situations known to the supervisor

47. A supervisor is conducting a special meeting with the assistant supervisors under her supervision to read and discuss some major complex changes in the rules and procedures. She notices that one of the assistant supervisors who is normally attentive at meetings seems to be paying no attention to what is being said. The supervisor stops reading the rules and asks the assistant supervisor a couple of questions about the changed procedure, to which she gets satisfactory answers.
The BEST action of the following for the supervisor to take at the meeting is to
    A. advise the assistant supervisor gently but firmly that these changes are complex and that her undivided attention is required in order to fully comprehend them
    B. avoid further embarrassment to the assistant supervisor by asking the group as a whole to pay more attention to what is being read
    C. discontinue the questioning and resume reading the procedure
    D. politely request the assistant supervisor to stop giving those present the impression that she is uninterested in what goes on about her

48. A supervisor becomes aware that one of her very competent experienced workers never takes notes during an interview with a client except to note an occasional name, address, or date. When asked about this practice by the supervisor, the worker states that she has a good memory for important details and has always been able to satisfactorily record an interview after the client has left.
It would generally be BEST for the supervisor to handle this situation by
    A. discussing with her that more extensive note-taking may sometimes be desirable with a client who believes note-taking to be evidence that his problem will receive serious consideration
    B. agreeing with this practice since note-taking interferes with the establishment of a proper worker-client relationship
    C. explaining that, since interviewing is an art form rather than an exact science, a good worker must devise her own personal rules for interviewing and not be bound by general principles

D. warning the worker that memory is too uncertain a thing to be relied upon and, therefore, notes should be taken during an interview of all matters

49. When an experienced subordinate who has the authority and information necessary to make a decision on a certain difficult matter brings the matter to his supervisor without having made the decision, it would generally be BEST for the supervisor to
   A. agree to make the decision for the subordinate after the subordinate has explained why he finds it difficult to make the decision and after he has made a recommendation
   B. make the decision for the subordinate, explaining to him the reasons for arriving at the decision
   C. refuse to make the decision, but discuss the various alternatives with the subordinate in order to clarify the issues involved
   D. refuse to make the decision, explaining to the subordinate that he is deemed to be fully qualified and competent to make the decision

50. The one of the following instances when it is MOST important for an upper level supervisor to follow the chain of command is when he is
   A. communicating decisions   B. communicating information
   C. receiving suggestions   D. seeking information

KEY (CORRECT ANSWERS)

1. C	11. D	21. C	31. A	41. A
2. D	12. B	22. B	32. B	42. A
3. D	13. B	23. B	33. C	43. B
4. A	14. C	24. B	34. C	44. B
5. D	15. D	25. D	35. A	45. B
6. A	16. B	26. D	36. D	46. D
7. D	17. C	27. D	37. B	47. C
8. C	18. D	28. C	38. A	48. A
9. D	19. B	29. B	39. D	49. C
10. B	20. D	30. D	40. A	50. A

TEST 3

DIRECTIONS: Each question or incomplete statement is followed by several suggested answers or completions. Select the one that BEST answers the question or completes the statement. *PRINT THE LETTER OF THE CORRECT ANSWER IN THE SPACE AT THE RIGHT.*

1. Experts in the field of personnel relations feel that it is generally bad practice for subordinate employees to become aware of pending or contemplated changes in policy or organizational set-up via the "grapevine" CHIEFLY because
    A. evidence that one or more responsible officials have proved untrustworthy will undermine confidence in the agency
    B. the information disseminated by this method is seldom entirely accurate and generally spreads needless unrest among the subordinate staff
    C. the subordinate staff may conclude that the administration feels the staff cannot be trusted with the true information
    D. the subordinate staff may conclude that the administration lacks the courage to make an unpopular announcement through officials channels

1.____

2. In order to maintain a proper relationship with a worker who is assigned to staff rather than line functions, a line supervisor should
    A. accept all recommendations of the staff worker
    B. include the staff worker in the conferences called by the supervisor for his subordinates
    C. keep the staff worker informed of developments in the area of his staff assignment
    D. require that the staff worker's recommendations be communicated to the supervisor through the supervisor's own superior

2.____

3. Of the following, the GREATEST disadvantage of placing a worker in a staff position under the direct supervision of the supervisor whom he advises is the possibility that the
    A. staff worker will tend to be insubordinate because of a feeling of superiority over the supervisor
    B. staff worker will tend to give advice of the type which the supervisor wants to hear or finds acceptable
    C. supervisor will tend to be mistrustful of the advice of a worker of subordinate rank
    D. supervisor will tend to derive little benefit from the advice because to supervise properly he should know at least as much as his subordinate

3.____

4. One factor which might be given consideration in deciding upon the optimum span of control of a supervisor over his immediate subordinates is the position of the supervisor in the hierarchy of the organization. It is generally considered proper that the number of subordinates immediately supervised by a higher, upper echelon, supervisor
    A. is unrelated to and tends to form no pattern with the number supervised by lower level supervisors
    B. should be about the same as the number supervised by a lower level supervisor

4.____

C. should be larger than the number supervised by a lower level supervisor
D. should be smaller than the number supervised by a lower level supervisor

5. An important administrative problem is how precisely to define the limits on authority that is delegated to subordinate supervisors.
Such definition of limits of authority should be
   A. as precise as possible and practicable in all areas
   B. as precise as possible and practicable in areas of function, but should allow considerable flexibility in the area of personnel management
   C. as precise as possible and practicable in the area of personnel management, but should allow considerable flexibility in the areas of function
   D. in general terms so as to allow considerable flexibility both in the areas of function and in the areas of personnel management

6. The LEAST important of the following reasons why a particular activity should be assigned to a unit which performs activities dissimilar to it is that
   A. close coordination is needed between the particular activity and other activities performed by the unit
   B. it will enhance the reputation and prestige of the unit supervisor
   C. the unit makes frequent use of the results of this particular activity
   D. the unit supervisor has a sound knowledge and understanding of the particular activity

7. A supervisor is put in charge of a special unit. She is exceptionally well-qualified for this assignment by her training and experience. One of her very close personal friends has been working for some time as a field investigator in this unit. Both the supervisor and investigator are certain that the rest of the investigators in the unit, many of whom have been in the bureau for a long time, know of this close relationship.
Under these circumstances, the MOST advisable action for the supervisor to take is to
   A. ask that either she be allowed to return to her old assignment, or, if that cannot be arranged, that her friend be transferred to another unit in the center
   B. avoid any overt sign of favoritism by acting impartially and with greater reserve when dealing with this investigator than the rest of the staff
   C. discontinue any socializing with this investigator either inside or outside the office so as to eliminate any gossip or dissatisfaction
   D. talk the situation over with the other investigators and arrive at a mutually acceptable plan of proper office decorum

8. The one of the following causes of clerical error which is usually considered to be LEAST attributable to faulty supervision or inefficient management is
   A. inability to carry out instructions
   B. too much work to do
   C. an inappropriate record-keeping system
   D. continual interruptions

9. Assume that you are the supervisor of a clerical unit in a government agency. One of your subordinates violates a rule of the agency, a violation which requires that the employee be suspended from his work for one day. The violated rule is one that you have found to be unduly strict and you have recommended to the management of the agency that the rule be changed or abolished. The management has been considering your recommendation but has not yet reached a decision on the matter.
In these circumstances, you should
   A. not initiate disciplinary action, but, instead explain to the employee that the rule may be changed shortly
   B. delay disciplinary action on the violation until the management has reached a decision on changing the rule
   C. modify the disciplinary action by reprimanding the employee and informing him that further action may be taken when the management has reached a decision on changing the rule
   D. initiate the prescribed disciplinary action without commenting on the strictness of the rule or on your recommendation

10. Assume that a supervisor praises his subordinates for satisfactory aspects of their work only when he is about to criticize them for unsatisfactory aspects of their work.
Such a practice is undesirable PRIMARILY because
   A. his subordinates may expect to be praised for their work even if it is unsatisfactory
   B. praising his subordinates for some aspects of their work while criticizing other aspects will weaken the effects of the criticisms
   C. his subordinates would be more receptive to criticism if it were followed by praise
   D. his subordinates may come to disregard praise and wait for criticism to be given

11. The one of the following which would be the BEST reason for an agency to eliminate a procedure for obtaining and recording certain information is that
   A. it is no longer legally required to obtain the information
   B. there is an advantage in obtaining the information
   C. the information could be compiled on the basis of other information available
   D. the information obtained is sometimes incorrect

12. In determining the type and number of records to be kept in an agency, it is important to recognize that records are of value PRIMARILY as
   A. raw material to be used in statistical analysis
   B. sources of information about the agency's activities
   C. by-products of the activities carried on by the agency
   D. data for evaluating the effectiveness of the agency

Questions 13-17.

DIRECTIONS: Each of Questions 13 through 17 consists of a statement which contains one word that is incorrectly used because it is not in keeping with the meaning that the statement is evidently intended to convey. For each of these questions, you are to select the incorrectly used word and substitute for it one of the words lettered A, B, C, or D, which helps BEST to convey the meaning of the statement.

13. There has developed in recent years an increasing awareness of the need to measure the quality of management in all enterprises and to seek the principles that can serve as a basis for this improvement. 13.____
    A. growth   B. raise   C. efficiency   D. define

14. It is hardly an exaggeration to deny that the permanence, productivity, and humanity of any industrial system depend upon its ability to utilize the positive and constructive impulses of all who work and upon its ability to arouse and continue interest in the necessary activities. 14.____
    A. develop   B. efficiency   C. state   D. inspiration

15. The selection of managers on the basis of technical knowledge alone seems to recognize that the essential characteristic of management is getting things done through others, thereby demanding skills that are essential in coordinating the activities of subordinates. 15.____
    A. training   B. fails
    C. organization   D. improving

16. Only when it is deliberate and when it is clearly understood what impressions the ease of communication will probably create in the minds of employees and subordinate management, should top management refrain from commenting on a subject that is of general concern. 16.____
    A. obvious   B. benefit   C. doubt   D. absence

17. Scientific planning of work requires careful analysis of facts and a precise plan of action for the whims and fancies of executives that often provide only a vague indication of work to be done. 17.____
    A. substitutes   B. development
    C. preliminary   D. comprehensive

18. Assume that you are a supervisor. One of the workers under your supervision is careless about the routine aspects of his work. 18.____
    Of the following, the action MOST likely to develop in this worker a better attitude toward job routines is to demonstrate that
    A. it is just as easy to do his job the right way
    B. organization of his job will leave more time for field work
    C. the routine part of the job is essential to performing a good piece of work
    D. job routines are a responsibility of the worker

19. A supervisor can MOST effectively secure necessary improvement in a worker's office work by
    A. encouraging the worker to keep abreast of his work
    B. relating the routine part of his job to the total job to be done
    C. helping the worker to establish a good system for covering his office work and holding him to it
    D. informing the worker that he will be required to organize his work more efficiently

19._____

20. A supervisor should offer criticism in such a manner that the criticisms is helpful and not overwhelming.
    Of the following, the LEAST valid inference that can be drawn on the basis of the above statement is that a supervisor should
    A. demonstrate that the criticism is partial and not total
    B. give criticism in such a way that it does not undermine the worker's self-confidence
    C. keep his relationships with the worker objective
    D. keep criticism directed towards general work performance

20._____

21. The one of the following areas in which a worker may LEAST reasonably expect direct assistance from the supervisor is in
    A. building up rapport with all clients
    B. gaining insight into the unmet needs of clients
    C. developing an understanding of community resources
    D. interpreting agency policies and procedures

21._____

22. You are informed that a worker under your supervision has submitted a letter complaining of unfair service rating.
    Of the following, the MOST valid assumption for you to make concerning this worker is that he should be
    A. more adequately supervised in the future
    B. called in for a supervisory conference
    C. given a transfer to some other unit where he may be more happy
    D. given no more consideration than any other inefficient worker

22._____

23. Assume that you are a supervisor. You find that a somewhat bewildered worker, newly appointed to the department, hesitates to ask questions for fear of showing his ignorance and jeopardizing his position.
    Of the following, the BEST procedure for you to follow is to
    A. try to discover the reason for his evident fear of authority
    B. tell him that when he is in doubt about a procedure or a policy he should consult his fellow workers
    C. develop with the worker a plan for more frequent supervisory conferences
    D. explain why each staff member is eager to give him available information that will help him do a good job

23._____

24. Of the following, the MOST effective method of helping a newly-appointed employee adjust to his new job is to
    A. assure him that with experience his uncertain attitudes will be replaced by a professional approach
    B. help him, by accepting him as he is, to have confidence in his ability to handle the job
    C. help him to be on guard against the development of punitive attitudes
    D. help him to recognize the mutability of the agency's policies and procedures

25. Suppose that, as a supervisor, you have scheduled an individual conference with an experienced employee under your supervision.
    Of the following, the BEST plan of action for this conference is to
    A. discuss the work that the employee is most interested in
    B. plan with the employee to cover any problems that are difficult for him
    C. advise the employee that the conference is his to do with as he sees fit
    D. spot check the employee's work in advance and select those areas for discussion in which the employee has done poor work

26. Of the following, the CHIEF function of a supervisor should be to
    A. assist in the planning of new policies and the evaluation of existing ones
    B. promote congenial relationships among members of the staff
    C. achieve optimum functioning of each unit and each worker
    D. promote the smooth functioning of job routines

27. The competent supervisor must realize the importance of planning.
    Of the following, the aspect of planning which is LEAST appropriately considered a responsibility of the supervisor is
    A. long-range planning for the proper functioning of his unit
    B. planning to take care of peak and slack periods
    C. planning to cover agency policies in group conferences
    D. long-range planning to develop community resources

28. The one of the following objectives which should be of LEAST concern to the supervisor in the performance of his duties is to
    A. help the worker to make friends with all of his fellow employees
    B. be impartial and fair to all members of the staff
    C. stimulate the worker's growth on the job
    D. meet the needs of the individual employee

29. The one of the following which is LEAST properly considered a direct responsibility of the supervisor is
    A. liaison between the staff and the administrator
    B. interpreting administrative orders and procedures to the employees
    C. training new employees
    D. maintaining staff morale at a high level

30. In order to teach the employee to develop an objective approach, the BEST action for the supervisor to take is to help the worker to
    A. develop a sincere interest in his job
    B. understand the varied responsibilities that are an integral part of his job
    C. differentiate clearly between himself as a friend and as an employee
    D. find satisfaction in his work

31. If the employee shows excessive submission which indicates a need for dependence on the supervisor in handling an assignment, it would be MOST advisable for the supervisor to
    A. indicate firmly that the employee-supervisor relationship does not call for submission
    B. define areas of responsibility of employee and supervisor
    C. recognize the employee's need and of supervisor
    D. recognize the employee's need to be sustained and supported and help him by making decisions for him

32. Assume that, as a supervisor, you are conducting a group conference.
    Of the following, the BEST procedure for you to follow in order to stimulate group discussion is to
    A. permit the active participation of all members
    B. direct the discussion to an acceptable conclusion
    C. resolve conflicts of opinion among members of the group
    D. present a question for discussion on which the group members have some knowledge or experience

33. Suppose that, as a new supervisor, you wish to inform the staff under your supervision of your methods of operation.
    Of the following, the BEST procedure for you to follow is to
    A. advise the staff that they will learn gradually from experience
    B. inform each employee in an individual conference
    C. call a group conference for this purpose
    D. distribute a written memorandum among all members of the staff

34. The MOST constructive and effective method of correcting an employee who has made a mistake is, in general, to
    A. explain that his evaluation is related to his errors
    B. point out immediately where he erred and tell him how it should have been done
    C. show him how to readjust his methods so as to avoid similar errors in the future
    D. try to discover by an indirect method why the error was made

35. The MOST effective method for the supervisor to follow in order to obtain the cooperation of an employee under his supervision is, wherever possible, to
    A. maintain a careful record of performance in order to keep the employee on his toes
    B. give the employee recognition in order to promote greater effort and give him more satisfaction in his work

C. try to gain the employee's cooperation for the good of the service
D. advise the employee that his advancement on the job depends on his cooperation

36. Of the following, the MOST appropriate initial course for an employee to take when he is unable to clarify a policy with his supervisor is to
    A. bring up the problem at the next group conference
    B. discuss the policy immediately with his fellow employees
    C. accept the supervisor's interpretation as final
    D. determine what responsibility he has for putting the policy into effect

37. Good administration allows for different treatment of different workers. Of the following, the CHIEF implication of this statement is that
    A. it would be unfair for the supervisor not to treat all staff members alike
    B. fear of favoritism tends to undermine staff morale
    C. best results are obtained by individualization within the limits of fair treatment
    D. difficult problems call for a different kind of approach

38. The MOST effective and appropriate method of building efficiency and morale in a group of employees is, in general,
    A. by stressing the economic motive
    B. through use of the authority inherent in the position
    C. by a friendly approach to all
    D. by a discipline that is fair but strict

39. Of the following, the LEAST valid basis for the assignment of work to an employee is the
    A. kind of service to be rendered
    B. experience and training of the employee
    C. health and capacity of the employee
    D. racial composition of the community where the office is located

40. The CHIEF justification for staff education, consisting of in-service training, lies in its contribution to
    A. improvement in the quality of work performed
    B. recruitment of a better type of employee
    C. employee morale, accruing from a feeling of growth on the job
    D. the satisfaction that the employee gets on his job

41. Suppose that you are a supervisor. An employee no longer with your department requests you, as his former supervisor, to write a letter recommending him for a position with a private organization.
    Of the following the BEST procedure for you to follow is to include in the letter only information that
    A. will help the applicant get the job
    B. is clear, factual, and substantiated
    C. is known to you personally
    D. can readily be corroborated by personal interview

42. Of the following, the MOST important item on which to base the efficiency evaluation of an employee under your supervision is
    A. the nature of the relationship that he has built up with his fellow employees
    B. how he gets along with his supervisors
    C. his personal habits and skills
    D. the effectiveness of his control over his work

43. According to generally accepted personnel practice, the MOST effective method of building morale in a new employee is to
    A. exercise caution in praising the employee, lest he become overconfident
    B. give sincere and frank recommendation whenever possible in order to stimulate interest and effort
    C. praise the employee highly even for mediocre performance so that he will be stimulated to do better
    D. warn the employee frequently that he cannot hope to succeed unless he puts forth his best efforts

44. Errors made by newly-appointed employees often follow a predictable pattern. The one of the following errors likely to have LEAST serious consequences is the tendency of a new employee to
    A. discuss problems that are outside his province with the client
    B. persuade the client to accept the worker's solution of a problem
    C. be two strict in carrying out departmental policy and procedure
    D. depend upon the use of authority due to his inexperience and lack of skill in working with people

45. The MOST effective way for a supervisor to break down a worker's defensive stand against supervisory guidance is to
    A. come to an understanding with him on the mutual responsibilities involved in the job of the employee and that of the supervisor
    B. tell him he must feel free to express his opinions and to discuss basic problems
    C. show him how to develop toward greater objectivity, sensitivity, and understanding
    D. advise him that it is necessary to carry out agency policy and procedures in order to do a good job

46. Of the following, the LEAST essential function of the supervisor who is conducting a group conference should be to
    A. keep attention focused on the purpose of the conference
    B. encourage discussion of controversial points
    C. make certain that all possible viewpoints are discussed
    D. be thoroughly prepared in advance

47. When conducting a group conference, the supervisor should be LEAST concerned with
    A. providing an opportunity for the free interchange of ideas
    B. imparting knowledge and understanding of the work

C. leading the discussion toward a planned goal
D. pointing out where individual workers have erred in work practice

48. If the participants in a group conference are unable to agree on the proper application of a concept to the work of a department, the MOST suitable temporary procedure for the supervisor to follow is to
   A. suggest that each member think the subject through before the next meeting
   B. tell the group to examine their differences for possible conflicts with present policies
   C. suggest that practices can be changed because of new conditions
   D. state the acceptable practice in the agency and whether deviations from such practice can be permitted

48.____

49. If an employee is to participate constructively in any group discussion, it is MOST important that he have
   A. advance notice of the agenda for the meeting
   B. long experience in the department
   C. knowledge and experience in the particular work
   D. the ability to assume a leadership role

49.____

50. Of the following, the MOST important principle for the supervisor to follow when conducting a group discussion is that he should
   A. move the discussion toward acceptance by the group of a particular point of view
   B. express his ideas clearly and succinctly
   C. lead the group to accept the authority inherent in his position
   D. contribute to the discussion from his knowledge and experience

50.____

KEY (CORRECT ANSWERS)

1.	B	11.	C	21.	A	31.	B	41.	B
2.	C	12.	B	22.	B	32.	D	42.	D
3.	B	13.	B	23.	C	33.	C	43.	B
4.	D	14.	C	24.	B	34.	C	44.	C
5.	A	15.	B	25.	B	35.	B	45.	A
6.	B	16.	D	26.	C	36.	D	46.	B
7.	A	17.	A	27.	D	37.	C	47.	D
8.	A	18.	D	28.	A	38.	D	48.	D
9.	D	19.	B	29.	A	39.	D	49.	A
10.	D	20.	D	30.	C	40.	A	50.	D

READING COMPREHENSION
UNDERSTANDING AND INTERPRETING WRITTEN MATERIAL
EXAMINATION SECTION
TEST 1

DIRECTIONS: Each question or incomplete statement is followed by several suggested answers or completions. Select the one that BEST answers the question or completes the statement. *PRINT THE LETTER OF THE CORRECT ANSWER IN THE SPACE AT THE RIGHT.*

Questions 1-4.

DIRECTIONS: Questions 1 through 4 are to be answered SOLELY on the basis of the following passage.

Those engaged in the exercise of First Amendment rights by pickets, marches, parades, and open-air assemblies are not exempted from obeying valid local traffic ordinances. In a recent pronouncement, Mr. Justice Baxter, speaking for the Supreme Court, wrote:

The rights of free speech and assembly, while fundamental to our democratic society, still do not mean that everyone with opinions or beliefs to express may address a group at any public place and at any time. The constitutional guarantee of liberty implies the existence of an organized society maintaining public order, without which liberty itself would be lost in the excesses of anarchy. The control of travel on the streets is a clear example of governmental responsibility to insure this necessary order. A restriction in that relation, designed to promote the public convenience in the interest of all, and not susceptible to abuses of discriminatory application, cannot be disregarded by the attempted exercise of some civil rights which, in other circumstances, would be entitled to protection. One would not be justified in ignoring the familiar red light because this was thought to be a means of social protest. Governmental authorities have the duty and responsibility to keep their streets open and available for movement. A group of demonstrators could not insist upon the right to cordon off a street, or entrance to a public or private building, and allow no one to pass who did not agree to listen to their exhortations.

1. Which of the following statements BEST reflects Mr. Justice Baxter's view of the relationship between liberty and public order?

    A. Public order cannot exist without liberty.
    B. Liberty cannot exist without public order.
    C. The existence of liberty undermines the existence of public order.
    D. The maintenance of public order insures the existence of liberty.

2. According to the above passage, local traffic ordinances result from

    A. governmental limitations on individual liberty
    B. governmental responsibility to insure public order
    C. majority rule as determined by democratic procedures
    D. restrictions on expression of dissent

3. The above passage suggests that government would be acting improperly if a local traffic ordinance

   A. was enforced in a discriminatory manner
   B. resulted in public inconvenience
   C. violated the right of free speech and assembly
   D. was not essential to public order

4. Of the following, the MOST appropriate title for the above passage is

   A. THE RIGHTS OF FREE SPEECH AND ASSEMBLY
   B. ENFORCEMENT OF LOCAL TRAFFIC ORDINANCES
   C. FIRST AMENDMENT RIGHTS AND LOCAL TRAFFIC ORDINANCES
   D. LIBERTY AND ANARCHY

Questions 5-8

DIRECTIONS: Questions 5 through 8 are to be answered SOLELY on the basis of the following passage

On November 8, 1976, the Supreme Court refused to block the payment of Medicaid funds for elective abortions. The Court's action means that a new Federal statute that bars the use of Federal funds for abortions unless abortion is necessary to save the life of the mother will not go into effect for many months, if at all.

A Federal District Court in Brooklyn ruled the following month that the statute was unconstitutional and ordered that Federal reimbursement for the costs of abortions continue on the same basis as reimbursements for the costs of pregnancy and childbirth-related services.

Technically, what the Court did today was to deny a request by Senator Howard Ramsdell and others for a stay blocking enforcement of the District Court order pending appeal. The Court's action was a victory for New York City. The City's Health and Hospitals Corporation initiated one of the two lawsuits challenging the new statute that led to the District Court's decision. The Corporation also opposed the request for a Supreme Court stay of that decision, telling the Court in a memorandum that a stay would subject the Corporation to a *grave and irreparable injury.*

5. According to the above passage, it would be CORRECT to state that the Health and Hospitals Corporation

   A. joined Senator Ramsdell in his request for a stay
   B. opposed the statute which limited reimbursement for the cost of abortions
   C. claimed that it would experience a loss if the District Court order was enforced
   D. appealed the District Court decision

6. The above passage indicates that the Supreme Court acted in DIRECT response to

   A. a lawsuit initiated by the Health and Hospitals Corporation
   B. a ruling by a Federal District Court
   C. a request for a stay
   D. the passage of a new Federal statute

7. According to the above passage, it would be CORRECT to state that the Supreme Court

   A. blocked enforcement of the District Court order
   B. refused a request for a stay to block enforcement of the Federal statute
   C. ruled that the new Federal statute was unconstitutional
   D. permitted payment of Federal funds for abortion to continue

8. Following are three statements concerning abortion that might be correct:
   I. Abortion costs are no longer to be Federally reimbursed on the same basis as those for pregnancy and childbirth
   II. Federal funds have not been available for abortions except to save the life of the mother
   III. Medicaid has paid for elective abortions in the past

   According to the passage above, which of the following CORRECTLY classifies the above statements into those that are true and those that are not true?

   A. I is true, but II and III are not.
   B. I and III are true, but II is not.
   C. I and II are true, but III is not.
   D. III is true, but I and II are not.

Questions 9-12.

DIRECTIONS: Questions 9 through 12 are to be answered SOLELY on the basis of the following passage.

A person may use physical force upon another person when and to the extent he reasonably believes such to be necessary to defend himself or a third person from what he reasonably believes to be the use or imminent use of unlawful physical force by such other person, unless (a) the latter's conduct was provoked by the actor himself with intent to cause physical injury to another person; or (b) the actor was the initial aggressor; or (c) the physical force involved is the product of a combat by agreement not specifically authorized by law.

A person may not use deadly physical force upon another person under the circumstances specified above unless (a) he reasonably believes that such other person is using or is about to use deadly physical force. Even in such case, however, the actor may not use deadly physical force if he knows he can, with complete safety, as to himself and others avoid the necessity of doing so by retreating; except that he is under no duty to retreat if he is in his dwelling and is not the initial aggressor; or (b) he reasonably believes that such other person is committing or attempting to commit a kidnapping, forcible rape, or forcible sodomy.

9. Jones and Smith, who have not met before, get into an argument in a tavern. Smith takes a punch at Jones, but misses. Jones then hits Smith on the chin with his fist. Smith falls to the floor and suffers minor injuries.
   According to the above passage, it would be CORRECT to state that _____ justified in using physical force.

   A. only Smith was
   B. only Jones was
   C. both Smith and Jones were
   D. neither Smith nor Jones was

10. While walking down the street, Brady observes Miller striking Mrs. Adams on the head with his fist in an attempt to steal her purse.
    According to the above passage, it would be CORRECT to state that Brady would

    A. not be justified in using deadly physical force against Miller since Brady can safely retreat
    B. be justified in using physical force against Miller but not deadly physical force
    C. not be justified in using physical force against Miller since Brady himself is not being attacked
    D. be justified in using deadly physical force

11. Winters is attacked from behind by Sharp, who attempts to beat up Winters with a blackjack. Winters disarms Sharp and succeeds in subduing him with a series of blows to the head. Sharp stops fighting and explains that he thought Winters was the person who had robbed his apartment a few minutes before, but now realizes his mistake.
    According to the above passage, it would be CORRECT to state that

    A. Winters was justified in using physical force on Sharp only to the extent necessary to defend himself
    B. Winters was not justified in using physical force on Sharp since Sharp's attack was provoked by what he believed to be Winters' behavior
    C. Sharp was justified in using physical force on Winters since he reasonably believed that Winters had unlawfully robbed him
    D. Winters was justified in using physical force on Sharp only because Sharp was acting mistakenly in attacking him

12. Roberts hears a noise in the cellar of his home, and, upon investigation, discovers an intruder, Welch. Welch moves towards Roberts in a threatening manner, thrusts his hand into a bulging pocket, and withdraws what appears to be a gun. Roberts thereupon strikes Welch over the head with a golf club. He then sees that the *gun* is a toy. Welch later dies of head injuries. According to the above passage, it would be CORRECT to state that Roberts was

    A. justified in using deadly physical force because he reasonably believed Welch was about to use deadly physical force
    B. not justified in using deadly physical force
    C. justified in using deadly physical force only because he did not provoke Welch's conduct
    D. justified in using deadly physical force only because he was not the initial aggressor

Questions 13-16.

DIRECTIONS: Questions 13 through 16 are to be answered SOLELY on the basis of the following passage.

From the beginning, the Supreme Court has supervised the fairness of trials conducted by the Federal government. But the Constitution, as originally drafted, gave the court no such general authority in state cases. The court's power to deal with state cases comes from the Fourteenth Amendment, which became part of the Constitution in 1868. The crucial provision forbids any state to *deprive any person of life, liberty, or property without due process of law.*

The guarantee of *due process* would seem, at the least, to require fair procedure in criminal trials. But curiously the Supreme Court did not speak on the question for many decades. During that time, however, the due process clause was interpreted to bar *unreasonable* state economic regulations, such as minimum wage laws.

In 1915, there came the case of Leo M. Frank, a Georgian convicted of murder in a trial that he contended was dominated by mob hysteria. Historians now agree that there was such hysteria, with overtones of anti-semitism.

The Supreme Court held that it could not look past the findings of the Georgia courts that there had been no mob atmosphere at the trial. Justices Oliver Wendell Holmes and Charles Evans Hughes dissented, arguing that the constitutional guarantee would be *a barren one* if the Federal courts could not make their own inferences from the facts.

In 1923, the case of Moore v. Dempsey involved five Arkansas Blacks convicted of murder and sentenced to death in a community so aroused against them that at one point they were saved from lynching only by Federal troops. Witnesses against them were said to have been beaten into testifying.

The court, though not actually setting aside the convictions, directed a lower Federal court to hold a habeas corpus hearing to find out whether the trial had been fair, or whether the whole proceeding had been *a mask—that counsel, jury, and judge were swept to the fatal end by an irresistible wave of public passion.*

13. According to the above passage, the Supreme Court's INITIAL interpretation of the Fourteenth Amendment

    A. protected state supremacy in economic matters
    B. increased the scope of Federal jurisdiction
    C. required fair procedures in criminal trials
    D. prohibited the enactment of minimum wage laws

14. According to the above passage, the Supreme Court in the Frank case

    A. denied that there had been mob hysteria at the trial
    B. decided that the guilty verdict was supported by the evidence
    C. declined to question the state court's determination of the facts
    D. found that Leo Frank had not received *due process*

15. According to the above passage, the dissenting judges in the Frank case maintained that

    A. due process was an empty promise in the circumstances of that case
    B. the Federal courts could not guarantee certain provisions of the Constitution
    C. the Federal courts should not make their own inferences from the facts in state cases
    D. the Supreme Court had rendered the Constitution *barren*

16. Of the following, the MOST appropriate title for the above passage is 16.___
    A. THE CONDUCT OF FEDERAL TRIALS
    B. THE DEVELOPMENT OF STATES' RIGHTS: 1868-1923
    C. MOORE V. DEMPSEY: A CASE STUDY IN CRIMINAL JUSTICE
    D. DUE PROCESS-THE EVOLUTION OF A CONSTITUTIONAL CORNERSTONE

Questions 17-20.

DIRECTIONS: Questions 17 through 20 are to be answered SOLELY on the basis of the following passage.

The difficulty experienced in determining which party has the burden of proving payment or non-payment is due largely to a lack of consistency between the rules of pleading and the rules of proof. In some cases, a plaintiff is obligated by a rule of pleading to allege non-payment on his complaint, yet is not obligated to prove non-payment on the trial. An action upon a contract for the payment of money will serve as an illustration. In such a case, the plaintiff must allege non-payment in his complaint, but the burden of proving payment on the trial is upon the defendant. An important and frequently cited case on this problem is Conkling v. Weatherwax. In that case, the action was brought to establish and enforce a legacy as a lien upon real property. The defendant alleged in her answer that the legacy had been paid. There was no witness competent to testify for the plaintiff to show that the legacy had not been paid. Therefore, the question of the burden of proof became of primary importance since, if the plaintiff had the burden of proving non-payment, she must fail in her action; whereas if the burden of proof was on the defendant to prove payment, the plaintiff might win. The Court of Appeals held that the burden of proof was on the plaintiff. In the course of his opinion, Judge Vann attempted to harmonize the conflicting cases on this subject, and for that purpose formulated three rules. These rules have been construed and applied to numerous subsequent cases. As so construed and applied, these may be summarized as follows:

Rule 1. In an action upon a contract for the payment of money only, where the complaint does not allege a balance due over and above all payments made, the plaintiff must allege nonpayment in his complaint, but the burden of proving payment is upon the defendant. In such a case, payment is an affirmative defense which the defendant must plead in his answer. If the defendant fails to plead payment, but pleads a general denial instead, he will not be permitted to introduce evidence of payment.

Rule 2. Where the complaint sets forth a balance in excess of all payments, owing to the structure of the pleading, burden is upon the plaintiff to prove his allegation. In this case, the defendant is not required to plead payment as a defense in his answer but may introduce evidence of payment under a general denial.

Rule 3. When the action is not upon contract for the payment of money, but is upon an obligation created by operation of law, or is for the enforcement of a lien where non-payment of the amount secured is part of the cause of action, it is necessary both to allege and prove the fact of nonpayment.

17. In the above passage, the case of Conkling v. Weatherwax was cited PRIMARILY to illustrate

    A. a case where the burden of proof was on the defendant to prove payment
    B. how the question of the burden of proof can affect the outcome of a case
    C. the effect of a legacy as a lien upon real property
    D. how conflicting cases concerning the burden of proof were harmonized

18. According to the above passage, the pleading of payment is a defense in Rule(s)

    A. 1, but not Rules 2 and 3
    B. 2, but not Rules 1 and 3
    C. 1 and 3, but not Rule 2
    D. 2 and 3, but not Rule 1

19. The facts in Conkling v. Weatherwax CLOSELY resemble the conditions described in

    A. Rule #1
    B. Rule #2
    C. Rule #3
    D. none of the rules

20. The MAJOR topic of the above passage may BEST be described as

    A. determining the ownership of property
    B. providing a legal definition
    C. placing the burden of proof
    D. formulating rules for deciding cases

Questions 21-25.

DIRECTIONS: Questions 21 through 25 are to be answered SOLELY on the basis of the following passage.

The law is quite clear that evidence obtained in violation of Section 605 of the Federal Communications Act is not admissible in Federal court. However, the law as to the admissibility of evidence in state court is far from clear. Had the Supreme Court of the United States made the wiretap exclusionary rule applicable to the states, such confusion would not exist.

In the case of Alton v. Texas, the Supreme Court was called upon to determine whether wiretapping by state and local officers came within the proscription of the Federal statute and, if so, whether Section 605 required the same remedies for its vindication in state courts. In answer to the first question, Mr. Justice Minton, speaking for the court, flatly stated that Section 605 made it a federal crime for anyone to intercept telephone messages and divulge what he learned. The court went on to say that a state officer who testified in state court concerning the existence, contents, substance, purport, effect, or meaning of an intercepted conversation violated the Federal law and committed a criminal act. In regard to the second question, how-ever, the Supreme Court felt constrained by due regard for federal-state relations to answer in the negative. Mr. Justice Minton stated that the court would not presume, in the absence of a clear manifestation of congressional intent, that Congress intended to supersede state rules of evidence.

Because the Supreme Court refused to apply the exclusionary rule to wiretap evidence that was being used in state courts, the states respectively made this decision for themselves. According to hearings held before a congressional committee in 1975, six states authorize wiretapping by statute, 33 states impose total bans on wiretapping, and 11 states have no definite statute on the subject. For examples of extremes, a statute in Pennsylvania will be compared with a statute in New York.

The Pennsylvania statute provides that no communications by telephone or telegraph can be intercepted without permission of both parties. It also specifically prohibits such interception by public officials and provides that evidence obtained cannot be used in court.

The lawmakers in New York, recognizing the need for legal wire-tapping, authorized wiretapping by statute. A New York law authorizes the issuance of an ex parte order upon oath or affirmation for limited wiretapping. The aim of the New York law is to allow court-ordered wiretapping and to encourage the testimony of state officers concerning such wiretapping in court. The New York law was found to be constitutional by the New York State Supreme Court in 1975. Other states, including Oregon, Maryland, Nevada, and Massachusetts, enacted similar laws which authorize court-ordered wiretapping.

To add to this legal disarray, the vast majority of the states, including New Jersey and New York, permit wiretapping evidence to be received in court even though obtained in violation of the state laws and of Section 605 of the Federal act. However, some states, such as Rhode Island, have enacted statutory exclusionary rules which provide that illegally procured wiretap evidence is incompetent in civil as well as criminal actions.

21. According to the above passage, a state officer who testifies in New York State court concerning the contents of a conversation he overheard through a court-ordered wire-tap is in violation of _____ law.

    A. state law but not federal
    B. federal law but not state
    C. federal law and state
    D. neither federal nor state

22. According to the above passage, which of the following statements concerning states statutes on wiretapping is CORRECT?

    A. The number of states that impose total bans on wiretapping is three times as great as the number of states with no definite statute on wiretapping.
    B. The number of states having no definite statute on wiretapping is more than twice the number of states authorizing wiretapping.
    C. The number of states which authorize wiretapping by statute and the number of states having no definite statute on wiretapping exceed the number of states imposing total bans on wiretapping.
    D. More states authorize wiretapping by statute than impose total bans on wiretapping.

23. Following are three statements concerning wiretapping that might be valid:
    I. In Pennsylvania, only public officials may legally intercept telephone communications.
    II. In Rhode Island, evidence obtained through an illegal wiretap is incompetent in criminal, but not civil, actions.
    III. Neither Massachusetts nor Pennsylvania authorizes wiretapping by public officials.

    According to the above passage, which of the following CORRECTLY classifies these statements into those that are valid and those that are not?

    A. I is valid, but II and III are not.
    B. II is valid, but I and III are not.
    C. II and III are valid, but I is not.
    D. None of the statements is valid.

24. According to the above passage, evidence obtained in violation of Section 605 of the Federal Communications Act is inadmissible in

    A. federal court but not in any state courts
    B. federal court and all state courts
    C. all state courts but not in federal court
    D. federal court and some state courts

25. In regard to state rules of evidence, Mr. Justice Minton expressed the Court's opinion that Congress

    A. intended to supersede state rules of evidence, as manifested by Section 605 of the Federal Communications Act
    B. assumed that federal statutes would govern state rules of evidence in all wiretap cases
    C. left unclear whether it intended to supersede state rules of evidence
    D. precluded itself from superseding state rules of evidence through its regard for federal-state relations

KEY (CORRECT ANSWERS)

1. B
2. B
3. A
4. C
5. B

6. C
7. D
8. D
9. B
10. B

11. A
12. A
13. D
14. C
15. A

16. D
17. B
18. A
19. C
20. C

21. B
22. A
23. D
24. D
25. C

TEST 2

DIRECTIONS: Each question or incomplete statement is followed by several suggested answers or completions. Select the one that BEST answers the question or completes the Statement. *PRINT THE LETTER OF THE CORRECT ANSWER IN THE SPACE AT THE RIGHT.*

Questions 1-3.

DIRECTIONS: Questions 1 through 3 are to be answered SOLELY on the basis of the following passage.

    The State Assembly has passed a bill that would require all state agencies, public authorities, and local governments to refuse bids in excess of $2,000 from any foreign firm or corporation. The only exceptions to this outright prohibition against public buying of foreign goods or services would be for products not available in this country, goods of a quality unobtainable from an American supplier, and products using foreign materials that are *substantially* manufactured in the United States.

    This bill is a flagrant violation of the United States' officially espoused trade principles. It would add to the costs of state and local governments. It could provoke retaliatory action from many foreign governments against the state and other American producers, and foreign governments would be fully entitled to take such retaliatory action under the General Agreement on Tariffs and Trade, which the United States has signed.

    The State Senate, which now has the Assembly bill before it, should reject this protectionist legislation out of enlightened regard for the interests of the taxpayers and producers of the State—as well as for those of the nation and its trading partners generally. In this time of unemployment and international monetary disorder, the State—with its reputation for intelligent and progressive law-making—should avoid contributing to what could become a tidal wave of protectionism here and overseas.

1. Under the requirements of the bill passed by the State Assembly, a bid from a foreign manufacturer in excess of $2,000 can be accepted by a state agency or local government only if it meets which one of the following requirements?
The

    A. bid is approved individually by the State Legislature
    B. bidder is willing to accept payment in United States currency
    C. bid is for an item of a quality unobtainable from an American supplier
    D. bid is for an item which would be more expensive if it were purchased from an American supplier

2. The author of the above passage feels that the bill passed by the State Assembly should be

    A. passed by the State Senate and put into effect
    B. passed by the State Senate but vetoed by the Governor
    C. reintroduced into the State Assembly and rejected
    D. rejected by the State Senate

3. The author of the above passage calls the practice of prohibiting purchase of products manufactured by foreign countries 3.___

   A. prohibition
   B. protectionism
   C. retaliatory action
   D. isolationism

Questions 4-7.

DIRECTIONS: Questions 4 through 7 are to be answered SOLELY on the basis of the following passage.

   Data processing is by no means a new invention. In one form or another, it has been carried on throughout the entire history of civilization. In its most general sense, data processing means organizing data so that it can be used for a specific purpose-a procedure commonly known simply as *record-keeping* or *paperwork*. With the development of modern office equipment, and particularly with the recent introduction of computers, the techniques of data processing have become highly elaborate and sophisticated, but the basic purpose remains the same: Turning raw data into useful information.

   The key concept here is usefulness. The data, or input, that is to be processed can be compared to the raw material that is to go into a manufacturing process. The information, or output, that results from data processing—like the finished product of a manufacturer—should be clearly usable. A collection of data has little value unless it is converted into information that serves a specific function.

4. The expression *paperwork,* as it is used in this passage, 4.___

   A. shows that the author regards such operations as a waste of time
   B. has the same general meaning as *data processing*
   C. refers to methods of record-keeping that are no longer in use
   D. indicates that the public does not understand the purpose of data processing

5. The above passage indicates that the use of computers has 5.___

   A. greatly simplified the clerical work in an office
   B. led to more complicated systems for the handling of data
   C. had no effect whatsoever on data processing
   D. made other modern office machines obsolete

6. Which of the following BEST expresses the basic principle of data processing as it is described in the above passage? 6.___

   A. Input-processing-output
   B. Historical record-keeping-modern techniques -specific functions
   C. Office equipment-computer-accurate data
   D. Raw material-manufacturer-retailer

7. According to the above passage, data processing may be described as 7.___

   A. a new management technique
   B. computer technology
   C. information output
   D. record-keeping

Questions 8-10.

DIRECTIONS: Questions 8 through 10 are to be answered SOLELY on the basis of the following passage.

A loan receipt is an instrument devised to permit the insurance company to bring an action against the wrongdoer in the name of the insured despite the fact that the insured no longer has any financial interest in the outcome. It provides, in effect, that the amount of the loss is advanced to the insured as a loan which is repayable only up to the extent of any recovery made from the wrongdoer. The insured further agrees to enter and prosecute suit against the wrongdoer in his own name. Such a receipt substitutes a loan for a payment for the purpose of permitting the insurance company to press its action against the wrongdoer in the name of the insured.

8. According to the above passage, the purpose behind the use of a loan receipt is to 8.____

   A. guarantee that the insurance company gets repayment from the person insured
   B. insure repayment of all expenditures to the named insured
   C. make it possible for the insurance company to sue in the name of the policyowner
   D. prevent the wrongdoer from escaping the natural consequences of his act

9. According to the above passage, the amount of the loan which must be paid back to the insurance company equals but does NOT exceed the amount 9.____

   A. of the loss
   B. on the face of the policy
   C. paid to the insured
   D. recovered from the wrongdoer

10. According to the above passage, by giving a loan receipt, the person insured agrees to 10.____

    A. a suit against the wrongdoer in his own name
    B. forego any financial gain from the outcome of the suit
    C. institute an action on behalf of the insurance company
    D. repay the insurance company for the loan received

Questions 11-12.

DIRECTIONS: Questions 11 and 12 are to be answered SOLELY on the basis of the following passage.

Open air markets originally came into existence spontaneously when groups of pushcart peddlers congregated in spots where business was good. Good business induced them to return to these spots daily and, thus, unofficial open air markets arose. These peddlers paid no fees, and the city received no revenue from them. Confusion and disorder reigned in these unsupervised markets; the earliest arrivals secured the best locations, unless or until forcibly ejected by stronger or tougher peddlers. Although the open air markets supplied a definite need in the community, there were many detrimental factors involved in their operation. They were unsightly, created unsanitary conditions in market streets by the deposit of garbage and waste and were a definite obstruction to traffic, as well as a fire hazard.

11. On the basis of the above passage, the MOST accurate of the following statements is:

    A. Each peddler in the original open air markets had his own fixed location.
    B. Open air markets were originally organized by means of agreements between groups of pushcart peddlers.
    C. The locations of these markets depended upon the amount of business the vendors were able to do.
    D. There was confusion and disorder in these open air markets because the peddlers were not required to pay any fees to the city.

12. Of the following, the MOST valid implication which can be made on the basis of the above passage is that the

    A. detrimental aspect of the operations of open air markets was the probable reason for the creation of enclosed markets under the supervision of the Department of Markets
    B. open air markets could not supply any community need without proper supervision
    C. original open air markets were good examples of the operation of fair competition in business
    D. possibility of obtaining a source of revenue was probably the most important reason for the city's ultimate undertaking of the supervision of open air markets

Questions 13-14.

DIRECTIONS: Questions 13 and 14 are to be answered SOLELY on the basis of the following passage.

A person who displays on his window, door, or in his place of business words or letters in Hebraic characters other than the word *kosher,* or any sign, emblem, insignia, six-pointed star, symbol or mark in simulation of same, without displaying in conjunction there-with in English letters of at least the same size as such characters, signs, emblems, insignia or marks, the words *we sell kosher meat and food only* or *we sell non-kosher meat and food only* or *we sell both kosher and non-kosher meat and food,* as the case may be, is guilty of a misdemeanor. Possession of non-kosher meat and food in any place of business advertising the sale of kosher meat and food only is presumptive evidence that the person in possession exposes the same for sale with intent to defraud, in violation of the provisions of this section.

13. Of the following, the MOST valid implication that can be made on the basis of the above passage is that a person who

    A. displays on his window a six-pointed star in addition to the word *kosher* in Hebraic letters is guilty of intent to defraud
    B. displays on his window the word *kosher* in Hebraic characters intends to indicate that he has only kosher food for sale
    C. sells both kosher and non-kosher food in the same place of business is guilty of a misdemeanor
    D. sells only that type of food which can be characterized as neither kosher nor non-kosher, such as fruit and vegetables, without an explanatory sign in English is guilty of intent to defraud

14. Of the following, the one which would constitute a violation of the rules of the above passage is a case in which a person 14.____

    A. displays the word *kosher* on his window in Hebraic letters has only kosher meat and food in the store but has some non-kosher meat in the rear of the establishment
    B. selling both kosher and non-kosher meat and food uses words in Hebraic letters, other than the word *kosher,* on his window and a sign of the same size letters in English stating *we sell both kosher and non-kosher meat and food*
    C. selling only kosher meat and food uses words in Hebraic letters, other than the word *kosher,* on his window and a sign of the same size letters in English stating *we sell kosher meat and food only*
    D. selling only non-kosher meat and food displays a six-pointed star on his window and a sign of the same size letters in English stating *we sell only non-kosher meat and food*

Questions 15-16.

DIRECTIONS: Questions 15 and 16 are to be answered SOLELY on the basis of the following passage.

COMMODITIES IN GLASS BOTTLES OR JARS

The contents of the bottle may be stated in terms of weight or of fluid measure, the weight being indicated in terms of pounds and ounces and the fluid measure being indicated in terms of gallons, quarts, pints, half-pints, gills, or fluid ounces. When contents are liquid, the amount should not be stated in terms of weight. The marking indicating content is to be on a tag attached to the bottle or upon a label. The letters shall be in bold-faced type at least one-ninth of an inch (1/9") in height for bottles or jars having a capacity of a gill, half-pint, pint, or multiples of a pint, and letters at least three-sixteenths of an inch (3/16") in height for bottles of other capacities, on a part of the tag or label free from other printing or ornamentation, leaving a clear space around the marking which indicates the contents.

15. Of the following, the one which does NOT meet the requirements of the above passage is a 15.____

    A. bottle of cooking oil with a label stating *contents—16 fluid ounces* in appropriate sized letters
    B. bottle of vinegar with a label stating *contents—8 ounces avoir.* in appropriate sized letters
    C. glass jar filled with instant coffee with a label stating *contents—1 lb. 3 ozs. avoir.* in appropriate sized letters
    D. glass jar filled with liquid bleach with a label stating *contents—1 quart* in appropriate sized letters

16. Of the following, the one which does meet the requirements of the above passage is a 16.____

    A. bottle filled with a low-calorie liquid sweetener with a label stating *contents—3 fluid ounces* in letters 1/12" high
    B. bottle filled with ammonia solution for cleaning with a label stating *contents—1 pint* in letters 1/10" high

C. jar filled with baking powder with a label stating *contents—$\frac{1}{2}$ pint* in letters $\frac{1}{4}$" high

D. jar filled with hard candy with a label stating *contents—1 lb. avoir.* in letters $\frac{1}{2}$" high

Question 17.

DIRECTIONS: Question 17 is to be answered SOLELY on the basis of the information contained in the following passage.

DEALERS IN SECOND HAND DEVICES

1. It shall be unlawful for any person to engage in or conduct the business of dealing in, trading in, selling, receiving, or repairing condemned, rebuilt, or used weighing or measuring devices without a permit therefor.

2. Such permit shall expire on the twenty-eighth day of February next succeeding the date of issuance thereof.

3. Every person engaged in the above business, within five days after the making of a repair, or the sale and delivery of a repaired, rebuilt, or used weighing or measuring device, shall serve notice in writing on the commissioner giving the name and address of the person for whom the repair has been made or to whom a repaired, rebuilt, or used weighing or measuring device has been sold or delivered, and shall include a statement that such device has been so altered, repaired, or rebuilt as to conform to the regulations of the department.

17. According to the above passage, the MOST accurate of the following statements is: 17.___

    A. A permit issued to engage in the business mentioned above, first issued on April 23, 1968, expired on February 28, 1969.
    B. A rebuilt or repaired weighing or measuring device should not operate with less error than the tolerances permitted by the regulations of the department.
    C. If a used scale in good condition is sold, it is not necessary for the seller to notify the commissioner of the name and address of the buyer.
    D. There is a difference in the time required to notify the commissioner of a repair or of a sale of a repaired device.

Questions 18-19.

DIRECTIONS: Questions 18 and 19 are to be answered SOLELY on the basis of the following passage.

A. It shall be unlawful for any person, firm, or corporation to sell or offer for sale at retail for use in internal combustion engines in motor vehicles any gasoline unless such seller shall post and keep continuously posted on the individual pump or other dispensing device from which such gasoline is sold or offered for sale a sign or placard not less than seven inches in height and eight inches in width nor larger than twelve inches in height and twelve inches in width and stating clearly in numbers of uniform size the selling price or prices per gallon of such gasoline so sold or offered for sale from such pump or other dispensing device.

B. The amount of governmental tax to be collected in connection with the sale of such gasoline shall be stated on such sign or placard and separately and apart from such selling price or prices.

18. The one of the following price signs posted on a gasoline pump which would be in violation of the above passage is a sign _____ square inches in size and _____ inches high.

    A. 144; 12   B. 84; 7   C. 72; 12   D. 60; 8

19. According to the above passage, the LEAST accurate of the following statements is:

    A. Gasoline may be sold from a dispensing device other than a pump.
    B. If two different pumps are used to sell the same grade of gasoline, a price sign must appear on each pump.
    C. The amount of governmental tax and the price of the gasoline must not be stated on the same sign.
    D. The sizes of the numbers used on a sign to indicate the price of gasoline must be the same.

Questions 20-21.

DIRECTIONS: Questions 20 and 21 are to be answered SOLELY on the basis of the following passage.

In all systems of weights and measures based on one or more arbitrary fundamental units, the concrete representation of the unit in the form of a standard is necessary, and the construction and preservation of such a standard is a matter of primary importance. Therefore, it is essential that the standard should be so constructed as to be as nearly permanent and invariable as human ingenuity can contrive. The reference of all measures to an original standard is essential for their correctness, and such a standard must be maintained and preserved in its integrity by some responsible authority which is thus able to provide against the use of false weights and measures. Accordingly, from earliest times, standards were constructed and preserved under the direction of kings and priests, and the temples were a favorite place for their deposit. Later, this duty was assumed by the government, and today we find the integrity of standards of weights and measures safeguarded by international agreement.

20. Of the following, the MOST valid implication which can be made on the basis of the above passage is that

    A. fundamental units of systems of weights and measures should be represented by quantities so constructed that they are specific and constant
    B. in the earliest times, standards were so constructed that they were as permanent and invariable as modern ones
    C. international agreement has practically relieved the U.S. government of the necessity of preserving standards of weights and measures
    D. the preservation of standards is of less importance than the ingenuity used in their construction

21. Of the following, the MOST appropriate title for the above passage is

    A. THE CONSTRUCTION AND PRESERVATION OF STANDARDS OF WEIGHTS AND MEASURES
    B. THE FIXING OF RESPONSIBILITY FOR THE ESTABLISHMENT OF STANDARDS OF WEIGHTS AND MEASURES
    C. THE HISTORY OF SYSTEMS OF WEIGHTS AND MEASURES
    D. THE VALUE OF PROPER STANDARDS IN PROVIDING CORRECT WEIGHTS AND MEASURES

Questions 22-23.

DIRECTIONS: Questions 22 and 23 are to be answered SOLELY on the basis of the following passage.

Accurate weighing and good scales insure that excess is not given just for the sake of good measure. No more striking example of the fundamental importance of correct weighing to the business man is found than in the simple and usual relation where a charge or value is obtained by multiplying a weight by a unit price. For example, a scale may weigh *light,* that is, the actual quantity delivered is in excess by 1 percent. The actual result is that the seller taxes himself. If his profit is supposed to be 10 percent of total sales, an overweight of 1 percent represents 10 percent of that profit. Under these conditions, the situation is as though the seller were required to pay a sales tax equivalent to what he is taxing himself.

22. Of the following, the MOST valid implication which can be made on the basis of the above passage is that

    A. consistent use of scales that weigh *light* will reduce sellers' profits
    B. no good businessman would give any buyer more than the weight required even if his scale is accurate
    C. the kind of situation described in the above passage could not arise if sales were being made of merchandise sold by the yard
    D. the use of incorrect scales is one of the reasons causing governments to impose sales taxes

23. According to the above passage, the MOST accurate of the following statements is:

    A. If his scale weighs *light* by an amount of 2 percent, the seller would deliver only 98 pounds when 100 pounds was the amount agreed upon.
    B. If the seller's scale weighs *heavy,* the buyer will receive an amount in excess of what he intended to purchase.
    C. If the seller's scale weighs *light* by an amount of 1 percent, a buyer who agreed to purchase 50 pounds of merchandise would actually receive $50\frac{1}{2}$ pounds.
    D. The use of a scale which delivers an amount which is in excess of that required is an example of deliberate fraud.

Questions 24-25.

DIRECTIONS: Questions 24 and 25 are to be answered SOLELY on the basis of the following passage.

Food shall be deemed to be misbranded:
1. If its labeling is false or misleading in any particular.

2. If any word, statement, or other information required by or under authority of this article to appear on the label or labeling is not prominently placed thereon with such conspicuousness (as compared with other words, statements, designs, or devices in the labeling) and in such terms as to render it likely to be read and understood by the ordinary individual under customary conditions of purchase and use.

3. If it purports to be or is represented as a food for which a standard of quality has been prescribed and its quality falls below such standard, unless its label bears a statement that it falls below such standard.

24. According to the above passage, the MOST accurate of the following statements is:

    A. A food may be considered misbranded if the label contains a considerable amount of information which is not required.
    B. If a consumer purchased one type of canned food, although he intended to buy another, the food is probably misbranded.
    C. If a food is used in large amounts by a group of people of certain foreign origin, it can be considered misbranded unless the label is in the foreign language with which they are familiar.
    D. The required information on a label is likely to be in larger print than other information which may appear on it.

25. According to the above passage, the one of the following foods which may be considered to be misbranded is a

    A. can of peaches with a label which carries the brand name of the packer but states *Below Standard in Quality*
    B. can of vegetables with a label on which is printed a shield which states *U.S. Grade B*
    C. package of frozen food which has some pertinent information printed on it in very small type which a customer cannot read and which the store manager cannot read when asked to do so by the customer
    D. package of margarine of the same size as the usual package of butter, kept near the butter, but clearly labeled as margarine

KEY (CORRECT ANSWERS)

1. C
2. D
3. B
4. B
5. B

6. A
7. D
8. C
9. D
10. A

11. C
12. A
13. B
14. A
15. B

16. D
17. A
18. C
19. C
20. A

21. D
22. A
23. C
24. D
25. C

PREPARING WRITTEN MATERIALS
EXAMINATION SECTION
TEST 1

DIRECTIONS: Each question or incomplete statement is followed by several suggested answers or completions. Select the one that BEST answers the question or completes the statement. *PRINT THE LETTER OF THE CORRECT ANSWER IN THE SPACE AT THE RIGHT.*

Questions 1-25.

DIRECTIONS: Questions 1 through 25 consist of sentences which may or may not be examples of good English usage. Consider grammar, punctuation, spelling, capitalization, awkwardness, etc. Examine each sentence and then choose the correct statement about it from the four choices below it. If the English usage in the sentence given is better than it would be with any of the changes suggested in options B, C, and D, choose option A. Do not choose an option that will change the meaning of the sentence.

1. According to Judge Frank, the grocer's sons found guilty of assault and sentenced last Thursday.
    A. This is an example of acceptable writing.
    B. A comma should be placed after the word *sentenced*.
    C. The word *were* should be placed after *sons*.
    D. The apostrophe in grocer's should be placed after the *s*.

1._____

2. The department heads assistant said that the stenographers should type duplicate copies of all contracts, leases, and bills.
    A. This is an example of acceptable writing,
    B. A comma should be placed before the word "*contracts*.
    C. An apostrophe should be placed before the *s* in *heads*.
    D. Quotation marks should be placed before the *stenographers* and after *bills*.

2._____

3. The lawyers questioned the men to determine who was the true property owner?
    A. This is an example of acceptable writing.
    B. The phrase *questioned the men* should be changed to *asked the men questions*.
    C. The word *was* should be changed to *were*.
    D. The question mark should be changed to a period.

3._____

4. The terms stated in the present contract are more specific than those stated in the previous contract.
   A. This is an example of acceptable writing,
   B. The word *are* should be changed to *is*.
   C. The word *than* should be changed to *then*.
   D. The word *specific* should be changed to *specified*.

   4._____

5. Of the few lawyers considered, the one who argued more skillful was chosen for the job.
   A. This is an example of acceptable writing.
   B. The word *more* should be replaced by the word *most*.
   C. The word *skillful* should be replaced by the word *skillfully*.
   D. The word *chosen* should be replaced by the word *selected*.

   5._____

6. Each of the states has a court of appeals; some states have circuit courts.
   A. This is an example of acceptable writing
   B. The semi-colon should be changed to a comma.
   C. The word *has* should be changed to *have*.
   D. The word *some* should be capitalized.

   6._____

7. The court trial has greatly effected the child's mental condition.
   A. This is an example of acceptable writing.
   B. The word *effected* should be changed to *affected*.
   C. The word *greatly* should be placed after *effected*.
   D. The apostrophe in *child's* should be placed after the *s*.

   7._____

8. Last week, the petition signed by all the officers was sent to the Better Business Bureau.
   A. This is an example of acceptable writing.
   B. The phrase *last week* should be placed after *officers*.
   C. A comma should be placed after *petition*.
   D. The word *was* should be changed to *were*.

   8._____

9. Mr. Farrell claims that he requested form A-12, and three booklets describing court procedures.
   A. This is an example of acceptable writing.
   B. The word *that* should be eliminated.
   C. A colon should be placed after *requested*.
   D. The comma after *A-12* should be eliminated.

   9._____

10. We attended a staff conference on Wednesday the new safety and fire rules were discussed.
    A. This is an example of acceptable writing.
    B. The words *safety*, *fire*, and *rules* should begin with capital letters.
    C. There should be a comma after the word *Wednesday*.
    D. There should be a period after the word *Wednesday*, and the word *the* should begin with a capital letter.

    10._____

11. Neither the dictionary or the telephone directory could be found in the office library.
    A. This is an example of acceptable writing.
    B. The word *or* should be changed to *nor*.
    C. The word *library* should be spelled *libery*.
    D. The word *neither* should be changed to *either*.

11.____

12. The report would have been typed correctly if the typist could read the draft.
    A. This is an example of acceptable writing.
    B. The word *would* should be removed.
    C. The word *have* should be inserted after the word *could*.
    D. The word *correctly* should be changed to *correct*.

12.____

13. The supervisor brought the reports and forms to an employees desk.
    A. This is an example of acceptable writing.
    B. The word *brought* should be changed to *took*.
    C. There should be a comma after the word *reports* and a comma after the word *forms*.
    D. The word *employees* should be spelled *employee's*.

13.____

14. It's important for all the office personnel to submit their vacation schedules on time.
    A. This is an example of acceptable writing.
    B. The word *It's* should be spelled *Its*.
    C. The word *their* should be spelled *they're*.
    D. The word *personnel* should be spelled *personal*.

14.____

15. The supervisor wants that all staff members report to the office at 9:00 A.M.
    A. This is an example of acceptable writing.
    B. The word *that* should be removed and the word *to* should be inserted after the word *members*.
    C. There should be a comma after the word *wants* and a comma after the word *office*.
    D. The word *wants* should be changed to *want* and the word *shall* should be inserted after the word *members*.

15.____

16. Every morning the clerk opens the office mail and distributes it.
    A. This is an example of acceptable writing.
    B. The word *opens* should be changed to *letters*.
    C. The word *mail* should be changed to *letters*.
    D. The word *it* should be changed to *them*.

16.____

17. The secretary typed more fast on a desktop computer than on a tablet.
    A. This is an example of acceptable writing.
    B. The words *more fast* should be changed to *faster*.
    C. There should be a comma after the words *desktop computer*.
    D. The word *than* should be changed to *then*.

17.____

18. The typist used an extention cord in order to connect her typewriter to the outlet nearest to her desks.   18._____
    A. This is an example of acceptable writing.
    B. A period should be placed after the word *cord*, and the word *in* should have a capital *I*.
    C. A comma should be placed after the word *typewriter*.
    D. The word *extention* should be spelled *extension*.

19. He would have went to the conference if he had received an invitation.   19._____
    A. This is an example of acceptable writing.
    B. The word *went* should be replaced by the word *gone*.
    C. The word *had* should be replaced by *would have*.
    D. The word *conference* should be spelled *conferance*.

20. In order to make the report neater, he spent many hours rewriting it.   20._____
    A. This is an example of acceptable writing.
    B. The word *more* should be inserted before the word *neater*.
    C. There should be a colon after the word *neater*,
    D. The word *spent* should be changed to *have spent*.

21. His supervisor told him that he should of read the memorandum more carefully.   21._____
    A. This is an example of acceptable writing.
    B. The word *memorandum* should be spelled *memorandom*.
    C. The word *of* should be replaced by the word *have*.
    D. The word *carefully* should be replaced by the word *careful*.

22. It was decided that two separate reports should be written.   22._____
    A. This is an example of acceptable writing.
    B. A comma should be inserted after the word *decided*.
    C. The word *be* should be replaced by the word *been*.
    D. A colon should be inserted after the word *that*.

23. She don't seem to understand that the work must be done as soon as possible.   23._____
    A. This is an example of acceptable writing.
    B. The word *doesn't* should replace the word *don't*.
    C. The word *why* should replace the word *that*.
    D. The word *as* before the word *soon* should be eliminated.

24. He excepted praise from his supervisor for a job well done.   24._____
    A. This is an example of acceptable writing.
    B. The word *excepted* should be spelled *accepted*.
    C. The order of the words *well done* should be changed to *done well*.
    D. There should be a comma after the word *supervisor*.

25. What appears to be intentional errors in grammar occur several times in the passage.
    A. This is an example of acceptable writing.
    B. The word *occur* should be spelled *occur*.
    C. The word *appears* should be changed to *appear*.
    D. The phrase *several times* should be changed to *from time to time*.

25.____

KEY (CORRECT ANSWERS)

1.	C	11.	B
2.	C	12.	C
3.	D	13.	D
4.	A	14.	A
5.	C	15.	B
6.	A	16.	A
7.	B	17.	B
8.	A	18.	D
9.	D	19.	B
10.	D	20.	A

21.	C
22.	A
23.	B
24.	B
25.	C

TEST 2

DIRECTIONS: Each question consists of a sentence which may or may not be an example of good formal English usage. Examine each sentence, considering grammar, punctuation, spelling, capitalization, and awkwardness. Then choose the CORRECT statement about it from the four options below it. If the English usage in the sentence given is better than any of the changes suggested in options B, C, or D, pick option A. Do not pick an option that will change the meaning of the sentence. *PRINT THE LETTER OF THE CORRECT ANSWER IN THE SPACE AT THE RIGHT.*

1. I don't know who could possibly of broken it.
   A. This is an example of acceptable writing.
   B. The word *who* should be replaced by the word *whom*.
   C. The word *of* should be replaced by the word *have*.
   D. The word *broken* should be replaced by the word *broke*.

2. Telephoning is easier than to write.
   A. This is an example of acceptable writing.
   B. The word *telephoning* should be spelled *telephoneing*.
   C. The word *than* should be replaced by the word *then*.
   D. The words *to write* should be replaced by the word *writing*.

3. The two operators who have been assigned to these consoles are on vacation.
   A. This is an example of acceptable writing.
   B. A comma should be placed after the word *operators*.
   C. The word *who* should be replaced by the word *whom*.
   D. The word *are* should be replaced by the word *is*.

4. You were suppose to teach me how to operate a plugboard.
   A. This is an example of acceptable writing,
   B. The word *were* should be replaced by the word *was*.
   C. The word *suppose* should be replaced by the word *supposed*.
   D. The word *teach* should be replaced by the word *team*.

5. If you had taken my advice; you would have spoken with him.
   A. This is an example of acceptable writing.
   B. The word *advice* should be spelled *advise*.
   C. The words *had taken* should be replaced by the word *take*.
   D. The semicolon should be changed to a comma.

6. The clerk could have completed the assignment on time if he knows where these materials were located.
   A. This is an example of acceptable writing.
   B. The word *knows* should be replaced by *had known*.
   C. The word "were" should be replaced by *had been*.
   D. The words *where these materials were located* should be replaced by *the location of these materials*.

7. All employees should be given safety training. Not just those who have accidents.
   A. This is an example of acceptable writing,
   B. The period after the word *training* should be changed to a colon.
   C. The period after the word *training* should be changed to a semicolon and the first letter of the word *Not* should be changed to a small *n*.
   D. The period after the word *training* should be changed to a comma, and the first letter of the word *Not* should be changed to a small *n*,

8. This proposal is designed to promote employee awareness of the suggestion program, to encourage employee participation in the program, and to increase the number of suggestions submitted.
   A. This is an example of acceptable writing.
   B. The word *proposal* should be spelled *proposal*.
   C. The words *to increase the number of suggestions submitted* should be changed to *an increase in the number of suggestions is expected*.
   D. The word *promote* should be changed to *enhance*, and the word *increase* should be changed to *add to*.

9. The introduction of inovative managerial techniques should be preceded by careful analysis of the specific circumstances and conditions in each department.
   A. This is an example of acceptable writing.
   B. The word *techniques* should be spelled *techneques*.
   C. The word *inovative* should be spelled *innovative*.
   D. A comma should be placed after the word *circumstances* and after the word *conditions*.

10. This occurrence indicates that such criticism embarrasses him.
    A. This is an example of acceptable writing.
    B. The word *occurrence* should be spelled *occurrence*.
    C. The word *criticism* should be spelled *creticism*.
    D. The word *embarrasses* should be spelled *embarasses*.

11. He can recommend a mechanic whose work is reliable.
    A. This is an example of acceptable writing.
    B. the word *reliable* should be spelled *relyable*.
    C. The word *whose* should be spelled *who's*.
    D. The word *mechanic* should be spelled *mecanic*.

12. She typed quickly; like someone who had not a moment to lose.
    A. This is an example of acceptable writing.
    B. The word *not* should be removed.
    C. The semicolon should be changed to a comma.
    D. The word *quickly* should be placed before instead of after the word *typed*.

13. She insisted that she had to much work to do. 13.____
    A. This is an example of acceptable writing.
    B. The word *insisted* should be spelled *insisted*.
    C. The word *to* used in front of *much* should be spelled *too*.
    D. The word *do* should be changed to *be done*.

14. The report, along with the accompanying documents, were submitted for 14.____
    review.
    A. This is an example of acceptable writing.
    B. The words *were submitted* should be changed to *was submitted*.
    C. The word *accompanying* should be spelled *accompaning*.
    D. The comma after the word *report* should be taken out.

15. If others must use your files, be certain that they understand how the system 15.____
    works, but insist that you do all the filing and refiling.
    A. This is an example of acceptable writing.
    B. There should be a period after the word *works*, and the word *but* should start a new sentence.
    C. The words *filing* and *refiling* should be spelled *fileing* and *refileing*.
    D. There should be a comma after the word *but*.

16. The appeal was not considered because of its late arrival. 16.____
    A. This is an example of acceptable writing.
    B. The word *its* should be changed to *it's*.
    C. The word *its* should be changed to *the*.
    D. The words *late arrival* should be changed to *arrival late*.

17. The letter must be read carefully to determine under which subject it should 17.____
    be filed.
    A. This is an example of acceptable writing.
    B. The word *under* should be changed to *at*.
    C. The word *determine* should be spelled *determin*.
    D. The word *carefully* should be spelled *carefuly*.

18. He showed potential as an office manager, but he lacked skill in delegating 18.____
    work.
    A. This is an example of acceptable writing.
    B. The word *delegating* should be spelled *delagating*.
    C. The word *potential* should be spelled *potencial*.
    D. The words *he lacked* should be changed to *was lacking*.

19. His supervisor told him that it would be all right to receive personal mail at 19.____
    the office.
    A. This is an example of acceptable writing.
    B. The words *all right* should be changed to *alright*.
    C. The word *personal* should be spelled *personel*.
    D. The word *mail* should be changed to *letters*.

20. The report, along with the accompanying documents, were submitted for review. 20.____
    A. This is an example of acceptable writing.
    B. The words *were submitted* should be changed to *was submitted*.
    C. The word *accompanying* should be spelled *accompaning*.
    D. The comma after the word *report* should be taken out.

KEY (CORRECT ANSWERS)

1. C	11. A
2. D	12. C
3. A	13. C
4. C	14. B
5. D	15. A
6. B	16. A
7. D	17. D
8. A	18. A
9. C	19. A
10. A	20. B

PREPARING WRITTEN MATERIAL

PARAGRAPH REARRANGEMENT
COMMENTARY

The sentences that follow are in scrambled order. You are to rearrange them in proper order and indicate the letter choice containing the correct answer at the space at the right.

Each group of sentences in this section is actually a paragraph presented in scrambled order. Each sentence in the group has a place in that paragraph; no sentence is to be left out. You are to read each group of sentences and decide upon the best order in which to put the sentences so as to form a well-organized paragraph.

The questions in this section measure the ability to solve a problem when all the facts relevant to its solution are not given.

More specifically, certain positions of responsibility and authority require the employee to discover connection between events sometimes, apparently, unrelated. In order to do this, the employee will find it necessary to correctly infer that unspecified events have probably occurred or are likely to occur. This ability becomes especially important when action must be taken on incomplete information.

Accordingly, these questions require competitors to choose among several suggested alternatives, each of which presents a different sequential arrangement of the events. Competitors must choose the MOST logical of the suggested sequences.

In order to do so, they may be required to draw on general knowledge to infer missing concepts or events that are essential to sequencing the given events. Competitors should be careful to infer only what is essential to the sequence. The plausibility of the wrong alternatives will always require the inclusion of unlikely events or of additional chains of events which are NOT essential to sequencing the given events.

It's very important to remember that you are looking for the best of the four possible choices, and that the best choice of all may not even be one of the answers you're given to choose from.

There is no one right way to solve these problems. Many people have found it helpful to first write out the order of the sentences, as they would have arranged them, on their scrap paper before looking at the possible answers. If their optimum answer is there, this can save them some time. If it isn't, this method can still give insight into solving the problem. Others find it most helpful to just go through each of the possible choices, contrasting each as they go along. You should use whatever method feels comfortable and works for you.

While most of these types of questions are not that difficult, we've added a higher percentage of the difficult type, just to give you more practice. Usually there are only one or two questions on this section that contain such subtle distinctions that you're unable to answer confidently. And you then may find yourself stuck deciding between two possible choices, neither of which you're sure about.

EXAMINATION SECTION
TEST 1

DIRECTIONS: The sentences that follow are in scrambled order. You are to rearrange them in proper order and indicate the letter choice containing the correct answer. *PRINT THE LETTER OF THE CORRECT ANSWER IN THE SPACE AT THE RIGHT.*

1. Below are four statements labeled W, X, Y and Z.
   W. He was a strict and fanatic drillmaster.
   X. The word is always used in a derogatory sense and generally shows resentment and anger on the part of the user.
   Y. It is from the name of this Frenchman that we derive our English word, martinet.
   Z. Jean Martinet was the Inspector-General of Infantry during the reign of King Louis XIV.
   The PROPER order in which these sentences should be placed in a paragraph is:
   A. X, Z, W, Y   B. X, Z, Y, W   C. Z, W, Y, X   D. Z, Y, W, X

   1.____

2. In the following paragraph, the sentences, which are numbered, have been jumbled.
   I. Since then it has undergone changes.
   II. It was incorporated in 1955 under the laws of the State of New York.
   III. Its primary purposes, a cleaner city, has, however, remained the same.
   IV. The Citizens Committee works in cooperation with the Mayor's Inter-departmental Committee for a Clean City.
   The order in which these sentences should be arranged to form a well-organized paragraph is:
   A. II, IV, I, III   B. III, IV, I, II   C. IV, II, I, III   D. IV, III, II, I

   2.____

   3.____

Questions 3-5.

DIRECTIONS: The sentences listed below are part of a meaningful paragraph but they are not given in their proper order. You are to decide what would be the BEST order in which to put the sentences so as to form a well-organized paragraph. Each sentence has a place in the paragraph; there are no extra sentences. You are then to answer Questions 3 through 5 inclusive on the basis of your rearrangements of these scrambled sentences into a properly organized paragraph.

In 1887 some insurance companies organized an Inspection Department to advise their clients on all phases of fire prevention and protection. Probably this has been due to the smaller annual fire losses in Great Britain than in the United States. It tests various fire prevention devices and appliances and determines manufacturing hazards and their safeguards. Fire research began earlier in the United States and is more advanced than in Great Britain. Later they established a laboratory specializing in electrical, mechanical, hydraulic, and chemical fields.

251

2 (#1)

3. When the five sentences are arranged in proper order, the paragraph starts with the sentence which begins
   A. "In 1887…"
   B. "Probably this…"
   C. "It tests…"
   D. "Fire research…"
   E. "Later they…"

   3._____

4. In the last sentence listed above, "they" refers to
   A. the insurance companies
   B. the United States and Great Britain
   C. the Inspection Department
   D. clients
   E. technicians

   4._____

5. When the above paragraph is properly arranged, it ends with the words
   A. "…and protection."
   B. "…the United States."
   C. "…their safeguards."
   D. "…in Great Britain."
   E. "…chemical fields."

   5._____

KEY (CORRECT ANSWERS)

1. C
2. C
3. D
4. A
5. C

TEST 2

DIRECTIONS: In each of the questions numbered I through V, several sentences are given. For each question, choose as your answer the group of number that represents the MOST logical order of these sentences if they were arranged in paragraph form. *PRINT THE LETTER OF THE CORRECT ANSWER IN THE SPACE AT THE RIGHT.*

1.
   I. It is established when one shows that the landlord has prevented the tenant's enjoyment of his interest in the property leased.
   II. Constructive eviction is the result of a breach of the covenant of quiet enjoyment implied in all leases.
   III. In some parts of the United States, it is not complete until the tenant vacates within a reasonable time.
   IV. Generally, the acts must be of such serious and permanent character as to deny the tenant the enjoyment of his possessing rights.
   V. In this event, upon abandonment of the premises, the tenant's liability for that ceases.
   The CORRECT answer is:
   A. II, I, IV, III, V
   B. V, II, III, I, IV
   C. IV, III, I, II, V
   D. I, III, V, IV, II

   1.____

2.
   I. The powerlessness before private and public authorities that is the typical experience of the slum tenant is reminiscent of the situation of blue-collar workers all through the nineteenth century.
   II. Similarly, in recent years, this chapter of history has been reopened by anti-poverty groups which have attempted to organize slum tenants to enable them to bargain collectively with their landlords about the conditions of their tenancies.
   III. It is familiar history that many of the worker remedied their condition by joining together and presenting their demands collectively.
   IV. Like the workers, tenants are forced by the conditions of modern life into substantial dependence on these who possess great political aid and economic power.
   V. What's more, the very fact of dependence coupled with an absence of education and self-confidence makes them hesitant and unable to stand up for what they need from those in power.
   The CORRECT answer is:
   A. V, IV, I, II, III
   B. II, III, I, V, IV
   C. III, I, V, IV, II
   D. I, IV, V, III, II

   2.____

3.
   I. A railroad, for example, when not acting as a common carrier may contract away responsibility for its own negligence.
   II. As to a landlord, however, no decision has been found relating to the legal effect of a clause shifting the statutory duty of repair to the tenant.
   III. The courts have not passed on the validity of clauses relieving the landlord of this duty and liability.
   IV. They have, however, upheld the validity of exculpatory clauses in other types of contracts.

   3.____

253

V. Housing regulations impose a duty upon the landlord to maintain leased premises in safe condition.
VI. As another example, a bailee may limit his liability except for gross negligence, willful acts, or fraud.

The CORRECT answer is:
- A. II, I, VI, IV, III, V
- B. I, III, IV, V, VI, II
- C. III, V, I, IV, II, VI
- D. V, III, IV, I, VI, II

4.
I. Since there are only samples in the building, retail or consumer sales are generally eschewed by mart occupants, and in some instances, rigid controls are maintained to limit entrance to the mart only to those persons engaged in retailing.
II. Since World War I, in many larger cities, there has developed a new type of property, called the mart building.
III. It can, therefore, be used by wholesalers and jobbers for the display of sample merchandise.
IV. This type of building is most frequently a multi-storied, finished interior property which is a cross between a retail arcade and a loft building.
V. This limitation enables the mart occupants to ship the orders from another location after the retailer or dealer makes his selection from the samples.

The CORRECT answer is:
- A. II, IV, III, I, V
- B. IV, III, V, I, II
- C. I, III, II, IV, V
- D. I, IV, II, III, V

5.
I. In general, staff-line friction reduces the distinctive contribution of staff personnel.
II. The conflicts, however, introduce an uncontrolled element into the managerial system.
III. On the other hand, the natural resistance of the line to staff innovations probably usefully restrains over-eager efforts to apply untested procedures on a large scale.
IV. Under such conditions, it is difficult to know when valuable ideas are being sacrificed.
V. The relatively weak position of staff, requiring accommodation to the line, tends to restrict their ability to engage in free, experimental innovation.

The CORRECT answer is:
- A. IV, II, III, I, V
- B. I, V, III, II, IV
- C. V, III, I, II, IV
- D. II, I, IV, V, III

KEY (CORRECT ANSWERS)

1. A
2. D
3. D
4. A
5. B

TEST 3

DIRECTIONS: Questions 1 through 4 consist of six sentences which can be arranged in a logical sequence. For each question, select the choice which places the numbered sentences in the MOST logical sequent. *PRINT THE LETTER OF THE CORRECT ANSWER IN THE SPACE AT THE RIGHT.*

1.
   I. The burden of proof as to each issue is determined before trial and remains upon the same party throughout the trial.
   II. The jury is at liberty to believe one witness' testimony as against a number of contradictory witnesses.
   III. In a civil case, the party bearing the burden of proof is required to prove his contention by a fair preponderance of the evidence.
   IV. However, it must be noted that a fair preponderance of evidence does not necessarily mean a greater number of witnesses.
   V. The burden of proof is the burden which rests upon one of the parties to an action to persuade the trier of the facts, generally the jury, that a proposition he asserts is true.
   VI. If the evidence is equally balanced, or if it leaves the jury in such doubt as to be unable to decide the controversy either way, judgment must be given against the party upon whom the burden of proof rests.
   The CORRECT answer is:
   A. III, II, V, IV, I, VI
   B. I, II, VI, V, III, IV
   C. III, IV, V, I, II, VI
   D. V, I, III, VI, IV, II

   1.____

2.
   I. If a parent is without assets and is unemployed, he cannot be convicted of the crime of non-support of a child.
   II. The term "sufficient ability" has been held to mean sufficient financial ability.
   III. It does not matter if his unemployment is by choice or unavoidable circumstances.
   IV. If he fails to take any steps at all, he may be liable to prosecution for endangering the welfare of a child.
   V. Under the penal law, a parent is responsible for the support of his minor child only if the parent is "of sufficient ability."
   VI. An indigent parent may meet his obligation by borrowing money or by seeking aid under the provisions of the Social Welfare Law.
   The CORRECT answer is:
   A. VI, I, V, III, II, IV
   B. I, III, V, II, IV, VI
   C. V, II, I, III, VI, IV
   D. I, VI, IV, V, II, III

   2.____

3.
   I. Consider, for example, the case of a rabble rouser who urges a group of twenty people to go out and break the windows of a nearby factory.
   II. Therefore, the law fills the indicated gap with the crime of inciting to riot.
   III. A person is considered guilty of inciting to riot when he urges ten or more persons to engage in tumultuous and violent conduct of a kind likely to create public alarm.
   IV. However, if he has not obtained the cooperation of at least four people, he cannot be charged with unlawful assembly.

   3.____

255

V. The charge of inciting to riot was added to the law to cover types of conduct which cannot be classified as either the crime of "riot" or the crime of "unlawful assembly."
VI. If he acquires the acquiescence of at least four of them, he is guilty of unlawful assembly even if the project does not materialize.

The CORRECT answer is:
A. III, V, I, VI, IV, II
B. V, I, IV, VI, II, III
C. III, IV, I, V, II, VI
D. V, I, IV, VI, III, II

4.
I. If, however, the rebuttal evidence presents an issue of credibility, it is for the jury to determine whether the presumption has, in fact, been destroyed.
II. Once sufficient evidence to the contrary is introduced, the presumption disappears from the trial.
III. The effect of a presumption is to place the burden upon the adversary to come forward with evidence to rebut the presumption.
IV. When a presumption is overcome and ceases to exist in the case, the fact or facts which gave rise to the presumption still remain.
V. Whether a presumption has been overcome is ordinarily a question for the court.
VI. Such information may furnish a basis for a logical inference.

The CORRECT answer is:
A. IV, VI, II, V, I, III
B. III, II, V, I, IV, VI
C. V, III, VI, IV, II, I
D. V, IV, I, II, VI, III

4._____

KEY (CORRECT ANSWERS)

1. D
2. C
3. A
4. B

GLOSSARY OF LEGAL TERMS

TABLE OF CONTENTS

	Page
Action ... Affiant	1
Affidavit ... At Bar	2
At Issue ... Burden of Proof	3
Business ... Commute	4
Complainant ... Conviction	5
Cooperative ... Demur (v.)	6
Demurrage ... Endorsement	7
Enjoin ... Facsimile	8
Factor ... Guilty	9
Habeas Corpus ... Incumbrance	10
Indemnify ... Laches	11
Landlord and Tenant ... Malice	12
Mandamus ... Obiter Dictum	13
Object (v.) ... Perjury	14
Perpetuity ... Proclamation	15
Proffered Evidence ... Referee	16
Referendum ... Stare Decisis	17
State ... Term	18
Testamentary ... Warrant (Warranty) (v.)	19
Warrant (n.) ... Zoning	20

GLOSSARY OF LEGAL TERMS

A

ACTION - "Action" includes a civil action and a criminal action.
A FORTIORI - A term meaning you can reason one thing from the existence of certain facts.
A POSTERIORI - From what goes after; from effect to cause.
A PRIORI - From what goes before; from cause to effect.
AB INITIO - From the beginning.
ABATE - To diminish or put an end to.
ABET - To encourage the commission of a crime.
ABEYANCE - Suspension, temporary suppression.
ABIDE - To accept the consequences of.
ABJURE - To renounce; give up.
ABRIDGE - To reduce; contract; diminish.
ABROGATE - To annul, repeal, or destroy.
ABSCOND - To hide or absent oneself to avoid legal action.
ABSTRACT - A summary.
ABUT - To border on, to touch.
ACCESS - Approach; in real property law it means the right of the owner of property to the use of the highway or road next to his land, without obstruction by intervening property owners.
ACCESSORY - In criminal law, it means the person who contributes or aids in the commission of a crime.
ACCOMMODATED PARTY - One to whom credit is extended on the strength of another person signing a commercial paper.
ACCOMMODATION PAPER - A commercial paper to which the accommodating party has put his name.
ACCOMPLICE - In criminal law, it means a person who together with the principal offender commits a crime.
ACCORD - An agreement to accept something different or less than that to which one is entitled, which extinguishes the entire obligation.
ACCOUNT - A statement of mutual demands in the nature of debt and credit between parties.
ACCRETION - The act of adding to a thing; in real property law, it means gradual accumulation of land by natural causes.
ACCRUE - To grow to; to be added to.
ACKNOWLEDGMENT - The act of going before an official authorized to take acknowledgments, and acknowledging an act as one's own.
ACQUIESCENCE - A silent appearance of consent.
ACQUIT - To legally determine the innocence of one charged with a crime.
AD INFINITUM - Indefinitely.
AD LITEM - For the suit.
AD VALOREM - According to value.
ADJECTIVE LAW - Rules of procedure.
ADJUDICATION - The judgment given in a case.
ADMIRALTY - Court having jurisdiction over maritime cases.
ADULT - Sixteen years old or over (in criminal law).
ADVANCE - In commercial law, it means to pay money or render other value before it is due.
ADVERSE - Opposed; contrary.
ADVOCATE - (v.) To speak in favor of;
               (n.) One who assists, defends, or pleads for another.
AFFIANT - A person who makes and signs an affidavit.

AFFIDAVIT - A written and sworn to declaration of facts, voluntarily made.
AFFINITY - The relationship between persons through marriage with the kindred of each other; distinguished from consanguinity, which is the relationship by blood.
AFFIRM - To ratify; also when an appellate court affirms a judgment, decree, or order, it means that it is valid and right and must stand as rendered in the lower court.
AFOREMENTIONED; AFORESAID - Before or already said.
AGENT - One who represents and acts for another.
AID AND COMFORT - To help; encourage.
ALIAS - A name not one's true name.
ALIBI - A claim of not being present at a certain place at a certain time.
ALLEGE - To assert.
ALLOTMENT - A share or portion.
AMBIGUITY - Uncertainty; capable of being understood in more than one way.
AMENDMENT - Any language made or proposed as a change in some principal writing.
AMICUS CURIAE - A friend of the court; one who has an interest in a case, although not a party in the case, who volunteers advice upon matters of law to the judge. For example, a brief amicus curiae.
AMORTIZATION - To provide for a gradual extinction of (a future obligation) in advance of maturity, especially, by periodical contributions to a sinking fund which will be adequate to discharge a debt or make a replacement when it becomes necessary.
ANCILLARY - Aiding, auxiliary.
ANNOTATION - A note added by way of comment or explanation.
ANSWER - A written statement made by a defendant setting forth the grounds of his defense.
ANTE - Before.
ANTE MORTEM - Before death.
APPEAL - The removal of a case from a lower court to one of superior jurisdiction for the purpose of obtaining a review.
APPEARANCE - Coming into court as a party to a suit.
APPELLANT - The party who takes an appeal from one court or jurisdiction to another (appellate) court for review.
APPELLEE - The party against whom an appeal is taken.
APPROPRIATE - To make a thing one's own.
APPROPRIATION - Prescribing the destination of a thing; the act of the legislature designating a particular fund, to be applied to some object of government expenditure.
APPURTENANT - Belonging to; accessory or incident to.
ARBITER - One who decides a dispute; a referee.
ARBITRARY - Unreasoned; not governed by any fixed rules or standard.
ARGUENDO - By way of argument.
ARRAIGN - To call the prisoner before the court to answer to a charge.
ASSENT - A declaration of willingness to do something in compliance with a request.
ASSERT - Declare.
ASSESS - To fix the rate or amount.
ASSIGN - To transfer; to appoint; to select for a particular purpose.
ASSIGNEE - One who receives an assignment.
ASSIGNOR - One who makes an assignment.
AT BAR - Before the court.

AT ISSUE - When parties in an action come to a point where one asserts something and the other denies it.

ATTACH - Seize property by court order and sometimes arrest a person.

ATTEST - To witness a will, etc.; act of attestation.

AVERMENT - A positive statement of facts.

B

BAIL - To obtain the release of a person from legal custody by giving security and promising that he shall appear in court; to deliver (goods, etc.) in trust to a person for a special purpose.

BAILEE - One to whom personal property is delivered under a contract of bailment.

BAILMENT - Delivery of personal property to another to be held for a certain purpose and to be returned when the purpose is accomplished.

BAILOR - The party who delivers goods to another, under a contract of bailment.

BANC (OR BANK) - Bench; the place where a court sits permanently or regularly; also the assembly of all the judges of a court.

BANKRUPT - An insolvent person, technically, one declared to be bankrupt after a bankruptcy proceeding.

BAR - The legal profession.

BARRATRY - Exciting groundless judicial proceedings.

BARTER - A contract by which parties exchange goods for other goods.

BATTERY - Illegal interfering with another's person.

BEARER - In commercial law, it means the person in possession of a commercial paper which is payable to the bearer.

BENCH - The court itself or the judge.

BENEFICIARY - A person benefiting under a will, trust, or agreement.

BEST EVIDENCE RULE, THE - Except as otherwise provided by statute, no evidence other than the writing itself is admissible to prove the content of a writing. This section shall be known and may be cited as the best evidence rule.

BEQUEST - A gift of personal property under a will.

BILL - A formal written statement of complaint to a court of justice; also, a draft of an act of the legislature before it becomes a law; also, accounts for goods sold, services rendered, or work done.

BONA FIDE - In or with good faith; honestly.

BOND - An instrument by which the maker promises to pay a sum of money to another, usually providing that upon performances of a certain condition the obligation shall be void.

BOYCOTT - A plan to prevent the carrying on of a business by wrongful means.

BREACH - The breaking or violating of a law, or the failure to carry out a duty.

BRIEF - A written document, prepared by a lawyer to serve as the basis of an argument upon a case in court, usually an appellate court.

BURDEN OF PRODUCING EVIDENCE - The obligation of a party to introduce evidence sufficient to avoid a ruling against him on the issue.

BURDEN OF PROOF - The obligation of a party to establish by evidence a requisite degree of belief concerning a fact in the mind of the trier of fact or the court. The burden of proof may require a party to raise a reasonable doubt concerning the existence of nonexistence of a fact or that he establish the existence or nonexistence of a fact by a preponderance of the evidence, by clear and convincing proof, or by proof beyond a reasonable doubt.

Except as otherwise provided by law, the burden of proof requires proof by a preponderance of the evidence.

BUSINESS, A - Shall include every kind of business, profession, occupation, calling or operation of institutions, whether carried on for profit or not.

BY-LAWS - Regulations, ordinances, or rules enacted by a corporation, association, etc., for its own government.

C

CANON - A doctrine; also, a law or rule, of a church or association in particular.

CAPIAS - An order to arrest.

CAPTION - In a pleading, deposition or other paper connected with a case in court, it is the heading or introductory clause which shows the names of the parties, name of the court, number of the case on the docket or calendar, etc.

CARRIER - A person or corporation undertaking to transport persons or property.

CASE - A general term for an action, cause, suit, or controversy before a judicial body.

CAUSE - A suit, litigation or action before a court.

CAVEAT EMPTOR - Let the buyer beware. This term expresses the rule that the purchaser of an article must examine, judge, and test it for himself, being bound to discover any obvious defects or imperfections.

CERTIFICATE - A written representation that some legal formality has been complied with.

CERTIORARI - To be informed of; the name of a writ issued by a superior court directing the lower court to send up to the former the record and proceedings of a case.

CHANGE OF VENUE - To remove place of trial from one place to another.

CHARGE - An obligation or duty; a formal complaint; an instruction of the court to the jury upon a case.

CHARTER - (n.) The authority by virtue of which an organized body acts;
   (v.) in mercantile law, it means to hire or lease a vehicle or vessel for transportation.

CHATTEL - An article of personal property.

CHATTEL MORTGAGE - A mortgage on personal property.

CIRCUIT - A division of the country, for the administration of justice; a geographical area served by a court.

CITATION - The act of the court by which a person is summoned or cited; also, a reference to legal authority.

CIVIL (ACTIONS) - It indicates the private rights and remedies of individuals in contrast to the word "criminal" (actions) which relates to prosecution for violation of laws.

CLAIM (n.) - Any demand held or asserted as of right.

CODICIL - An addition to a will.

CODIFY - To arrange the laws of a country into a code.

COGNIZANCE - Notice or knowledge.

COLLATERAL - By the side; accompanying; an article or thing given to secure performance of a promise.

COMITY - Courtesy; the practice by which one court follows the decision of another court on the same question.

COMMIT - To perform, as an act; to perpetrate, as a crime; to send a person to prison.

COMMON LAW - As distinguished from law created by the enactment of the legislature (called statutory law), it relates to those principles and rules of action which derive their authority solely from usages and customs of immemorial antiquity, particularly with reference to the ancient unwritten law of England. The written pronouncements of the common law are found in court decisions.

COMMUTE - Change punishment to one less severe.

COMPLAINANT - One who applies to the court for legal redress.
COMPLAINT - The pleading of a plaintiff in a civil action; or a charge that a person has committed a specified offense.
COMPROMISE - An arrangement for settling a dispute by agreement.
CONCUR - To agree, consent.
CONCURRENT - Running together, at the same time.
CONDEMNATION - Taking private property for public use on payment therefor.
CONDITION - Mode or state of being; a qualification or restriction.
CONDUCT - Active and passive behavior; both verbal and nonverbal.
CONFESSION - Voluntary statement of guilt of crime.
CONFIDENTIAL COMMUNICATION BETWEEN CLIENT AND LAWYER - Information transmitted between a client and his lawyer in the course of that relationship and in confidence by a means which, so far as the client is aware, discloses the information to no third persons other than those who are present to further the interest of the client in the consultation or those to whom disclosure is reasonably necessary for the transmission of the information or the accomplishment of the purpose for which the lawyer is consulted, and includes a legal opinion formed and the advice given by the lawyer in the course of that relationship.
CONFRONTATION - Witness testifying in presence of defendant.
CONSANGUINITY - Blood relationship.
CONSIGN - To give in charge; commit; entrust; to send or transmit goods to a merchant, factor, or agent for sale.
CONSIGNEE - One to whom a consignment is made.
CONSIGNOR - One who sends or makes a consignment.
CONSPIRACY - In criminal law, it means an agreement between two or more persons to commit an unlawful act.
CONSPIRATORS - Persons involved in a conspiracy.
CONSTITUTION - The fundamental law of a nation or state.
CONSTRUCTION OF GENDERS - The masculine gender includes the feminine and neuter.
CONSTRUCTION OF SINGULAR AND PLURAL - The singular number includes the plural; and the plural, the singular.
CONSTRUCTION OF TENSES - The present tense includes the past and future tenses; and the future, the present.
CONSTRUCTIVE - An act or condition assumed from other parts or conditions.
CONSTRUE - To ascertain the meaning of language.
CONSUMMATE - To complete.
CONTIGUOUS - Adjoining; touching; bounded by.
CONTINGENT - Possible, but not assured; dependent upon some condition.
CONTINUANCE - The adjournment or postponement of an action pending in a court.
CONTRA - Against, opposed to; contrary.
CONTRACT - An agreement between two or more persons to do or not to do a particular thing.
CONTROVERT - To dispute, deny.
CONVERSION - Dealing with the personal property of another as if it were one's own, without right.
CONVEYANCE - An instrument transferring title to land.
CONVICTION - Generally, the result of a criminal trial which ends in a judgment or sentence that the defendant is guilty as charged.

COOPERATIVE - A cooperative is a voluntary organization of persons with a common interest, formed and operated along democratic lines for the purpose of supplying services at cost to its members and other patrons, who contribute both capital and business.

CORPUS DELICTI - The body of a crime; the crime itself.

CORROBORATE - To strengthen; to add weight by additional evidence.

COUNTERCLAIM - A claim presented by a defendant in opposition to or deduction from the claim of the plaintiff.

COUNTY - Political subdivision of a state.

COVENANT - Agreement.

CREDIBLE - Worthy of belief.

CREDITOR - A person to whom a debt is owing by another person, called the "debtor."

CRIMINAL ACTION - Includes criminal proceedings.

CRIMINAL INFORMATION - Same as complaint.

CRITERION (sing.)

CRITERIA (plural) - A means or tests for judging; a standard or standards.

CROSS-EXAMINATION - Examination of a witness by a party other than the direct examiner upon a matter that is within the scope of the direct examination of the witness.

CULPABLE - Blamable.

CY-PRES - As near as (possible). The rule of *cy-pres* is a rule for the construction of instruments in equity by which the intention of the party is carried out *as near as may be*, when it would be impossible or illegal to give it literal effect.

D

DAMAGES - A monetary compensation, which may be recovered in the courts by any person who has suffered loss, or injury, whether to his person, property or rights through the unlawful act or omission or negligence of another.

DECLARANT - A person who makes a statement.

DE FACTO - In fact; actually but without legal authority.

DE JURE - Of right; legitimate; lawful.

DE MINIMIS - Very small or trifling.

DE NOVO - Anew; afresh; a second time.

DEBT - A specified sum of money owing to one person from another, including not only the obligation of the debtor to pay, but the right of the creditor to receive and enforce payment.

DECEDENT - A dead person.

DECISION - A judgment or decree pronounced by a court in determination of a case.

DECREE - An order of the court, determining the rights of all parties to a suit.

DEED - A writing containing a contract sealed and delivered; particularly to convey real property.

DEFALCATION - Misappropriation of funds.

DEFAMATION - Injuring one's reputation by false statements.

DEFAULT - The failure to fulfill a duty, observe a promise, discharge an obligation, or perform an agreement.

DEFENDANT - The person defending or denying; the party against whom relief or recovery is sought in an action or suit.

DEFRAUD - To practice fraud; to cheat or trick.

DELEGATE (v.)- To entrust to the care or management of another.

DELICTUS - A crime.

DEMUR (v.) - To dispute the sufficiency in law of the pleading of the other side.

DEMURRAGE - In maritime law, it means, the sum fixed or allowed as remuneration to the owners of a ship for the detention of their vessel beyond the number of days allowed for loading and unloading or for sailing; also used in railroad terminology.
DENIAL - A form of pleading; refusing to admit the truth of a statement, charge, etc.
DEPONENT - One who gives testimony under oath reduced to writing.
DEPOSITION - Testimony given under oath outside of court for use in court or for the purpose of obtaining information in preparation for trial of a case.
DETERIORATION - A degeneration such as from decay, corrosion or disintegration.
DETRIMENT - Any loss or harm to person or property.
DEVIATION - A turning aside.
DEVISE - A gift of real property by the last will and testament of the donor.
DICTUM (sing.)
DICTA (plural) - Any statements made by the court in an opinion concerning some rule of law not necessarily involved nor essential to the determination of the case.
DIRECT EVIDENCE - Evidence that directly proves a fact, without an inference or presumption, and which in itself if true, conclusively establishes that fact.
DIRECT EXAMINATION - The first examination of a witness upon a matter that is not within the scope of a previous examination of the witness.
DISAFFIRM - To repudiate.
DISMISS - In an action or suit, it means to dispose of the case without any further consideration or hearing.
DISSENT - To denote disagreement of one or more judges of a court with the decision passed by the majority upon a case before them.
DOCKET (n.) - A formal record, entered in brief, of the proceedings in a court.
DOCTRINE - A rule, principle, theory of law.
DOMICILE - That place where a man has his true, fixed and permanent home to which whenever he is absent he has the intention of returning.
DRAFT (n.) - A commercial paper ordering payment of money drawn by one person on another.
DRAWEE - The person who is requested to pay the money.
DRAWER - The person who draws the commercial paper and addresses it to the drawee.
DUPLICATE - A counterpart produced by the same impression as the original enlargements and miniatures, or by mechanical or electronic re-recording, or by chemical reproduction, or by other equivalent technique which accurately reproduces the original.
DURESS - Use of force to compel performance or non-performance of an act.

E

EASEMENT - A liberty, privilege, or advantage without profit, in the lands of another.
EGRESS - Act or right of going out or leaving; emergence.
EIUSDEM GENERIS - Of the same kind, class or nature. A rule used in the construction of language in a legal document.
EMBEZZLEMENT - To steal; to appropriate fraudulently to one's own use property entrusted to one's care.
EMBRACERY - Unlawful attempt to influence jurors, etc., but not by offering value.
EMINENT DOMAIN - The right of a state to take private property for public use.
ENACT - To make into a law.
ENDORSEMENT - Act of writing one's name on the back of a note, bill or similar written instrument.

ENJOIN - To require a person, by writ of injunction from a court of equity, to perform or to abstain or desist from some act.
ENTIRETY - The whole; that which the law considers as one whole, and not capable of being divided into parts.
ENTRAPMENT - Inducing one to commit a crime so as to arrest him.
ENUMERATED - Mentioned specifically; designated.
ENURE - To operate or take effect.
EQUITY - In its broadest sense, this term denotes the spirit and the habit of fairness, justness, and right dealing which regulate the conduct of men.
ERROR - A mistake of law, or the false or irregular application of law as will nullify the judicial proceedings.
ESCROW - A deed, bond or other written engagement, delivered to a third person, to be delivered by him only upon the performance or fulfillment of some condition.
ESTATE - The interest which any one has in lands, or in any other subject of property.
ESTOP - To stop, bar, or impede.
ESTOPPEL - A rule of law which prevents a man from alleging or denying a fact, because of his own previous act.
ET AL. (alii) - And others.
ET SEQ. (sequential) - And the following.
ET UX. (uxor) - And wife.
EVIDENCE - Testimony, writings, material objects, or other things presented to the senses that are offered to prove the existence or non-existence of a fact.
Means from which inferences may be drawn as a basis of proof in duly constituted judicial or fact finding tribunals, and includes testimony in the form of opinion and hearsay.
EX CONTRACTU
EX DELICTO - In law, rights and causes of action are divided into two classes, those arising *ex contractu* (from a contract) and those arising *ex delicto* (from a delict or tort).
EX OFFICIO - From office; by virtue of the office.
EX PARTE - On one side only; by or for one.
EX POST FACTO - After the fact.
EX POST FACTO LAW - A law passed after an act was done which retroactively makes such act a crime.
EX REL. (relations) - Upon relation or information.
EXCEPTION - An objection upon a matter of law to a decision made, either before or after judgment by a court.
EXECUTOR (male)
EXECUTRIX (female) - A person who has been appointed by will to execute the will.
EXECUTORY - That which is yet to be executed or performed.
EXEMPT - To release from some liability to which others are subject.
EXONERATION - The removal of a burden, charge or duty.
EXTRADITION - Surrender of a fugitive from one nation to another.

F

F.A.S.- "Free alongside ship"; delivery at dock for ship named.
F.O.B.- "Free on board"; seller will deliver to car, truck, vessel, or other conveyance by which goods are to be transported, without expense or risk of loss to the buyer or consignee.
FABRICATE - To construct; to invent a false story.
FACSIMILE - An exact or accurate copy of an original instrument.

FACTOR - A commercial agent.
FEASANCE - The doing of an act.
FELONIOUS - Criminal, malicious.
FELONY - Generally, a criminal offense that may be punished by death or imprisonment for more than one year as differentiated from a misdemeanor.
FEME SOLE - A single woman.
FIDUCIARY - A person who is invested with rights and powers to be exercised for the benefit of another person.
FIERI FACIAS - A writ of execution commanding the sheriff to levy and collect the amount of a judgment from the goods and chattels of the judgment debtor.
FINDING OF FACT - Determination from proof or judicial notice of the existence of a fact. A ruling implies a supporting finding of fact; no separate or formal finding is required unless required by a statute of this state.
FISCAL - Relating to accounts or the management of revenue.
FORECLOSURE (sale) - A sale of mortgaged property to obtain satisfaction of the mortgage out of the sale proceeds.
FORFEITURE - A penalty, a fine.
FORGERY - Fabricating or producing falsely, counterfeited.
FORTUITOUS - Accidental.
FORUM - A court of justice; a place of jurisdiction.
FRAUD - Deception; trickery.
FREEHOLDER - One who owns real property.
FUNGIBLE - Of such kind or nature that one specimen or part may be used in the place of another.

G

GARNISHEE - Person garnished.
GARNISHMENT - A legal process to reach the money or effects of a defendant, in the possession or control of a third person.
GRAND JURY - Not less than 16, not more than 23 citizens of a county sworn to inquire into crimes committed or triable in the county.
GRANT - To agree to; convey, especially real property.
GRANTEE - The person to whom a grant is made.
GRANTOR - The person by whom a grant is made.
GRATUITOUS - Given without a return, compensation or consideration.
GRAVAMEN - The grievance complained of or the substantial cause of a criminal action.
GUARANTY (n.) - A promise to answer for the payment of some debt, or the performance of some duty, in case of the failure of another person, who, in the first instance, is liable for such payment or performance.
GUARDIAN - The person, committee, or other representative authorized by law to protect the person or estate or both of an incompetent (or of a *sui juris* person having a guardian) and to act for him in matters affecting his person or property or both. An incompetent is a person under disability imposed by law.
GUILTY - Establishment of the fact that one has committed a breach of conduct; especially, a violation of law.

H

HABEAS CORPUS - You have the body; the name given to a variety of writs, having for their object to bring a party before a court or judge for decision as to whether such person is being lawfully held prisoner.
HABENDUM - In conveyancing; it is the clause in a deed conveying land which defines the extent of ownership to be held by the grantee.
HEARING - A proceeding whereby the arguments of the interested parties are heared.
HEARSAY - A type of testimony given by a witness who relates, not what he knows personally, but what others have told hi, or what he has heard said by others.
HEARSAY RULE, THE - (a) "Hearsay evidence" is evidence of a statement that was made other than by a witness while testifying at the hearing and that is offered to prove the truth of the matter stated; (b) Except as provided by law, hearsay evidence is inadmissible; (c) This section shall be known and may be cited as the hearsay rule.
HEIR - Generally, one who inherits property, real or personal.
HOLDER OF THE PRIVILEGE - (a) The client when he has no guardian or conservator; (b) A guardian or conservator of the client when the client has a guardian or conservator; (c) The personal representative of the client if the client is dead; (d) A successor, assign, trustee in dissolution, or any similar representative of a firm, association, organization, partnership, business trust, corporation, or public entity that is no longer in existence.
HUNG JURY - One so divided that they can't agree on a verdict.
HUSBAND-WIFE PRIVILEGE - An accused in a criminal proceeding has a privilege to prevent his spouse from testifying against him.
HYPOTHECATE - To pledge a thing without delivering it to the pledgee.
HYPOTHESIS - A supposition, assumption, or toehry.

I

I.E. (id est) - That is.
IB., OR IBID.(ibidem) - In the same place; used to refer to a legal reference previously cited to avoid repeating the entire citation.
ILLICIT - Prohibited; unlawful.
ILLUSORY - Deceiving by false appearance.
IMMUNITY - Exemption.
IMPEACH - To accuse, to dispute.
IMPEDIMENTS - Disabilities, or hindrances.
IMPLEAD - To sue or prosecute by due course of law.
IMPUTED - Attributed or charged to.
IN LOCO PARENTIS - In place of parent, a guardian.
IN TOTO - In the whole; completely.
INCHOATE - Imperfect; unfinished.
INCOMMUNICADO - Denial of the right of a prisoner to communicate with friends or relatives.
INCOMPETENT - One who is incapable of caring for his own affairs because he is mentally deficient or undeveloped.
INCRIMINATION - A matter will incriminate a person if it constitutes, or forms an essential part of, or, taken in connection with other matters disclosed, is a basis for a reasonable inference of such a violation of the laws of this State as to subject him to liability to punishment therefor, unless he has become for any reason permanently immune from punishment for such violation.
INCUMBRANCE - Generally a claim, lien, charge or liability attached to and binding real property.

INDEMNIFY - To secure against loss or damage; also, to make reimbursement to one for a loss already incurred by him.
INDEMNITY - An agreement to reimburse another person in case of an anticipated loss falling upon him.
INDICIA - Signs; indications.
INDICTMENT - An accusation in writing found and presented by a grand jury charging that a person has committed a crime.
INDORSE - To write a name on the back of a legal paper or document, generally, a negotiable instrument
INDUCEMENT - Cause or reason why a thing is done or that which incites the person to do the act or commit a crime; the motive for the criminal act.
INFANT - In civil cases one under 21 years of age.
INFORMATION - A formal accusation of crime made by a prosecuting attorney.
INFRA - Below, under; this word occurring by itself in a publication refers the reader to a future part of the publication.
INGRESS - The act of going into.
INJUNCTION - A writ or order by the court requiring a person, generally, to do or to refrain from doing an act.
INSOLVENT - The condition of a person who is unable to pay his debts.
INSTRUCTION - A direction given by the judge to the jury concerning the law of the case.
INTERIM - In the meantime; time intervening.
INTERLOCUTORY - Temporary, not final; something intervening between the commencement and the end of a suit which decides some point or matter, but is not a final decision of the whole controversy.
INTERROGATORIES - A series of formal written questions used in the examination of a party or a witness usually prior to a trial.
INTESTATE - A person who dies without a will.
INURE - To result, to take effect.
IPSO FACTO - By the fact iself; by the mere fact.
ISSUE (n.) The disputed point or question in a case,

J

JEOPARDY - Danger, hazard, peril.
JOINDER - Joining; uniting with another person in some legal steps or proceeding.
JOINT - United; combined.
JUDGE - Member or members or representative or representatives of a court conducting a trial or hearing at which evidence is introduced.
JUDGMENT - The official decision of a court of justice.
JUDICIAL OR JUDICIARY - Relating to or connected with the administration of justice.
JURAT - The clause written at the foot of an affidavit, stating when, where and before whom such affidavit was sworn.
JURISDICTION - The authority to hear and determine controversies between parties.
JURISPRUDENCE - The philosophy of law.
JURY - A body of persons legally selected to inquire into any matter of fact, and to render their verdict according to the evidence.

L

LACHES - The failure to diligently assert a right, which results in a refusal to allow relief.

LANDLORD AND TENANT - A phrase used to denote the legal relation existing between the owner and occupant of real estate.

LARCENY - Stealing personal property belonging to another.

LATENT - Hidden; that which does not appear on the face of a thing.

LAW - Includes constitutional, statutory, and decisional law.

LAWYER-CLIENT PRIVILEGE - (1) A "client" is a person, public officer, or corporation, association, or other organization or entity, either public or private, who is rendered professional legal services by a lawyer, or who consults a lawyer with a view to obtaining professional legal services from him; (2) A "lawyer" is a person authorized, or reasonably believed by the client to be authorized, to practice law in any state or nation; (3) A "representative of the lawyer" is one employed to assist the lawyer in the rendition of professional legal services; (4) A communication is "confidential" if not intended to be disclosed to third persons other than those to whom disclosure is in furtherance of the rendition of professional legal services to the client or those reasonably necessary for the transmission of the communication.

General rule of privilege - A client has a privilege to refuse to disclose and to prevent any other person from disclosing confidential communications made for the purpose of facilitating the rendition of professional legal services to the client, (1) between himself or his representative and his lawyer or his lawyer's representative, or (2) between his lawyer and the lawyer's representative, or (3) by him or his lawyer to a lawyer representing another in a matter of common interest, or (4) between representatives of the client or between the client and a representative of the client, or (5) between lawyers representing the client.

LEADING QUESTION - Question that suggests to the witness the answer that the examining party desires.

LEASE - A contract by which one conveys real estate for a limited time usually for a specified rent; personal property also may be leased.

LEGISLATION - The act of enacting laws.

LEGITIMATE - Lawful.

LESSEE - One to whom a lease is given.

LESSOR - One who grants a lease

LEVY - A collecting or exacting by authority.

LIABLE - Responsible; bound or obligated in law or equity.

LIBEL (v.) - To defame or injure a person's reputation by a published writing.

(n.) - The initial pleading on the part of the plaintiff in an admiralty proceeding.

LIEN - A hold or claim which one person has upon the property of another as a security for some debt or charge.

LIQUIDATED - Fixed; settled.

LIS PENDENS - A pending civil or criminal action.

LITERAL - According to the language.

LITIGANT - A party to a lawsuit.

LITATION - A judicial controversy.

LOCUS - A place.

LOCUS DELICTI - Place of the crime.

LOCUS POENITENTIAE - The abandoning or giving up of one's intention to commit some crime before it is fully completed or abandoning a conspiracy before its purpose is accomplished.

M

MALFEASANCE - To do a wrongful act.

MALICE - The doing of a wrongful act Intentionally without just cause or excuse.

MANDAMUS - The name of a writ issued by a court to enforce the performance of some public duty.
MANDATORY (adj.) Containing a command.
MARITIME - Pertaining to the sea or to commerce thereon.
MARSHALING - Arranging or disposing of in order.
MAXIM - An established principle or proposition.
MINISTERIAL - That which involves obedience to instruction, but demands no special discretion, judgment or skill.
MISAPPROPRIATE - Dealing fraudulently with property entrusted to one.
MISDEMEANOR - A crime less than a felony and punishable by a fine or imprisonment for less than one year.
MISFEASANCE - Improper performance of a lawful act.
MISREPRESENTATION - An untrue representation of facts.
MITIGATE - To make or become less severe, harsh.
MITTIMUS - A warrant of commitment to prison.
MOOT (adj.) Unsettled, undecided, not necessary to be decided.
MORTGAGE - A conveyance of property upon condition, as security for the payment of a debt or the performance of a duty, and to become void upon payment or performance according to the stipulated terms.
MORTGAGEE - A person to whom property is mortgaged.
MORTGAGOR - One who gives a mortgage.
MOTION - In legal proceedings, a "motion" is an application, either written or oral, addressed to the court by a party to an action or a suit requesting the ruling of the court on a matter of law.
MUTUALITY - Reciprocation.

N

NEGLIGENCE - The failure to exercise that degree of care which an ordinarily prudent person would exercise under like circumstances.
NEGOTIABLE (instrument) - Any instrument obligating the payment of money which is transferable from one person to another by endorsement and delivery or by delivery only.
NEGOTIATE - To transact business; to transfer a negotiable instrument; to seek agreement for the amicable disposition of a controversy or case.
NOLLE PROSEQUI - A formal entry upon the record, by the plaintiff in a civil suit or the prosecuting officer in a criminal action, by which he declares that he "will no further prosecute" the case.
NOLO CONTENDERE - The name of a plea in a criminal action, having the same effect as a plea of guilty; but not constituting a direct admission of guilt.
NOMINAL - Not real or substantial.
NOMINAL DAMAGES - Award of a trifling sum where no substantial injury is proved to have been sustained.
NONFEASANCE - Neglect of duty.
NOVATION - The substitution of a new debt or obligation for an existing one.
NUNC PRO TUNC - A phrase applied to acts allowed to be done after the time when they should be done, with a retroactive effect.("Now for then.")

O

OATH - Oath includes affirmation or declaration under penalty of perjury.
OBITER DICTUM - Opinion expressed by a court on a matter not essentially involved in a case and hence not a decision; also called dicta, if plural.

OBJECT (v.) - To oppose as improper or illegal and referring the question of its propriety or legality to the court.
OBLIGATION - A legal duty, by which a person is bound to do or not to do a certain thing.
OBLIGEE - The person to whom an obligation is owed.
OBLIGOR - The person who is to perform the obligation.
OFFER (v.) - To present for acceptance or rejection.
 (n.) - A proposal to do a thing, usually a proposal to make a contract.
OFFICIAL INFORMATION - Information within the custody or control of a department or agency of the government the disclosure of which is shown to be contrary to the public interest.
OFFSET - A deduction.
ONUS PROBANDI - Burden of proof.
OPINION - The statement by a judge of the decision reached in a case, giving the law as applied to the case and giving reasons for the judgment; also a belief or view.
OPTION - The exercise of the power of choice; also a privilege existing in one person, for which he has paid money, which gives him the right to buy or sell real or personal property at a given price within a specified time.
ORDER - A rule or regulation; every direction of a court or judge made or entered in writing but not including a judgment.
ORDINANCE - Generally, a rule established by authority; also commonly used to designate the legislative acts of a municipal corporation.
ORIGINAL - Writing or recording itself or any counterpart intended to have the same effect by a person executing or issuing it. An "original" of a photograph includes the negative or any print therefrom. If data are stored in a computer or similar device, any printout or other output readable by sight, shown to reflect the data accurately, is an "original."
OVERT - Open, manifest.

P

PANEL - A group of jurors selected to serve during a term of the court.
PARENS PATRIAE - Sovereign power of a state to protect or be a guardian over children and incompetents.
PAROL - Oral or verbal.
PAROLE - To release one in prison before the expiration of his sentence, conditionally.
PARITY - Equality in purchasing power between the farmer and other segments of the economy.
PARTITION - A legal division of real or personal property between one or more owners.
PARTNERSHIP - An association of two or more persons to carry on as co-owners a business for profit.
PATENT (adj.) - Evident.
 (n.) - A grant of some privilege, property, or authority, made by the government or sovereign of a country to one or more individuals.
PECULATION - Stealing.
PECUNIARY - Monetary.
PENULTIMATE - Next to the last.
PER CURIAM - A phrase used in the report of a decision to distinguish an opinion of the whole court from an opinion written by any one judge.
PER SE - In itself; taken alone.
PERCEIVE - To acquire knowledge through one's senses.
PEREMPTORY - Imperative; absolute.
PERJURY - To lie or state falsely under oath.

PERPETUITY - Perpetual existence; also the quality or condition of an estate limited so that it will not take effect or vest within the period fixed by law.

PERSON - Includes a natural person, firm, association, organization, partnership, business trust, corporation, or public entity.

PERSONAL PROPERTY - Includes money, goods, chattels, things in action, and evidences of debt.

PERSONALTY - Short term for personal property.

PETITION - An application in writing for an order of the court, stating the circumstances upon which it is founded and requesting any order or other relief from a court.

PLAINTIFF - A person who brings a court action.

PLEA - A pleading in a suit or action.

PLEADINGS - Formal allegations made by the parties of their respective claims and defenses, for the judgment of the court.

PLEDGE - A deposit of personal property as a security for the performance of an act.

PLEDGEE - The party to whom goods are delivered in pledge.

PLEDGOR - The party delivering goods in pledge.

PLENARY - Full; complete.

POLICE POWER - Inherent power of the state or its political subdivisions to enact laws within constitutional limits to promote the general welfare of society or the community.

POLLING THE JURY - Call the names of persons on a jury and requiring each juror to declare what his verdict is before it is legally recorded.

POST MORTEM - After death.

POWER OF ATTORNEY - A writing authorizing one to act for another.

PRECEPT - An order, warrant, or writ issued to an officer or body of officers, commanding him or them to do some act within the scope of his or their powers.

PRELIMINARY FACT - Fact upon the existence or nonexistence of which depends the admissibility or inadmissibility of evidence. The phrase "the admissibility or inadmissibility of evidence" includes the qualification or disqualification of a person to be a witness and the existence or nonexistence of a privilege.

PREPONDERANCE - Outweighing.

PRESENTMENT - A report by a grand jury on something they have investigated on their own knowledge.

PRESUMPTION - An assumption of fact resulting from a rule of law which requires such fact to be assumed from another fact or group of facts found or otherwise established in the action.

PRIMA FACUE - At first sight.

PRIMA FACIE CASE - A case where the evidence is very patent against the defendant.

PRINCIPAL - The source of authority or rights; a person primarily liable as differentiated from "principle" as a primary or basic doctrine.

PRO AND CON - For and against.

PRO RATA - Proportionally.

PROBATE - Relating to proof, especially to the proof of wills.

PROBATIVE - Tending to prove.

PROCEDURE - In law, this term generally denotes rules which are established by the Federal, State, or local Governments regarding the types of pleading and courtroom practice which must be followed by the parties involved in a criminal or civil case.

PROCLAMATION - A public notice by an official of some order, intended action, or state of facts.

PROFFERED EVIDENCE - The admissibility or inadmissibility of which is dependent upon the existence or nonexistence of a preliminary fact.
PROMISSORY (NOTE) - A promise in writing to pay a specified sum at an expressed time, or on demand, or at sight, to a named person, or to his order, or bearer.
PROOF - The establishment by evidence of a requisite degree of belief concerning a fact in the mind of the trier of fact or the court.
PROPERTY - Includes both real and personal property.
PROPRIETARY (adj.) - Relating or pertaining to ownership; usually a single owner.
PROSECUTE - To carry on an action or other judicial proceeding; to proceed against a person criminally.
PROVISO - A limitation or condition in a legal instrument.
PROXIMATE - Immediate; nearest
PUBLIC EMPLOYEE - An officer, agent, or employee of a public entity.
PUBLIC ENTITY - Includes a national, state, county, city and county, city, district, public authority, public agency, or any other political subdivision or public corporation, whether foreign or domestic.
PUBLIC OFFICIAL - Includes an official of a political dubdivision of such state or territory and of a municipality.
PUNITIVE - Relating to punishment.

Q

QUASH - To make void.
QUASI - As if; as it were.
QUID PRO QUO - Something for something; the giving of one valuable thing for another.
QUITCLAIM (v.) - To release or relinquish claim or title to, especially in deeds to realty.
QUO WARRANTO - A legal procedure to test an official's right to a public office or the right to hold a franchise, or to hold an office in a domestic corporation.

R

RATIFY - To approve and sanction.
REAL PROPERTY - Includes lands, tenements, and hereditaments.
REALTY - A brief term for real property.
REBUT - To contradict; to refute, especially by evidence and arguments.
RECEIVER - A person who is appointed by the court to receive, and hold in trust property in litigation.
RECIDIVIST - Habitual criminal.
RECIPROCAL - Mutual.
RECOUPMENT - To keep back or get something which is due; also, it is the right of a defendant to have a deduction from the amount of the plaintiff's damages because the plaintiff has not fulfilled his part of the same contract.
RECROSS EXAMINATION - Examination of a witness by a cross-examiner subsequent to a redirect examination of the witness.
REDEEM - To release an estate or article from mortgage or pledge by paying the debt for which it stood as security.
REDIRECT EXAMINATION - Examination of a witness by the direct examiner subsequent to the cross-examination of the witness.
REFEREE - A person to whom a cause pending in a court is referred by the court, to take testimony, hear the parties, and report thereon to the court.

REFERENDUM - A method of submitting an important legislative or administrative matter to a direct vote of the people.
RELEVANT EVIDENCE - Evidence including evidence relevant to the credulity of a witness or hearsay declarant, having any tendency in reason to prove or disprove any disputed fact that is of consequence to the determination of the action.
REMAND - To send a case back to the lower court from which it came, for further proceedings.
REPLEVIN - An action to recover goods or chattels wrongfully taken or detained.
REPLY (REPLICATION) - Generally, a reply is what the plaintiff or other person who has instituted proceedings says in answer to the defendant's case.
RE JUDICATA - A thing judicially acted upon or decided.
RES ADJUDICATA - Doctrine that an issue or dispute litigated and determined in a case between the opposing parties is deemed permanently decided between these parties.
RESCIND (RECISSION) - To avoid or cancel a contract.
RESPONDENT - A defendant in a proceeding in chancery or admiralty; also, the person who contends against the appeal in a case.
RESTITUTION - In equity, it is the restoration of both parties to their original condition (when practicable), upon the rescission of a contract for fraud or similar cause.
RETROACTIVE (RETROSPECTIVE) - Looking back; effective as of a prior time.
REVERSED - A term used by appellate courts to indicate that the decision of the lower court in the case before it has been set aside.
REVOKE - To recall or cancel.
RIPARIAN (RIGHTS) - The rights of a person owning land containing or bordering on a water course or other body of water, such as lakes and rivers.

S

SALE - A contract whereby the ownership of property is transferred from one person to another for a sum of money or for any consideration.
SANCTION - A penalty or punishment provided as a means of enforcing obedience to a law; also, an authorization.
SATISFACTION - The discharge of an obligation by paying a party what is due to him; or what is awarded to him by the judgment of a court or otherwise.
SCIENTER - Knowingly; also, it is used in pleading to denote the defendant's guilty knowledge.
SCINTILLA - A spark; also the least particle.
SECRET OF STATE - Governmental secret relating to the national defense or the international relations of the United States.
SECURITY - Indemnification; the term is applied to an obligation, such as a mortgage or deed of trust, given by a debtor to insure the payment or performance of his debt, by furnishing the creditor with a resource to be used in case of the debtor's failure to fulfill the principal obligation.
SENTENCE - The judgment formally pronounced by the court or judge upon the defendant after his conviction in a criminal prosecution.
SET-OFF - A claim or demand which one party in an action credits against the claim of the opposing party.
SHALL and MAY - "Shall" is mandatory and "may" is permissive.
SITUS - Location.
SOVEREIGN - A person, body or state in which independent and supreme authority is vested.
STARE DECISIS - To follow decided cases.

STATE - "State" means this State, unless applied to the different parts of the United States. In the latter case, it includes any state, district, commonwealth, territory or insular possession of the United States, including the District of Columbia.

STATEMENT - (a) Oral or written verbal expression or (b) nonverbal conduct of a person intended by him as a substitute for oral or written verbal expression.

STATUTE - An act of the legislature. Includes a treaty.

STATUTE OF LIMITATION - A statute limiting the time to bring an action after the right of action has arisen.

STAY - To hold in abeyance an order of a court.

STIPULATION - Any agreement made by opposing attorneys regulating any matter incidental to the proceedings or trial.

SUBORDINATION (AGREEMENT) - An agreement making one's rights inferior to or of a lower rank than another's.

SUBORNATION - The crime of procuring a person to lie or to make false statements to a court.

SUBPOENA - A writ or order directed to a person, and requiring his attendance at a particular time and place to testify as a witness.

SUBPOENA DUCES TECUM - A subpoena used, not only for the purpose of compelling witnesses to attend in court, but also requiring them to bring with them books or documents which may be in their possession, and which may tend to elucidate the subject matter of the trial.

SUBROGATION - The substituting of one for another as a creditor, the new creditor succeeding to the former's rights.

SUBSIDY - A government grant to assist a private enterprise deemed advantageous to the public.

SUI GENERIS - Of the same kind.

SUIT - Any civil proceeding by a person or persons against another or others in a court of justice by which the plaintiff pursues the remedies afforded him by law.

SUMMONS - A notice to a defendant that an action against him has been commenced and requiring him to appear in court and answer the complaint.

SUPRA - Above; this word occurring by itself in a book refers the reader to a previous part of the book.

SURETY - A person who binds himself for the payment of a sum of money, or for the performance of something else, for another.

SURPLUSAGE - Extraneous or unnecessary matter.

SURVIVORSHIP - A term used when a person becomes entitled to property by reason of his having survived another person who had an interest in the property.

SUSPEND SENTENCE - Hold back a sentence pending good behavior of prisoner.

SYLLABUS - A note prefixed to a report, especially a case, giving a brief statement of the court's ruling on different issues of the case.

T

TALESMAN - Person summoned to fill a panel of jurors.

TENANT - One who holds or possesses lands by any kind of right or title; also, one who has the temporary use and occupation of real property owned by another person (landlord), the duration and terms of his tenancy being usually fixed by an instrument called "a lease."

TENDER - An offer of money; an expression of willingness to perform a contract according to its terms.

TERM - When used with reference to a court, it signifies the period of time during which the court holds a session, usually of several weeks or months duration.

TESTAMENTARY - Pertaining to a will or the administration of a will.
TESTATOR (male)
TESTATRIX (female) - One who makes or has made a testament or will.
TESTIFY (TESTIMONY) - To give evidence under oath as a witness.
TO WIT - That is to say; namely.
TORT - Wrong; injury to the person.
TRANSITORY - Passing from place to place.
TRESPASS - Entry into another's ground, illegally.
TRIAL - The examination of a cause, civil or criminal, before a judge who has jurisdiction over it, according to the laws of the land.
TRIER OF FACT - Includes (a) the jury and (b) the court when the court is trying an issue of fact other than one relating to the admissibility of evidence.
TRUST - A right of property, real or personal, held by one party for the benefit of another.
TRUSTEE - One who lawfully holds property in custody for the benefit of another.

U

UNAVAILABLE AS A WITNESS - The declarant is (1) Exempted or precluded on the ground of privilege from testifying concerning the matter to which his statement is relevant; (2) Disqualified from testifying to the matter; (3) Dead or unable to attend or to testify at the hearing because of then existing physical or mental illness or infirmity; (4) Absent from the hearing and the court is unable to compel his attendance by its process; or (5) Absent from the hearing and the proponent of his statement has exercised reasonable diligence but has been unable to procure his attendance by the court's process.
ULTRA VIRES - Acts beyond the scope and power of a corporation, association, etc.
UNILATERAL - One-sided; obligation upon, or act of one party.
USURY - Unlawful interest on a loan.

V

VACATE - To set aside; to move out.
VARIANCE - A discrepancy or disagreement between two instruments or two aspects of the same case, which by law should be consistent.
VENDEE - A purchaser or buyer.
VENDOR - The person who transfers property by sale, particularly real estate; the term "seller" is used more commonly for one who sells personal property.
VENIREMEN - Persons ordered to appear to serve on a jury or composing a panel of jurors.
VENUE - The place at which an action is tried, generally based on locality or judicial district in which an injury occurred or a material fact happened.
VERDICT - The formal decision or finding of a jury.
VERIFY - To confirm or substantiate by oath.
VEST - To accrue to.
VOID - Having no legal force or binding effect.
VOIR DIRE - Preliminary examination of a witness or a juror to test competence, interest, prejudice, etc.

W

WAIVE - To give up a right.
WAIVER - The intentional or voluntary relinquishment of a known right.
WARRANT (WARRANTY) (v.) - To promise that a certain fact or state of facts, in relation to the subject matter, is, or shall be, as it is represented to be.

WARRANT (n.) - A writ issued by a judge, or other competent authority, addressed to a sheriff, or other officer, requiring him to arrest the person therein named, and bring him before the judge or court to answer or be examined regarding the offense with which he is charged.

WRIT - An order or process issued in the name of the sovereign or in the name of a court or judicial officer, commanding the performance or nonperformance of some act.

WRITING - Handwriting, typewriting, printing, photostating, photographing and every other means of recording upon any tangible thing any form of communication or representation, including letters, words, pictures, sounds, or symbols, or combinations thereof.

WRITINGS AND RECORDINGS - Consists of letters, words, or numbers, or their equivalent, set down by handwriting, typewriting, printing, photostating, photographing, magnetic impulse, mechanical or electronic recording, or other form of data compilation.

Y

YEA AND NAY - Yes and no.

YELLOW DOG CONTRACT - A contract by which employer requires employee to sign an instrument promising as condition that he will not join a union during its continuance, and will be discharged if he does join.

Z

ZONING - The division of a city by legislative regulation into districts and the prescription and application in each district of regulations having to do with structural and architectural designs of buildings and of regulations prescribing use to which buildings within designated districts may be put.